contents

acknowledgments

American Heart Association Consumer Publications

 Director: Jane Anneken Ruehl

 Senior Editor: Janice Roth Moss

 Editor: Jacqueline Fornerod Haigney

 Assistant Editor: Roberta Westcott Sullivan

 Senior Marketing Manager: Bharati Gaitonde

Recipe Developers

 Andy Broder

 Nancy S. Hughes

 Karen Levin

 Carol Ritchie

Nutrient Analyst

 Tammi Hancock, RD

Writer

 Sandy Szwarc, RN, BSN, CCP

American Heart Association®

Fighting Heart Disease and Stroke

One-Dish
meals

Also by the American Heart Association

The New American Heart Association Cookbook, 6th Edition

American Heart Association Low-Fat, Low-Cholesterol Cookbook, Second Edition

American Heart Association Low-Calorie Cookbook

American Heart Association Low-Salt Cookbook, Second Edition

American Heart Association Quick & Easy Cookbook

American Heart Association Meals in Minutes Cookbook

American Heart Association Low-Fat & Luscious Desserts

American Heart Association Kids' Cookbook

American Heart Association To Your Health! A Guide to Heart-Smart Living

American Heart Association 6 Weeks to Get Out the Fat

American Heart Association Fitting in Fitness

American Heart Association 365 Ways to Get Out the Fat

American Heart
Association®

Fighting Heart Disease and Stroke

One-Dish
m e a l s

Over 200 All-New, All-in-One Recipes

Clarkson Potter/Publishers
New York

Copyright © 2003 by the American Heart Association

All rights reserved.
Published by Clarkson Potter/Publishers, New York, New York.
Member of the Crown Publishing Group, a division of Random House, Inc.
www.clarksonpotter.com

Originally published in hardcover by Clarkson Potter/Publishers, a division of
Random House, Inc., in 2003.

Your contribution to the American Heart Association supports research that helps
make publications like this possible. For more information, call 1-800-AHA-USA1
(1-800-242-8721) or contact us online at www.americanheart.org.

Printed in the United States of America

Front cover: Greek-Style Chicken with Lemon-Pistachio Rice (pages 80–81)
Photograph by Ben Fink

Design by Jan Derevjanik

Illustrations by Iskra Johnson

Library of Congress Cataloging-in-Publication Data
American Heart Association one-dish meals: over 200 all-new, all-in-one recipes /
The American Heart Association.
    1. Casserole cookery.   2. Quick and easy cookery.   I. Title: One-dish meals.
II. American Heart Association.
TX693 .A53   2003
641.8'21—dc21   2003007642

ISBN 1-4000-8184-X

10 9 8 7 6 5 4 3 2 1

First Paperback Edition

one-dish meals— healthful home cooking for every day

Mmmm.... A hot, homecooked dinner is the perfect antidote to a hectic day.

Whether you're busy with school, with career and family, or in the prime of your life and hardly sitting on the sidelines, life today is revved up. It seems the busier and more complicated our lives become, the more our hearts yearn for the comforts of home. Increasingly, too, we hunger for real food—not just something gobbled from the dashboards of our cars or out of a cardboard box.

As we try to reconnect with the people and simple things that give meaning to our lives, we're treasuring the tradition of homecooked dinners as never before. And they're proving to be one of the best things we can do for ourselves and our loved ones.

Many of our most lasting memories are made while we're gathered around the table. Talking and sharing bring people closer and nurture our emotional well-being. Mealtimes really do strengthen the ties that bind.

Dinners at home are also surprisingly important for our physical health. Homecooked meals mean all of us—children and adults—are more likely to eat more fruits and vegetables and less fried foods and sodas and to get all the nutrients important for a lifetime of good health.

the magical solution to the mealtime dilemma

Regularly making homecooked meals a reality can feel like an impossible task, however. Are you enjoying them at your house as often as you'd like? Probably not, and you're not alone. We all have a multitude of reasons:

· **Finding the time and energy to cook at the end of the day is hard. Grabbing a fast-food burger or pizza seems quicker and easier.**

· **Juggling multiple dishes and getting them all on the table hot and ready to eat at the same time is a daunting task.**

· **Cooking feels too much like work.**

· **Cleaning up afterward is time-consuming.**

- Talking with loved ones or dinner guests is more fun than cooking in the kitchen while they visit in the family room.

- Eating healthful food is boring. It seems impossible to eat what's good for us and still love every bite.

If you're like us, you want meals that are wholesome and satisfying but also packed with flavor. And they must be fast and convenient, of course! With these challenges in mind, we set out to find a way to make it easy—virtually effortless—to dig into delicious homecooked meals anytime. And we found it!

The secret: one-dish meals.

The benefits impressed us and will you, too. Using the recipes and tips we've gathered in this cookbook, you'll be putting terrific dinners on the table for yourself, your family, and your friends—meals everyone will love coming home to! These delicious dinners practically cook themselves, are ready when you are, and can even save you money. You get not only a balanced, nutritious meal in one pot but also more time for all the things you want to do. As if by magic, eating well has never been simpler.

Neither has planning. Because almost every dish is cooked in just one pot or pan, timing is a snap. In addition, each recipe contains protein, carbohydrates, and at least one serving of fruit and/or vegetables, so coming up with a menu is super-simple. Some of the one-dish meals are so substantial that you won't want or need to supplement them. With others, a salad, whole-grain roll, or fruit-based dessert makes a fine complement.

a world of flavor and comfort in every pot

How do these dishes taste, though? Forget about those anemic, dated casseroles with pasty white cream sauces burying overcooked, unidentifiable objects, and those boring, mushy mixtures that passed for stews. The 200-plus recipes in this cookbook are based on many of the most-loved foods in the world. Some are clever and daring, while others offer old-fashioned solace. As any *bon vivant* knows, the finest cooking often can be found in the modest one-dish meals that home cooks have made for centuries.

These dishes ooze good taste and warm comfort: French beef bourguignon, coq au vin, salade niçoise, and cassoulet; Italian risottos, pastas, paninis, and pizzas; Mexican enchiladas, posoles, and quesadillas; Asian stir-fries and rice and noodle bowls; Spanish paellas and seafood stews; East Indian curries and tandoori; Middle Eastern couscous- and tabbouleh-based dishes; Moroccan tagines; Greek phyllo pies and stuffed pitas; all-American stews, pot roast, and meat loaf; plus Cajun gumbo and catfish sandwiches, Texas chili, and New England crab cakes. You'll find recipes for these treats and many more on the following pages.

Sound enticing? With the terrific variety you'll find among our updated recipes, there's something for everyone and every occasion. The meat-and-potatoes crowd, the fussiest eater in the house, and the diehard fast-food fans will all be won over. You'll find recipes for casual weekday family suppers to special weekend dinners for company.

nutrition—it's in there!

You know that, coming from the American Heart Association, these are also heart-smart meals that all of us can enjoy for optimum health. That's the beauty of one-dish meals. They make it a no-brainer to put together the foods recommended for healthful eating. (See Appendix A: Eating for a Healthy Heart, page 273.) Everything's in there—fruits and vegetables, lean protein, and grains, pastas, or starchy vegetables—and in proper portions. With all-in-one cooking, you can control saturated fat, cholesterol, calories, and sodium while creating foods rich in flavor. In Appendix B: Meal Planning, starting on page 285, you'll discover more about how the one-dish meal approach can mean a more healthful way of eating for you and your loved ones.

convenience that saves you time, trouble, and money

One-dish cooking is easy—so easy, it's perfect for the novice cook or anyone who doesn't want to be bothered with complicated cooking. Its convenience is great for frazzled weeknights but just as welcome when you want a foolproof company meal that won't banish you to the kitchen.

You'll love how one-dish cooking can simplify your life and save you time and money:

· **Many recipes require little more than assembling the ingredients—and even those can be freely varied depending on your tastes, what you have on hand, or what's on sale at the market. They also let you take advantage of time-saving convenience products, if you like.**

· **You can forget about having to coordinate multiple dishes and get everything on the table at the same time. All you have to manage is one pot. You can do that!**

- It can be faster to prepare one-dish meals than wait for pizza delivery or pick up takeout.

- Some meals cook unattended in the oven, in the slow cooker, or on the stovetop. Genuine slow food, these meals give you the gift of time. While they fill your house with tantalizing aromas, you can be at work, working out, or doing whatever else you feel like. No need to slave over a hot stove!

- Some of the meals are cooked in and served from the same pot they're prepared in. No need to dirty every pot in the house. With less mess and just one pot to wash, cleanup's a snap.

- Lots of one-dish meals aren't fussy about timing and can be held and kept warm so dinner is ready when you are.

- Many can be readied ahead and refrigerated or frozen. Lots of the dishes reheat well too, meaning the leftovers are tasty.

- You don't need a lot of fancy or expensive cookware. Much one-dish cookware is multipurpose, going from the oven or stove to the table; other types may go from the freezer or refrigerator to the microwave.

- These meals are great for tiny kitchens—in apartments, galleys, and even RVs.

- The tradition of one-dish meals extends costly protein or combines modest ingredients into tasty dishes that will allow you to stretch your food dollars. Turn to Appendix B: Meal Planning, page 285, for more time- and budget-saving ideas.

Wouldn't a nice homecooked meal taste great tonight? You deserve it. So grab a pot and bring comfort back into your day.

how to use this book

nutritional analyses

A nutritional analysis accompanies each recipe in this cookbook. These analyses can help you learn how well a certain dish will fit into your eating plan. Or if dinner usually means grabbing a burger and fries, these analyses can help you learn which foods make healthier choices. Think of them as training wheels or bumper pads on your road to heart-smart eating!

Each analysis lists the number of calories and the amount of protein, total fat (and breaks down the fats into their saturated, polyunsaturated, and monounsaturated amounts), cholesterol, fiber, sodium, carbohydrates, and sugar **in each serving.** Because a good eating plan is based on balance, variety, and moderation, these analyses can help you budget your saturated fat, cholesterol, calories, and sodium for the day.

Here's a more detailed explanation of how we calculated those numbers, plus tips that may help you use them:

- Each analysis is based on one serving. Note the serving sizes at the top of each recipe. If you eat more or less than a single serving, you'll need to adjust the numbers proportionately.

- Optional ingredients and garnishes aren't included in the numbers, unless we've specially noted them. If you need to keep close track of numbers, remember to add up *everything* you eat. We encourage you to add colorful fruit and vegetable garnishes to create beautiful meals that will be all the more appealing and nutritious.

- When several choices are offered for an ingredient, such as fat-free or low-fat sour cream, we use the first option for the analysis.

- When a recipe calls for a range for the amount of an ingredient, such as a 1^1/2- to 2-pound pork tenderloin, we use the average of the measurements.

- If a dash is shown for a value, an accurate nutrient value isn't available for at least one ingredient in the recipe.

- The total fat listed may not exactly equal the sum of the saturated, monounsaturated, and polyunsaturated fats. That's because we round off numbers and because values for other fatty substances, such as trans fats and glycerol, aren't yet available.

- Only the amount of marinade that would be absorbed by meats, poultry, and seafood, based on U.S. Department of Agriculture data, is included in our analyses. Of course, if the marinade is boiled and used as a sauce, the full amount is included.

- Meat figures are based on cooked lean meat with all the visible fat removed. We use 90 percent fat-free for lean ground beef.

- For recipes that use alcohol, our nutritional analyses estimate that most of the alcohol calories evaporate during cooking.

- When we call for "acceptable vegetable oil," we used canola oil in our analyses. You can use any monounsaturated-rich oil you prefer, such as olive, peanut, almond, or walnut, or a polyunsaturated-rich oil, such as corn, soybean, sunflower, sesame, flaxseed, or safflower. In case you were wondering, all olive oils have the same nutritional breakdown regardless of their variety or price. (Light olive oil is no lighter in fat than other olive oil.) Refer to Appendix A: Eating for a Healthy Heart (page 273) for more information on fats and oils.

- If a recipe calls for "acceptable stick margarine," we used corn oil margarine in our analyses. If you prefer, you can substitute any margarine that lists liquid vegetable oil as the first ingredient.

- Although the vitamin content of the same foods doesn't differ whether they are fresh, frozen, or canned, read labels carefully, especially with canned foods. They're typically lower in fiber and, more important, often have added sugars and salt. Such additions can dramatically change their sodium and calorie counts. For our analyses, we call for no-salt versions if possible. If not, we rinse and drain canned vegetables and beans. That reduces their sodium content by 25 to 30 percent. See Appendix B: Meal Planning (page 285) for tips on making your own salt-free convenience foods.

- We call for fresh citrus juices, but if you use frozen or canned without sugar added, you won't need to make any adjustments in the numbers.

- The reduced-fat cheeses we used in our analyses had no more than 3 grams fat per serving. See Appendix C: Shopping Information (page 292) for helpful information on what the labels "reduced-fat," "light," and "low-fat" on dairy and other products mean.

- We use the abbreviations *g* for gram and *mg* for milligram.

special ingredients we use

When you're watching your calorie, saturated fat, cholesterol, or salt intake, it can be hard to find recipes that meet your needs and still taste terrific. The American Heart Association to the rescue! Our recipes and nutritional analyses use ingre-

WHAT IS THAT LOW-SODIUM INGREDIENT?

When your medical needs go beyond preventive balance and moderation, keeping close track of sodium could be critical for you. The products listed below typically are high in sodium. Our analyses use the lowest-sodium products we know of that are widely available. If the sodium in the products you use differs from these amounts, adjust the analyses accordingly.

Barbecue sauce = 210 mg sodium per 2 tablespoons

Fat-free, no-salt-added beef broth = 74 mg sodium per 1 cup

Fat-free, low-sodium chicken broth = 60 mg sodium per 1 cup

Fat-free flour tortillas = 340 mg sodium per 8-inch tortilla

Low-fat, lower-sodium ham = 235 mg sodium per ounce

Light Italian salad dressing = 270 mg sodium per 2 tablespoons

No-salt-added ketchup = 3 mg sodium per 1 tablespoon

Salsa = 140 mg sodium per 2 tablespoons

Low-salt soy sauce = 390 mg sodium per 1 tablespoon

Fat-free, low-sodium spaghetti sauce = 168 mg sodium per ½ cup

Steak sauce = 90 mg sodium per 1 tablespoon

Light teriyaki sauce = 280 mg sodium per 1 tablespoon

No-salt-added vegetable broth = 47 mg sodium per 1 cup

Very low sodium Worcestershire sauce = 7 mg sodium per 1 teaspoon

dients with the lowest amounts of saturated fat and sodium possible for the dish. But finding the right products requires careful shopping. To make matters challenging, sometimes the low-fat or low-sodium versions you do locate aren't the lowest in sodium, fat, or calories! For example, it's possible that a product that's much lower in sodium than the competition may not say "reduced sodium" on the label.

Extra sodium, fats, sugars, and calories can hide in the most unexpected ingredients. Would you have guessed that some breads, crackers, and flour tortillas are loaded with saturated or hydrogenated fats and sodium? Or that commercial sauces (such as barbecue sauce, chile sauce, salsa, hoisin and other Asian sauces, spaghetti sauce, pizza sauce, Worcestershire sauce—well, you get the idea), imitation bacon bits, and salad dressings may contain fats or heaping spoonfuls of sugar and salt? We all know that soy sauce and seasoning salts are salty, but so are many canned broths and bouillons, processed meats and cheeses, pickles, and capers. We probably don't even need to mention chips and other crunchy snacks, do we?

It's important to become an astute label reader and compare items to make the best selection. For more notes on checking labels when shopping, turn to Appendix C: Shopping Information (page 292).

making substitutions

Think of our recipes as paint-by-number kits for cooking delicious, healthful meals. That doesn't mean you can't color outside the lines—that's the fun of cooking! We encourage you to ad lib and make these recipes your own, even if you're watching those nutritional analysis numbers closely. You can still make additions, or substitute ingredients with similar nutritional profiles, that won't affect the numbers. You can endlessly mix and match herbs and spices, vinegars, citrus juices, and even certain fruits, vegetables, meats, and fish to give variety and customize these recipes to your tastes, budget, what's in your pantry, or what's at its seasonal best.

Most times, the form of an ingredient—fresh or dried herbs, fresh-squeezed or bottled juice, fresh or frozen vegetables, and canned no-salt-added beans and stocks or homemade—won't affect the analyses either.

cook's tips

We've scattered helpful Cook's Tips throughout this cookbook. They will give you ideas on where to find or how to use unusual ingredients, what to do with leftovers, cooking shortcuts, and many more useful hints. Also, check out Appendix B: Meal Planning (page 285), to find creative ideas for making one-dish meals more fun and exciting, easier, faster, more nutritious, and less expensive.

one-dish cookware

One-dish cooking uses simple, practical cookware. Not every pot is cut out for one-dish cooking or every recipe, however. Read the recipe and use the type of pan suggested for the cooking method, factoring in your own plans to freeze or refrigerate the dish before or after cooking. If a recipe says to spray nonstick cookware with vegetable oil spray but the manufacturer says not to, follow your manufacturer's instructions.

Try to match the size of the pan called for in the recipe because pan size affects the outcome of the dish. For long-cooking covered casseroles and stews, volume (a 5- to 6-quart pot) is more important than the pot's dimensions. For baking, broiling, or short stovetop cooking, the pan dimensions determine the surface area reaching the heat and thus affect cooking times. A pan that's too shallow or too wide may cook food faster than the recipe intended, maybe burning it or drying it out. Always favor heavy-gauge and thick-bottomed pans because they are the most durable and cook evenly without burning.

Do you want meals that literally cook themselves while you're not even home? Simply switch cookware. Let your slow cooker do the cooking for you, and you won't have to hang around the kitchen.

To convert long-cooking stovetop and oven recipes for a slow cooker: Eliminate the multiple additions of ingredients, putting in everything except dairy ingredients at the same time. (Add the dairy products just before serving.) Liquids won't evaporate as much, so you may want to use slightly less of them.

To determine the timing: The low setting on a slow cooker cooks foods half as fast as the high, so you can coordinate your cooking with the rest of your schedule. If you want to have dinner ready when you get home from work, most recipes will cook to perfection all day on low. For recipes that cook in under an hour, allow 1^1/$_2$ hours on high in the slow cooker for every 15 minutes of cooking time using other methods. For longer-cooking recipes, allow 4 to 6 hours on high or 8 to 12 hours on low.

recipes

seafood

Thai Curry Catfish
with Jasmine Rice

❖

Cajun Catfish Sandwiches

❖

South-of-the-Border Fish
and Chips

❖

Stir-Fried Fish and Snow Peas
with Spicy Ginger Curry

❖

Spinach and Red Pepper
Flounder with Feta

❖

Halibut with Asian Vegetables
and Noodles

❖

Herb-Crusted Halibut with
Potatoes and Artichokes

❖

Seafood Tortilla Soup

❖

Orange Roughy with Green Beans
and Penne Pasta

❖

Parchment-Baked Orange Roughy
with Aromatic Vegetables

❖

Parchment-Baked Salmon
and Vegetables

❖

Salmon and Pasta
with Baby Spinach

❖

Salmon and Snow Peas
with Ginger-Lime Rice

❖

Salmon and Tortellini Salad
with Artichokes

❖

Salmon on Spring Greens
with Citrus-Soy Dressing

❖

Salmon-Topped Tomato-Zucchini
Risotto

❖

Salmon Niçoise

❖

Peppery Salmon
with Braised Vegetables

❖

Caribbean Salmon and Sweet
Potatoes with Papaya Salsa

❖

Italian-Style Salmon
and White Bean Salad

❖

Cioppino (Italian Fish Stew)

❖

Broiled Snapper
and Pear Bruschetta

❖

Poblano Snapper
with Black Beans

❖

Snapper in Mango Curry

❖

(continued on following page)

Tex-Mex Red Snapper
with Coriander

❖

Broiled Sole Mediterranean

❖

Sole Rolls with Lemon Sauce
and Couscous

❖

Caribbean Tilapia

❖

Grilled Tuna and Vegetables
with Balsamic Dressing

❖

Greek-Style Tuna Steaks
with Roasted Vegetables

❖

Grilled Tuna on Panzanella Salad

❖

Piled-High Tuna Salad
Sandwiches

❖

Tuna Linguini with Mushrooms

❖

Tuna Tostada with Jícama Slaw

❖

Tuna with Orzo
and Baby Spinach

❖

Creamy Crab
and Red Pepper Chowder

❖

Crab Cake Salad with
Orange-Tarragon Dressing

❖

Crab Quesadillas with
Avocado Salsa

❖

Angel Hair Pasta
with Mussels and Tomatoes

❖

Potato-Leek Soup
with Poached Oysters

❖

Seafood Jambalaya

❖

Inferno-Roasted Vegetable
and Scallop Casserole

❖

Shrimp-and-Pasta Caesar Salad

❖

Dilled Shrimp Salad

❖

Lemon-Tarragon Shrimp
Vermicelli

❖

Mediterranean-Style
Seafood Stir-Fry

❖

Seafood Paella

❖

Shrimp and Papaya
with Chutney

thai curry catfish
with jasmine rice

Lemongrass stalks impart their soothing flavor to catfish, vegetables, and rice.

> 2 stalks of lemongrass, 2 teaspoons grated lemon zest, or 1 teaspoon ground dried lemongrass
>
> 1 pound catfish fillets
>
> 1 teaspoon acceptable vegetable oil
>
> ^{1}/$_2$ medium onion, sliced
>
> 1 large carrot, thinly sliced
>
> 1 cup cauliflower florets
>
> 1^1/$_2$ cups fat-free, low-sodium chicken broth
>
> 1 cup frozen green peas
>
> 1 to 2 teaspoons Thai red curry paste
>
> ^{1}/$_2$ teaspoon coconut extract
>
> ^{3}/$_4$ cup uncooked jasmine rice
>
> ^{1}/$_4$ teaspoon salt

Trim about 6 inches from the slender, green end of the lemongrass stalks and discard. Remove the outer layer of leaves from the roots of the stalks. Cut the stalks in half lengthwise. Set aside. Rinse the fish and pat dry with paper towels. Cut the fish into ^{3}/$_4$-inch pieces.

Heat a large saucepan over medium-high heat. Pour the oil into the saucepan and swirl to coat the bottom. Cook the onion for 1 minute, stirring occasionally. Add the carrot and cauliflower. Cook for 2 to 3 minutes, or until the vegetables are tender-crisp, stirring occasionally.

Stir in the broth, peas, curry paste, and coconut extract. If using lemongrass stalks or dried lemongrass, add now. Bring to a simmer.

Stir in the catfish. Stir in the rice, salt, and lemon zest, if using. Bring to a simmer, stirring occasionally.

Reduce the heat and simmer, covered, for 20 minutes, or until the rice is tender. If using lemongrass stalks, remove the lid and let cool for 2 to 3 minutes. Remove the stalks before serving the dish. (Tongs work well for this.)

PER SERVING	
Calories 301	Cholesterol 66 mg
Total Fat 4.5 g	Sodium 305 mg
Saturated 1.0 g	Carbohydrates 39 g
Polyunsaturated 1.5 g	Fiber 4 g
Monounsaturated 1.5 g	Sugar 5 g
	Protein 24 g

cajun catfish sandwiches

Serve this Cajun-style sandwich with iced tea and a fresh fruit salad for a light summertime meal.

White of 1 large egg

1 teaspoon water

2 tablespoons all-purpose flour

2 tablespoons yellow cornmeal

2 teaspoons salt-free Cajun or Creole seasoning blend

1/2 teaspoon salt

4 catfish fillets (about 4 ounces each)

Vegetable oil spray (olive oil preferred)

2 teaspoons acceptable vegetable oil

2 cups packaged shredded coleslaw mix or 1 1/2 cups shredded cabbage and 1/2 cup shredded carrots

1 tablespoon fat-free or light Italian or honey Dijon salad dressing

1 tablespoon fat-free or low-fat mayonnaise dressing

1/4 teaspoon salt-free Cajun or Creole seasoning blend

4 whole-wheat hamburger buns

4 thick slices of a large tomato

In a shallow bowl, using a fork, beat the egg white and water.

On a large plate, combine the flour, cornmeal, 2 teaspoons seasoning blend, and salt. Set the plate next to the bowl, assembly-line fashion.

Rinse the fish and pat dry with paper towels. Dip each fillet in the egg mixture, then in the flour mixture, turning and patting to coat lightly. Shake off any excess flour mixture.

Heat a large nonstick skillet over medium heat. Lightly spray with vegetable oil spray. Pour the oil into the skillet and swirl to coat the bottom. Cook the fish for 3 to 4 minutes on each side, or until it flakes easily when tested with a fork.

Meanwhile, in a medium bowl, stir together the coleslaw mix, salad dressing, mayonnaise, and 1/4 teaspoon seasoning blend.

PER SERVING	
Calories 301	Cholesterol 66 mg
Total Fat 8.0 g	Sodium 655 mg
Saturated 1.5 g	Carbohydrates 33 g
Polyunsaturated 2.5 g	Fiber 5 g
Monounsaturated 3.0 g	Sugar 5 g
	Protein 25 g

Split and toast the hamburger buns.

To assemble, put each fillet on the bottom half of a bun. Spoon the coleslaw mixture over the fish. Add the tomato. Top with the remaining buns.

COOK'S TIP ON CAJUN OR CREOLE SEASONING BLEND

Salt-free versions of this zesty seasoning blend may be hard to find. If so, you can easily make your own. In a small bowl, combine 1 tablespoon each chili powder, ground cumin, garlic powder, onion powder, and paprika. You can store the seasoning tightly covered at room temperature for about 6 months.

south-of-the-border fish and chips

SERVES 4; 1²/₃ CUPS PER SERVING

A slow-cooked, onion-dense sauce turns tortilla chips soft and slightly chewy. Cod seasoned with lemon juice and chili powder tops the mixture before baking.

> **Vegetable oil spray**
>
> 2 large onions, cut into matchstick-size strips (about 4 cups)
>
> 1 pound cod fillets, rinsed and patted dry with paper towels
>
> 3 medium garlic cloves, minced
>
> 10 medium pimiento-stuffed green olives, minced
>
> 1/3 cup white wine vinegar
>
> 1/4 teaspoon pepper
>
> Juice of 1 medium lemon (about 2 tablespoons)
>
> 2 tablespoons sugar
>
> 1/4 teaspoon chili powder
>
> 2¹/4 cups hot water
>
> 4 ounces baked tortilla chips (about 5¹/2 cups)

Heat a deep 12-inch skillet over medium heat. Remove from the heat and lightly spray with vegetable oil spray (being careful not to spray near a gas flame). Cook the onions for 10 minutes, stirring frequently.

Meanwhile, cut the fish into 1-inch pieces.

Stir the garlic into the onions. Cook for 3 minutes, stirring frequently. Stir in the olives, vinegar, and pepper. Cook for 10 minutes, stirring occasionally.

Meanwhile, in a medium bowl, stir together the lemon juice, sugar, and chili powder. Add the fish and 1/2 cup of the onion mixture, gently stirring to coat.

Preheat the oven to 375°F.

Pour the water into the skillet with the remaining onion mixture. Bring to a boil over high heat. Remove from the heat. Gently fold in the tortilla chips. In the next 2 to 3 minutes, fold 4 or 5 times, until the chips absorb most of the liquid and become soft. Spread the mixture evenly in the skillet.

PER SERVING	
Calories 264	Cholesterol 49 mg
Total Fat 3.0 g	Sodium 476 mg
Saturated 0.5 g	Carbohydrates 36 g
Polyunsaturated 1.0 g	Fiber 4 g
Monounsaturated 1.0 g	Sugar 6 g
	Protein 24 g

Using a slotted spoon, remove the cod and onions from the marinade. Arrange them on the chips so the pieces of fish do not touch one another. Discard the marinade.

Bake for 10 minutes, or until the fish flakes easily when tested with a fork. Using a pancake turner, divide the mixture into quarters and transfer to plates. Serve immediately.

stir-fried fish and
snow peas with
spicy ginger curry

Wondering what to do with the catch of the day? Give it a quick toss with a spicy ginger curry marinade, then add tender pea pods and nutty brown rice.

1 tablespoon fresh lime juice

2 teaspoons olive oil

2 teaspoons minced peeled gingerroot

1 teaspoon curry powder

2 medium garlic cloves, minced

¹/₂ to 1 teaspoon crushed red pepper flakes

1 pound firm-fleshed fish fillets, such as cod, halibut, or salmon, cut into ³/₄-inch cubes, or 1 pound bay scallops

6 ounces fresh snow peas, trimmed

2 green onions (green and white parts), thinly sliced

1¹/₄ cups fat-free, low-sodium chicken broth

1 cup uncooked instant brown rice

¹/₄ teaspoon salt

In a large airtight bag, combine the lime juice, olive oil, ginger, curry powder, garlic, and red pepper flakes. Rinse the fish and pat dry with paper towels. Put the fish in the bag. Reseal; gently turn the bag over several times to coat the fish. Refrigerate for 15 minutes to 1 hour.

Heat a large, deep nonstick skillet or nonstick wok over medium-high heat. Cook the fish with the marinade for 3 to 4 minutes (scallops for 1 to 2 minutes), or until the fish is almost cooked through (scallops should be solid white and slightly firm), stirring constantly.

Stir in the snow peas and green onions. Cook for 1 minute, or until the snow peas are just tender-crisp, stirring constantly.

Stir in the broth, rice, and salt. Bring to a simmer, stirring once. Reduce the heat and simmer, covered, for 10 minutes, or until the rice is tender.

PER SERVING	
Calories 227	Cholesterol 49 mg
Total Fat 4.0 g	Sodium 234 mg
Saturated 0.5 g	Carbohydrates 22 g
Polyunsaturated 1.0 g	Fiber 3 g
Monounsaturated 2.0 g	Sugar 2 g
	Protein 24 g

spinach and red pepper
flounder with feta

This is an ideal shove-in-the-oven dinner that's on the table in 30 minutes flat.

4 flounder, tilapia, or other white fish fillets (about 4 ounces each)

10-ounce package frozen chopped spinach, thawed and squeezed dry

1 cup chopped roasted red bell peppers, rinsed and drained if bottled

1 teaspoon dried basil, crumbled

1/4 teaspoon salt

2 teaspoons olive oil (extra virgin preferred)

2 ounces feta cheese, crumbled

1 cup uncooked couscous

1/8 teaspoon salt

1 teaspoon olive oil

Preheat the oven to 350°F.

Rinse the fish and pat dry with paper towels. Place the fish fillets in a single layer in a 13 × 9 × 2-inch baking pan. Top each piece with a thin layer of spinach and a single layer of roasted peppers. Sprinkle with the basil and 1/4 teaspoon salt. Drizzle with 2 teaspoons oil. Sprinkle with the feta.

Bake for 10 to 12 minutes for flounder, 13 to 15 minutes for tilapia, or until the fish flakes easily when tested with a fork.

Meanwhile, prepare the couscous using the package directions. Using a fork, mix in 1/8 teaspoon salt and 1 teaspoon oil.

To serve, spoon the couscous onto plates. Place the fish on the couscous.

COOK'S TIP ON THAWING SPINACH

To thaw a box of spinach quickly, remove the outer wrapper. Put the box of spinach on a microwaveable plate. Microwave on 100 percent power (high) for 3 1/2 to 4 minutes.

PER SERVING	
Calories 383	Cholesterol 61 mg
Total Fat 8.0 g	Sodium 553 mg
Saturated 2.5 g	Carbohydrates 46 g
Polyunsaturated 1.0 g	Fiber 4 g
Monounsaturated 3.0 g	Sugar 2 g
	Protein 31 g

halibut with asian
vegetables and noodles

SERVES 4; 1 FISH FILLET AND ABOUT 1¹/₃ CUPS VEGETABLE
AND NOODLE MIXTURE PER SERVING

This brothy, quick-cooking noodle dish will wow the whole family.

1 tablespoon all-purpose flour

2 teaspoons five-spice powder or ground ginger

4 skinless halibut fillets (about 4 ounces each)

2 teaspoons toasted sesame oil

Vegetable oil spray

2 cups thinly sliced bok choy (stems and leaves)

2 cups fresh snow peas, trimmed, halved diagonally if large

1 cup matchstick-size or thinly sliced carrots

2 14.5-ounce cans fat-free, low-sodium chicken broth

¹/₄ teaspoon crushed red pepper flakes (optional)

5 ounces Chinese curly noodles (chukka soba) or dried thin pasta

¹/₄ cup light teriyaki sauce

Combine the flour and five-spice powder in a plastic or paper bag.

Rinse the fish and pat dry with paper towels. Put one fish fillet in the bag and shake to coat lightly. Repeat with the remaining fillets.

Heat a large, deep skillet or Dutch oven over medium heat. Pour the oil into the skillet and swirl to coat the bottom. Cook the halibut for 3 minutes on each side, or until the fish flakes easily when tested with a fork. Using a large spatula, transfer the fish to a plate. Set aside.

Lightly spray the same skillet with vegetable oil spray. Cook the bok choy, pea pods, and carrots for 1 minute, stirring constantly.

Stir in the broth and red pepper flakes. Bring to a simmer.

Break the noodles into chunks. Stir the noodles and teriyaki sauce into the broth mixture. Reduce the heat and simmer, covered, for 2 minutes. Stir well. Simmer for 4 minutes, or until the vegetables and noodles are tender.

Return the fish to the skillet. Turn off the heat. Let stand, covered, for 2 minutes, or until the fish is heated through.

PER SERVING	
Calories 324	Cholesterol 36 mg
Total Fat 6.0 g	Sodium 406 mg
Saturated 1.0 g	Carbohydrates 38 g
Polyunsaturated 2.0 g	Fiber 7 g
Monounsaturated 2.0 g	Sugar 5 g
	Protein 31 g

herb-crusted halibut with potatoes and artichokes

SERVES 4; 1 FILLET, 1 CUP POTATOES, AND $^{1}/_{2}$ CUP ARTICHOKES PER SERVING

Mayonnaise infused with fresh herbs makes a decadently rich tasting, creamy coating for meaty-textured halibut or salmon.

Vegetable oil spray

3 large red potatoes (about 1 pound), unpeeled, cut into $^{1}/_{8}$-inch slices

$^{1}/_{4}$ teaspoon pepper

$^{1}/_{4}$ cup fat-free or reduced-fat mayonnaise dressing

2 tablespoons chopped fresh rosemary or 2 teaspoons dried, crushed

2 tablespoons chopped fresh thyme or 2 teaspoons dried, crumbled

1 tablespoon chopped fresh oregano or 1 teaspoon dried, crumbled

4 halibut or salmon fillets (about 4 ounces each)

14.5-ounce can artichoke quarters, rinsed and drained

1 cup halved cherry tomatoes

1 tablespoon fresh lemon juice

2 teaspoons olive oil

Preheat the oven to 400°F.

Lightly spray a rimmed baking sheet with vegetable oil spray. Arrange the potatoes in a single layer. Lightly spray with vegetable oil spray. Sprinkle with the pepper.

Bake for 18 to 20 minutes (no stirring needed), or until the potatoes are tender and lightly browned.

Meanwhile, in a small bowl, stir together the mayonnaise, rosemary, thyme, and oregano. Cover and refrigerate while the potatoes bake or for up to 8 hours.

Rinse the fish and pat dry with paper towels. Arrange the fish fillets about 2 inches apart on the cooked potatoes. Scatter the artichokes and tomatoes over the potatoes. Drizzle the lemon juice and oil over the vegetables. Lightly spray the tops of the vegetables with vegetable oil spray. Spoon the mayonnaise mixture over the tops and sides of the fillets.

Bake for 12 to 15 minutes, or until the fish flakes easily when tested with a fork and the vegetables are warmed through.

PER SERVING	
Calories 257	Cholesterol 36 mg
Total Fat 5.0 g	Sodium 355 mg
Saturated 0.5 g	Carbohydrates 25 g
Polyunsaturated 1.0 g	Fiber 3 g
Monounsaturated 2.5 g	Sugar 6 g
	Protein 28 g

seafood tortilla soup

This Mexican soup showcases fresh halibut in a rich-tasting, spicy broth. The sweet potato isn't traditional, but because it makes the soup prettier and adds beta-carotene, maybe it should be!

4 6-inch corn tortillas

1 tablespoon plus 2 teaspoons acceptable vegetable oil or olive oil, divided use

1 large onion, chopped

3 medium garlic cloves, minced

14.5-ounce can fat-free, low-sodium chicken broth

14.5-ounce can no-salt-added diced tomatoes, undrained

1 large sweet potato, peeled, cut into $1/2$-inch pieces (about $1^1/2$ cups)

1 tablespoon pureed or minced canned chipotle pepper in adobo sauce

1 large or 2 small zucchini

1 pound boneless, skinless halibut or red snapper

$1/4$ teaspoon salt

$1/4$ cup snipped fresh cilantro

1 lime, quartered

Cut the tortillas in half; stack the halves. Cut crosswise into $1/8$- to $1/4$-inch strips.

Heat a large saucepan over medium heat. Pour 1 tablespoon oil into the saucepan and swirl to coat the bottom. Heat until the oil is hot but not smoking. Cook the tortillas until golden brown and crisp, 4 to 5 minutes, stirring occasionally. Transfer to paper towels. Set aside.

Pour the remaining 2 teaspoons oil into the saucepan. Cook the onions for 5 minutes, stirring occasionally.

Add the garlic. Cook for 30 seconds, stirring occasionally.

Stir in the broth, tomatoes, sweet potato, and chipotle pepper. Bring to a boil. Reduce the heat and simmer for 10 minutes.

Meanwhile, cut the zucchini into $1/2$-inch pieces. Rinse the fish and pat dry with paper towels. Cut the fish into 1-inch pieces.

PER SERVING	
Calories 318	Cholesterol 36 mg
Total Fat 9.0 g	Sodium 369 mg
Saturated 1.0 g	Carbohydrates 32 g
Polyunsaturated 3.0 g	Fiber 6 g
Monounsaturated 4.5 g	Sugar 10 g
	Protein 28 g

When the broth mixture has simmered, stir in the zucchini and salt. Simmer for 5 minutes.

Gently stir in the halibut to avoid breaking it up. Simmer for 5 minutes, or until the fish flakes easily when tested with a fork and the vegetables are tender, gently stirring once.

To serve, ladle into bowls. Top with the cilantro and tortilla strips. Serve with the lime wedges.

COOK'S TIP ON CHIPOTLE PEPPERS

Chipotle peppers canned in adobo sauce are in the ethnic section of the supermarket. You can refrigerate the leftovers in an airtight nonmetal container for several months or freeze them for longer storage.

orange roughy with green beans and penne pasta

SERVES 4; 1³/4 CUPS PER SERVING

SERVES 4; 1³/₄ CUPS PER SERVING

While penne pasta cooks in a carrot and ginger-flavored broth, layers of mild orange roughy and green beans steam in the same pan.

1 cup fat-free, low-sodium chicken broth

1 cup uncooked penne pasta (about 4 ounces)

4 orange roughy fillets or other mild fish fillets (about 4 ounces each)

1 cup carrot juice

1 tablespoon minced peeled gingerroot

¹/₂ teaspoon salt-free all-purpose seasoning blend

8 ounces fresh or frozen green beans, trimmed if fresh (about 2 cups)

In a large, deep nonstick skillet, bring the chicken broth and pasta to a simmer over medium-high heat, stirring occasionally. Reduce the heat and simmer, covered, for 8 to 10 minutes, or until the pasta is partially cooked and somewhat tender.

Meanwhile, rinse the fish and pat dry with paper towels.

Stir the carrot juice, ginger, and seasoning blend into the partially cooked pasta. Place the green beans in an even layer on the pasta. Lay the fish fillets over the green beans. Increase the heat to medium-high and bring to a simmer. Reduce the heat and simmer, covered, for 15 to 20 minutes, or until the pasta is tender and the fish flakes easily when tested with a fork.

PER SERVING	
Calories 216	Cholesterol 23 mg
Total Fat 1.5 g	Sodium 119 mg
Saturated 0 g	Carbohydrates 28 g
Polyunsaturated 0 g	Fiber 3 g
Monounsaturated 0.5 g	Sugar 2 g
	Protein 22 g

parchment-baked
orange roughy with aromatic vegetables

SERVES 4; 1³/₄ CUPS PER SERVING

Tempting aromas waft from the oven while this meal-in-a-package bakes.

> 2 cups frozen nonfat shredded hash brown potatoes
>
> 4 orange roughy fillets or other mild fish fillets (about 4 ounces each)
>
> 4 medium ribs of celery, cut into matchstick-size pieces (about 2 cups)
>
> 2 medium leeks (white part only) or 1 medium onion, thinly sliced
>
> 4 medium garlic cloves, thinly sliced
>
> 2 teaspoons salt-free lemon-dill herb seasoning blend

Preheat the oven to 425°F (450°F if using aluminum foil instead of parchment paper).

Let the hash browns stand at room temperature for 5 to 10 minutes to partially thaw. Rinse the fish and pat dry with paper towels.

Meanwhile, to make the packets, measure 4 sheets of 15-inch-square parchment paper or aluminum foil. Fold each in half, creasing the fold with your fingers. Open one sheet and lay it on a rimmed baking sheet. On one half of the sheet, place one fourth each of the celery, leeks, and garlic. Place a fish fillet on top. Sprinkle the fish with ¹/₂ teaspoon seasoning. Top with ¹/₂ cup potatoes. Fold the other half of the sheet over the mixture; fold or crimp the edges to seal completely. Repeat with the remaining ingredients. Space the packages evenly on the baking sheet.

Bake for 18 to 20 minutes, or until the vegetables are tender and the fish flakes easily when tested with a fork. Be careful to avoid a steam burn when you open the packages.

To serve, carefully cut an *X* on top of each packet.

PER SERVING	
Calories 199	Cholesterol 23 mg
Total Fat 1.0 g	Sodium 139 mg
Saturated 0 g	Carbohydrates 28 g
Polyunsaturated 0 g	Fiber 3 g
Monounsaturated 0.5 g	Sugar 2 g
	Protein 20 g

parchment-baked salmon and vegetables

SERVES 4; 3 OUNCES SALMON, $1/2$ CUP CORN,
AND $1^{1}/2$ CUPS BROCCOLI-CAULIFLOWER MIX PER SERVING

Who says quick and easy can't be a little fancy? This salmon dinner looks and tastes as if you fussed in the kitchen all day.

1 small fresh jalapeño pepper, ribs and seeds discarded, coarsely chopped

2 tablespoons all-fruit orange marmalade

Juice of 1 medium lime

$1/4$ teaspoon salt

4 skinless salmon fillets (about 4 ounces each), rinsed and patted dry with paper towels

1 medium tomato, diced

$1/2$ teaspoon ground cumin

$1/8$ teaspoon pepper

3 cups broccoli florets, cut into $3/4$-inch pieces

3 cups cauliflower florets, cut into $3/4$-inch pieces

4 medium ears of corn, cobs discarded, or 2 cups frozen corn

In a food processor (small preferred) or blender, puree the jalapeño, marmalade, lime juice, and salt. Spread on top of the salmon fillets. Do not clean the processor or blender.

Preheat the oven to 400°F. Place one rack in the top third of the oven, one in the bottom third.

In the processor or blender, puree the tomato, cumin, and pepper. Pour into a medium bowl. Stir in the broccoli, cauliflower, and corn.

Cut four sheets of cooking parchment into ovals 20 inches long and 12 to 14 inches wide. With the long sides at the top and bottom, fold each sheet in half, from left to right. Unfold the sheets. For each packet, place a salmon fillet about $1^{1}/2$ inches to the right of the crease. Spoon one fourth of the vegetables around the top, bottom, and right side of the salmon. Fold the left half of the parchment over the fish and vegetables. Seal the parchment by folding both layers toward

PER SERVING	Cholesterol 65 mg
Calories 286	Sodium 282 mg
Total Fat 6.0 g	Carbohydrates 32 g
Saturated 1.0 g	Fiber 7 g
Polyunsaturated 2.5 g	Sugar 13 g
Monounsaturated 1.5 g	Protein 31 g

the food, making pleatlike folds about every 2 inches. Be sure the parchment is securely folded together. Place 2 parchment packets on each of two baking sheets.

Bake for 8 minutes. Switch the placement of the baking sheets so the one on top is on the bottom, and vice versa. Bake for 8 minutes. Opening the parchment carefully to avoid steam burns, check for doneness. The salmon should flake easily with a fork and the vegetables should be tender. If not done, reseal the parchment and bake for 1 to 2 minutes.

To serve, slide each packet onto a plate. Allow each person to carefully open his or her own.

COOK'S TIP ON PARCHMENT PAPER

Check the baking section or plastic wrap/aluminum foil section of the grocery store when looking for parchment paper, also called *cooking parchment.* In addition to sealing in moisture and flavor, as in this dish, it can be used to line cookie sheets and baking pans for easy-release baked goods that aren't burned on the bottom.

COOK'S TIP ON HANDLING HOT CHILE PEPPERS

Hot chile peppers contain oils that can burn your skin, lips, and eyes. Wear rubber or plastic disposable gloves while handling peppers, or wash your hands thoroughly with warm, soapy water immediately after handling them. Rinsing the peppers under water makes removing the seeds and ribs (the hottest parts) easier. Examples of hot peppers are Anaheim, ancho, cascabel, cayenne, cherry, chipotle, habanero, Hungarian wax, jalapeño, poblano, Scotch bonnet, serrano, and Thai. A rule of thumb is the smaller the pepper, the hotter it is.

salmon and pasta
with baby spinach

A lemony dill-caper sauce is the crowning glory of this delightful dish featuring canned salmon.

   2 teaspoons olive oil

   2 medium carrots, thinly sliced

   2 medium ribs of celery, chopped

   4 medium leeks (white part only), thinly sliced, or 1 large onion, sliced

   2 medium garlic cloves, minced

1¹/₂ cups fat-free, low-sodium chicken broth

7.5-ounce can salmon, drained, bones discarded if desired and skin discarded

   2 tablespoons capers, rinsed and drained

¹/₂ teaspoon dried dillweed, crumbled

¹/₄ teaspoon pepper

   4 ounces dried angel hair pasta

   8 cups fresh baby spinach

   1 teaspoon grated lemon zest

   1 tablespoon fresh lemon juice

Heat a large, deep nonstick skillet over medium heat. Pour the oil into the skillet and swirl to coat the bottom. Cook the carrots, celery, leeks, and garlic for 3 to 4 minutes, or until tender, stirring occasionally.

Stir in the broth, salmon, capers, dillweed, and pepper. Bring to a simmer over medium-high heat, stirring occasionally.

Stir in the pasta. Place the spinach leaves on top, pressing them slightly into the mixture (they will steam while the pasta cooks). Reduce the heat and simmer, covered, for 5 to 6 minutes, or until the pasta is tender.

Stir in the lemon zest and lemon juice; cook, uncovered, for 1 to 2 minutes, or until the flavors mingle, stirring occasionally to incorporate the spinach into the pasta.

PER SERVING	
Calories 259	Cholesterol 38 mg
Total Fat 5.0 g	Sodium 437 mg
Saturated 0.5 g	Carbohydrates 35 g
Polyunsaturated 0.5 g	Fiber 5 g
Monounsaturated 1.5 g	Sugar 6 g
	Protein 21 g

salmon and snow peas
with ginger-lime rice

SERVES 4; 3 OUNCES SALMON, 3/4 CUP SNOW PEAS,
AND 1/2 CUP RICE PER SERVING

Salmon glazed with honey and soy sauce cooks with gingered jasmine rice. Delicate snow peas are piled high on the salmon near the end of the cooking time so they stay crisp.

2^1/2 cups water

1 cup uncooked jasmine rice

1^1/2 tablespoons crystallized ginger, minced

Zest of 1 medium lime

1 tablespoon honey

1 teaspoon low-salt soy sauce

1-pound salmon fillet with skin, rinsed and patted dry with paper towels

8 ounces fresh snow peas, trimmed

In a Dutch oven, bring the water to a boil over high heat. Stir in the rice, ginger, and lime zest. Return to a boil. Reduce the heat and simmer, covered, for 5 minutes.

Meanwhile, in a small bowl, stir together the honey and soy sauce. Spread on the top and sides of the salmon.

After 5 minutes, stir the rice. Place the salmon with the skin side down on the rice. Cook, covered, for 8 minutes.

Place the peas on the salmon. Cook, covered, for 8 minutes, or until the salmon flakes easily when tested with a fork and the peas are slightly crunchy.

PER SERVING	
Calories 364	Cholesterol 61 mg
Total Fat 4.0 g	Sodium 117 mg
Saturated 0.5 g	Carbohydrates 51 g
Polyunsaturated 1.5 g	Fiber 3 g
Monounsaturated 1.0 g	Sugar 9 g
	Protein 28 g

salmon and tortellini salad with artichokes

A winning trio of salmon, tortellini, and artichoke hearts combines with fresh peppercorn-dill dressing seasoned with herbs and just a hint of lemon.

9-ounce package fresh cheese-filled spinach tortellini

2 tablespoons fat-free or reduced-fat mayonnaise dressing

2 tablespoons nonfat or light sour cream

1 tablespoon snipped fresh dillweed or 1 teaspoon dried, crumbled

1 tablespoon snipped fresh chives or 1 teaspoon dried

1 teaspoon grated lemon zest

¹/₂ teaspoon salt-free garlic and onion seasoning blend

¹/₄ teaspoon pepper

7.1-ounce package flaked boneless, skinless salmon, lightly rinsed and drained, or 1 cup flaked cooked salmon

2 9-ounce packages frozen artichoke hearts, thawed, drained, and coarsely chopped

¹/₂ small red onion, chopped

1 tablespoon capers, rinsed and drained

Prepare the tortellini using the package directions, omitting the salt and oil. Drain in a colander; let cool for at least 5 minutes, so the pasta won't be hot enough to curdle the sour cream in the dressing.

In a medium bowl, whisk together the mayonnaise, sour cream, dill, chives, lemon zest, seasoning blend, and pepper.

Gently stir in the remaining ingredients, including the tortellini. Cover and refrigerate for at least 30 minutes before serving.

COOK'S TIP ON SALMON

Look for new packaging of an old favorite. Vacuum-packed bags of flaked salmon save time because the skin, bones, and liquid have been removed for you. To help remove some of the sodium, put the salmon in a colander and gently rinse it under cold water.

PER SERVING	
Calories 278	Cholesterol 34 mg
Total Fat 6.0 g	Sodium 419 mg
Saturated 3.5 g	Carbohydrates 36 g
Polyunsaturated 0 g	Fiber 11 g
Monounsaturated 0 g	Sugar 4 g
	Protein 19 g

salmon on spring greens
with citrus-soy dressing

SERVES 4; 2 CUPS SALAD, $^1/_2$ CUP RICE,
AND $2^1/_2$ TABLESPOONS DRESSING PER SERVING

Tired of tuna? Switch to salmon for a refreshing salad full of omega-3s. The secret to great flavor and texture is to keep the salmon in chunks, so handle it gently.

6 cups mixed salad greens (spring mixture preferred)

2 cups cooked rice, room temperature

2 6-ounce cans salmon, drained, bones discarded if desired and skin discarded

4 thin slices red onion

1 medium red bell pepper, thinly sliced

4 medium oranges, peeled and sectioned

2 tablespoons snipped fresh cilantro

CITRUS-SOY DRESSING

$^1/_4$ cup low-salt soy sauce

3 tablespoons sugar

3 tablespoons cider vinegar

$1^1/_2$ tablespoons sesame oil

1 teaspoon grated orange zest

$^1/_2$ to $^3/_4$ teaspoon crushed red pepper flakes

Place $1^1/_2$ cups salad greens on each plate. Spoon $^1/_2$ cup rice in the center of each bed of salad greens. Arrange the salmon and onions on each serving. Place the bell pepper and oranges around the edges of the salad. Sprinkle with cilantro.

For the dressing, combine the ingredients in a small jar with a tight-fitting lid. Cover and shake vigorously until completely blended. Pour the dressing over all.

PER SERVING	
Calories 356	Cholesterol 61 mg
Total Fat 8.5 g	Sodium 747 mg
Saturated 1.0 g	Carbohydrates 46 g
Polyunsaturated 3.5 g	Fiber 4 g
Monounsaturated 3.0 g	Sugar 17 g
	Protein 27 g

salmon-topped
tomato-zucchini risotto

SERVES 6; 3 OUNCES SALMON AND 1 CUP RISOTTO-VEGETABLE MIXTURE PER SERVING

This robust risotto is the cure for that I-need-Italian-food craving. Unlike most other risottos, it needs almost no stirring.

Vegetable oil spray
1 teaspoon olive oil
1 small onion, minced
1 large carrot, grated
4 medium garlic cloves, thinly sliced
2 large zucchini, minced
2 14.5-ounce cans no-salt-added diced tomatoes, undrained
2¹/₂ cups hot water
1 tablespoon balsamic vinegar
¹/₂ teaspoon salt
¹/₄ teaspoon pepper
6 skinless salmon fillets (about 4 ounces each)
1¹/₃ cups uncooked arborio rice

Heat a Dutch oven over medium heat. Remove from the heat and lightly spray with vegetable oil spray (being careful not to spray near a gas flame). Pour in the oil. Swirl to coat the bottom. Cook the onion and carrot for 5 minutes, stirring occasionally.

Stir in the garlic. Cook for 1 minute, stirring constantly.

Stir in the zucchini, undrained tomatoes, water, vinegar, salt, and pepper. Increase the heat to high and bring to a boil. Reduce the heat and simmer for 10 minutes, stirring occasionally.

Meanwhile, rinse the salmon and pat dry with paper towels. Place the salmon in the sauce. Press gently to immerse the salmon. Reducing the heat if necessary, cook at a low simmer for 8 minutes. Using a spatula, transfer the salmon to a plate. Cover with aluminum foil, then cover the foil with a dish towel folded in half. The salmon will continue to cook.

PER SERVING	
Calories 385	Cholesterol 59 mg
Total Fat 5.0 g	Sodium 336 mg
Saturated 1.0 g	Carbohydrates 54 g
Polyunsaturated 1.5 g	Fiber 5 g
Monounsaturated 1.5 g	Sugar 9 g
	Protein 29 g

Stir the rice into the Dutch oven. Increase the heat to high and bring to a boil. Reduce the heat and simmer, covered, for 10 minutes. Stir the rice. Simmer, covered, for 5 minutes, or until the rice is tender but not mushy. Continue cooking, covered, for 3 to 4 minutes if the rice is not tender. Increase the heat to medium. Cook until all the liquid is absorbed, stirring constantly.

To serve, spoon the risotto onto plates and top with the salmon.

COOK'S TIP ON POACHING FISH

When poaching fish, use a liquid that is steaming hot but not bubbling. The delicate meat will break apart if the poaching liquid is boiling or at a rapid simmer.

COOK'S TIP ON GARLIC

Some grocery stores carry fresh peeled garlic cloves in the refrigerated area of the produce section. If you prefer to peel them yourself, you may want to buy a garlic peeler, which is a small rubber tube. Put the garlic clove inside the tube and, pressing lightly, roll the tube on a flat surface. The peel loosens from the clove and is easy to remove.

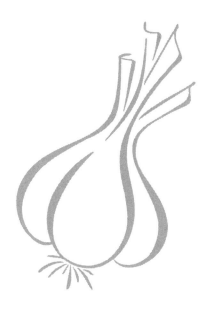

salmon niçoise

SERVES 4; 2 CUPS PER SERVING

Calcium-rich canned salmon takes the place of tuna in this version of the classic French salad.

 1 pound small (1-inch) red potatoes, such as red creamers, halved, or larger red potatoes, cut into chunks

 1 tablespoon water

 1/2 pound fresh green beans, trimmed, cut into 1 1/2-inch pieces

 1/3 cup light Italian or fat-free or light honey Dijon salad dressing

 1 tablespoon chopped fresh tarragon or 1 teaspoon dried, crumbled

 6 cups packed mixed salad greens or mesclun

 2 cups cherry tomatoes or yellow pear-shaped, or teardrop, tomatoes

 7.5-ounce can sockeye salmon, drained, bones and skin discarded, broken into chunks

 16 niçoise or kalamata olives

 1/8 teaspoon pepper, or to taste (optional)

Put the potatoes in a large microwave-safe bowl or casserole dish. Sprinkle with the water. Cover the bowl loosely with wax paper. Microwave on 100 percent power (high) for 5 minutes.

Stir in the green beans. Cover with wax paper. Microwave on 100 percent power for 3 to 5 minutes, or until the beans are tender-crisp and the potatoes are tender. Transfer the vegetables to a colander. Rinse with cold water to stop the cooking and cool the vegetables. Let stand in the colander to cool to room temperature. Drain well. Spread on paper towels and pat dry.

In a large bowl, combine the dressing and tarragon. Add the salad greens, tomatoes, potatoes, and green beans. Toss to coat.

To serve, arrange the salad on plates. Top with the salmon and olives. Sprinkle with the pepper.

PER SERVING	Cholesterol 23 mg
Calories 282	Sodium 742 mg
Total Fat 10.5 g	Carbohydrates 35 g
Saturated 2.0 g	Fiber 7 g
Polyunsaturated 1.5 g	Sugar 9 g
Monounsaturated 5.0 g	Protein 17 g

peppery salmon
with braised vegetables

Salmon fillets develop a velvety texture in this one-skillet meal, which is full of color and flavor.

14.5-ounce can low-sodium vegetable broth
1 pound red potatoes, cut into 1-inch pieces
1 large green or red bell pepper, cut into 1-inch pieces
1 cup baby carrots
3/4 teaspoon garlic powder
3/4 teaspoon paprika
3/4 teaspoon dried thyme, crumbled
1/4 teaspoon salt
1/4 teaspoon black pepper
1/8 to 1/4 teaspoon cayenne
4 skinless salmon fillets (center cut preferred) (about 4 ounces each)
1/4 cup snipped fresh parsley (optional)

In a large, deep skillet, stir together the vegetable broth, potatoes, bell pepper, and carrots. Cover; bring to a boil over high heat. Reduce the heat and simmer, covered, for 10 minutes.

Meanwhile, in a small bowl, stir together the garlic powder, paprika, thyme, salt, black pepper, and cayenne.

Stir the vegetables. Top with the salmon. Sprinkle the garlic powder mixture over the salmon and vegetables. Simmer, covered, for 8 to 10 minutes, or until the salmon flakes easily when tested with a fork and the vegetables are tender.

To serve, transfer to bowls. Sprinkle with the parsley.

PER SERVING	
Calories 244	Cholesterol 59 mg
Total Fat 4.5 g	Sodium 256 mg
Saturated 0.5 g	Carbohydrates 27 g
Polyunsaturated 1.5 g	Fiber 4 g
Monounsaturated 1.0 g	Sugar 5 g
	Protein 27 g

caribbean salmon
and sweet potatoes
with papaya salsa

SERVES 4; 3 OUNCES SALMON, 4 WEDGES SWEET POTATO,
AND $^1/_2$ CUP SALSA PER SERVING

Jerk seasoning is frequently used on poultry or pork but also can flavor just about anything from tofu to goat. Here it adds its sweet and hotly spicy gusto to baked salmon and sweet potatoes.

Vegetable oil spray

2 large sweet potatoes (unpeeled) (about $1^1/_4$ pounds), each cut lengthwise into 8 wedges

2 teaspoons Caribbean or Jamaican jerk seasoning blend

1 large papaya or mango, peeled, seeded, and diced, or 2 cups diced bottled papaya or mango

$^1/_4$ cup finely chopped red onion

$^1/_4$ cup snipped fresh cilantro

1 tablespoon minced fresh jalapeño pepper, ribs and seeds discarded if desired

1 tablespoon plain rice vinegar or white wine vinegar

2 teaspoons acceptable vegetable oil

4 salmon fillets with skin (4 to 5 ounces each), about $^1/_2$ inch thick

2 teaspoons Caribbean or Jamaican jerk seasoning blend

$1^1/_2$ tablespoons honey mustard

Preheat the oven to 400°F.

Lightly spray a large roasting pan or heavy rimmed baking sheet with vegetable oil spray. Arrange the sweet potato wedges with cut sides down in a single layer in the pan. Lightly spray with vegetable oil spray. Sprinkle with 2 teaspoons jerk seasoning.

Bake for 20 minutes.

Meanwhile, in a medium bowl, stir together the papaya, onion, cilantro, jalapeño, vinegar, and oil. Set aside.

PER SERVING	
Calories 365	Cholesterol 66 mg
Total Fat 7.0 g	Sodium 424 mg
Saturated 1.0 g	Carbohydrates 49 g
Polyunsaturated 2.5 g	Fiber 6 g
Monounsaturated 2.5 g	Sugar 14 g
	Protein 28 g

Rinse the salmon and pat dry with paper towels.

Using a large spatula, turn the potatoes over. Arrange them around the edges of the pan. Place the salmon with the skin side down in the center. Sprinkle 2 teaspoons jerk seasoning over the salmon. Spread the mustard over the salmon.

Bake for 10 minutes, or until the salmon flakes easily when tested with a fork and the potatoes are tender.

To serve, transfer the salmon and potatoes to plates. Spoon the papaya salsa over both.

COOK'S TIP ON PAPAYA OR MANGO SLICES

Look for jars of papaya or mango slices in the refrigerated produce section of the supermarket.

COOK'S TIP ON FISH FILLETS

Fish fillets are often sold with the skin on. Cooking with the skin side down helps hold the fish together.

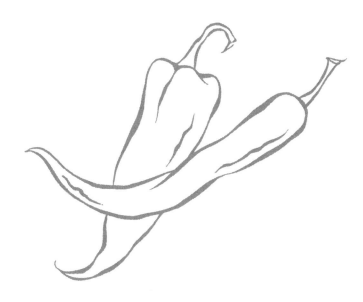

italian-style salmon and white bean salad

This main-dish salad is attractive, tastes good, and takes only minutes to prepare. It's a winner from every perspective.

6 cups packed torn romaine (about ³/4 large head or 10-ounce package) or mixed salad greens

15- to 16-ounce can reduced-sodium Great Northern or cannellini beans, rinsed and drained

¹/3 cup fat-free or light Italian or Caesar salad dressing

7.5-ounce can sockeye or pink salmon, drained, bones discarded if desired and skin discarded

4 Italian plum tomatoes, quartered

¹/4 cup garlic- or herb-seasoned croutons

Pepper to taste

In a large bowl, toss the romaine, beans, and dressing.

Break the salmon into chunks. Add to the romaine mixture. Toss lightly.

Arrange the salad on plates. Place the tomatoes around the salad. Top with croutons. Sprinkle with pepper.

COOK'S TIP ON CANNED SALMON

Sockeye salmon is more flavorful and contains more omega-3 fatty acids than pink salmon. It does, however, cost more.

PER SERVING	
Calories 181	Cholesterol 36 mg
Total Fat 2.5 g	Sodium 587 mg
Saturated 0 g	Carbohydrates 21 g
Polyunsaturated 0 g	Fiber 6 g
Monounsaturated 0.5 g	Sugar 5 g
	Protein 20 g

cioppino (italian fish stew)

Saffron adds both color and an exotic flavor to this fish stew. Feel free to substitute other seafood depending on availability and taste preferences.

     2 teaspoons olive oil
     3 medium garlic cloves, minced
14.5-ounce can fat-free, low-sodium chicken broth
     1 cup dried ditalini or small shell pasta
     2 14.5-ounce cans no-salt-added stewed tomatoes, undrained
     $1/4$ cup dry white wine (regular or nonalcoholic) or water
     $1/2$ teaspoon saffron threads (optional)
     1 teaspoon dried basil, crumbled
     1 teaspoon dried thyme, crumbled
     1 teaspoon red hot-pepper sauce or $1/2$ teaspoon crushed red pepper flakes
     1 pound littleneck clams or mussels, scrubbed, or $1/2$ pound of each
    12 ounces halibut or red snapper fillets, cut into $1^1/2$-inch pieces
     $1/4$ cup chopped fresh basil or snipped Italian, or flat-leaf, parsley

Heat a large, deep skillet over medium heat. Pour the oil into the skillet and swirl to coat the bottom. Cook the garlic for 2 minutes, stirring occasionally.

Stir in the broth and pasta. Bring to a simmer. Reduce the heat and simmer for 5 minutes.

Stir in the undrained tomatoes, wine, saffron, dried basil, thyme, and hot-pepper sauce. Increase the heat to high and bring to a simmer.

Stir in the clams or mussels. Lower the heat and simmer for 3 minutes.

Stir in the fish fillets. Simmer for 5 to 6 minutes, or until the fish flakes easily when tested with a fork, the mussels or clams have opened, and the pasta is tender. Discard any clams or mussels that did not open.

Ladle into soup bowls. Sprinkle with the fresh basil.

COOK'S TIP

Scrub clam or mussel shells under cold running water. Pull off any beards from the mussels. (Farm-raised mussels do not have beards.)

PER SERVING	
Calories 321	Cholesterol 39 mg
Total Fat 5.0 g	Sodium 183 mg
Saturated 0.5 g	Carbohydrates 38 g
Polyunsaturated 1.0 g	Fiber 4 g
Monounsaturated 2.5 g	Sugar 13 g
	Protein 28 g

broiled snapper
and pear bruschetta

SERVES 4; SCANT 1 1/2 CUPS PER SERVING

Bruschetta is Italian for "toast," and it's not just for breakfast anymore. Combined with juicy broiled pears and delicately seasoned red snapper fillets, it's ready for prime time.

1 pound skinless red snapper fillets

4 large slices sourdough bread (about 2 ounces each and about 3/4 inch thick)

4 medium pears, thinly sliced

Juice of 1 small orange

1 tablespoon olive oil (extra virgin preferred)

2 teaspoons chopped fresh rosemary

1/8 teaspoon salt

1/8 teaspoon pepper

1 large red bell pepper, finely diced

2 tablespoons sliced almonds

Preheat the broiler.

Rinse the fish and pat dry with paper towels. Cut the fish into 1/2-inch pieces. Set aside.

Put the bread on a baking sheet. Broil about 6 inches from the heat for 4 to 6 minutes, or until golden on both sides, turning over once halfway through the broiling time.

Remove the bread from the oven. Cover each slice with a layer of overlapping pears. Be sure the pears overhang the bread by 3/8 to 1/2 inch, or the sides of the bread will burn.

Broil for 5 to 7 minutes, or until the pears begin to bubble and brown.

Meanwhile, in a medium bowl, stir together the orange juice, oil, rosemary, salt, and pepper. Stir in the fish, bell pepper, and almonds. Spoon over the browned pears.

Broil for 4 to 6 minutes, or until the fish flakes easily when tested with a fork.

PER SERVING	
Calories 430	Cholesterol 40 mg
Total Fat 9.0 g	Sodium 468 mg
Saturated 1.5 g	Carbohydrates 60 g
Polyunsaturated 1.5 g	Fiber 7 g
Monounsaturated 4.5 g	Sugar 22 g
	Protein 29 g

poblano snapper
with black beans

SERVES 4; 3 OUNCES FISH AND 1 CUP BEAN AND VEGETABLE MIXTURE PER SERVING

The salsa-style topping of roasted peppers and beans in this recipe is loaded with flavors that ooze down to the tender fish below.

Vegetable oil spray

4 red snapper fillets with skin (about 6 ounces each)

$1/2$ teaspoon dried oregano, crumbled

$1/4$ teaspoon salt

Paprika to taste

2 medium poblano or green bell peppers, seeded and chopped

15-ounce can no-salt-added black beans, rinsed if desired and drained

1 medium tomato, seeded and diced

$1/4$ cup snipped fresh cilantro

3 tablespoons fresh lime juice

2 tablespoons olive oil (extra virgin preferred)

$1/4$ teaspoon salt

1 medium lime, quartered

Preheat the oven to 425°F. Lightly spray a nonstick rimmed baking sheet with vegetable oil spray.

Rinse the fish fillets and pat dry with paper towels. Place the fish with the skin side down on the baking sheet. Sprinkle with the oregano, salt, and paprika. Sprinkle the peppers around the fish.

Bake for 10 to 12 minutes, or until the fish flakes easily when tested with a fork.

Meanwhile, in a medium bowl, stir together the remaining ingredients except the lime wedges.

When the fish is done, transfer it to plates.

Using a slotted spoon, transfer the peppers to the bean mixture. Stir gently. Spoon the mixture over and around the fish. Serve with the lime wedges.

PER SERVING	
Calories 280	Cholesterol 40 mg
Total Fat 8.5 g	Sodium 343 mg
Saturated 1.0 g	Carbohydrates 22 g
Polyunsaturated 1.0 g	Fiber 5 g
Monounsaturated 5.5 g	Sugar 6 g
	Protein 29 g

snapper in mango curry

Swirling noodles, tender fish cubes, bright green beans, and chunky baby corn make this curry a feast for your eyes as well as your palate.

Vegetable oil spray

1 large shallot, minced

2 teaspoons curry powder (Madras preferred)

2 medium garlic cloves, minced

1 large mango, coarsely chopped

Juice of 1 large orange

Juice of 1 medium lime

4 cups hot water

2 teaspoons low-salt soy sauce

1 pound fresh green beans

1 pound red snapper, orange roughy, or rockfish fillets

3 ounces whole-wheat soba noodles (1 bundle) or very thin pasta, such as vermicelli

15-ounce can cut baby corn packed in water, rinsed and drained

1¹/₂ tablespoons chopped fresh mint

Heat a deep 12-inch skillet over medium heat (a paella pan works well). Remove from the heat and lightly spray with vegetable oil spray (being careful not to spray near a gas flame). Cook the shallot for 1 minute, stirring constantly. Add the curry powder and garlic. Cook for 1 minute, stirring constantly.

Stir in the mango, orange juice, and lime juice. Cook for 1 to 2 minutes, or until the curry powder no longer sticks to the skillet and the liquid is nearly evaporated, stirring constantly and scraping any dried curry powder from the skillet. Stop stirring and bring the mixture to a boil.

Stir in the water and soy sauce. Increase the heat to high. Cook for 10 to 12 minutes, or until the mixture is reduced by one third.

Meanwhile, trim the beans and cut into 1-inch pieces. Rinse the fish and pat dry with paper towels. Cut the fish into 1-inch pieces.

PER SERVING	
Calories 325	Cholesterol 42 mg
Total Fat 2.0 g	Sodium 373 mg
Saturated 0.5 g	Carbohydrates 47 g
Polyunsaturated 0.5 g	Fiber 11 g
Monounsaturated 0.5 g	Sugar 18 g
	Protein 31 g

After the curry sauce is reduced, stir in the green beans and soba noodles. Reduce the heat to medium. Cook for 1 to 2 minutes, or until the noodles are soft, stirring frequently.

Add the corn. Cook for 8 minutes, or until the liquid thickens, stirring frequently. (Stirring increases the amount of starch released by the noodles, and this thickens the curry.)

Add the fish, stirring just enough to distribute evenly. Push any floating pieces into the liquid. Cook for 5 minutes, or until the fish flakes easily when tested with a fork.

To serve, ladle into bowls and sprinkle with mint.

COOK'S TIP ON SOBA NOODLES

Soba noodles, available in many grocery stores and at Asian specialty markets, get their light brown color and distinctive flavor from buckwheat. They're Japanese in origin.

tex-mex red snapper
with coriander

Coriander seeds and enchilada sauce spice up this easy fish-and-vegetable medley.

2 medium chayote or zucchini squash

15-ounce can no-salt-added black beans, rinsed if desired and drained

1 cup fresh, no-salt-added canned, or frozen whole-kernel corn, rinsed if desired and drained if canned, thawed if frozen

1/2 cup roasted red bell peppers, rinsed and drained if bottled, diced

1/2 cup fat-free, low-sodium chicken broth

4 red snapper fillets (about 4 ounces each)

10-ounce can enchilada sauce

1 tablespoon coriander seeds, crushed

Preheat the oven to 400°F.

If using chayote squash, peel, cut in half, and remove the seeds. Cut into 1/2-inch cubes. If using zucchini, dice.

In a 13 × 9 × 2-inch nonstick baking pan, combine the squash, beans, corn, bell peppers, and broth. Cover tightly with aluminum foil.

Bake for 15 minutes, or until the squash is tender-crisp.

Place the fish on the squash mixture, spooning the mixture over the fish to partially cover. Pour the enchilada sauce over all. Sprinkle with the coriander seeds.

Bake for 13 to 15 minutes, or until the fish flakes easily when tested with a fork.

PER SERVING	Cholesterol 40 mg
Calories 294	Sodium 275 mg
Total Fat 3.5 g	Carbohydrates 34 g
Saturated 0.5 g	Fiber 8 g
Polyunsaturated 1.5 g	Sugar 6 g
Monounsaturated 1.0 g	Protein 32 g

broiled sole
mediterranean

SERVES 4; 3 OUNCES SOLE AND 1¹/₄ CUPS VEGETABLE AND BREAD MIX PER SERVING

A visual feast, this dish features delicate sole with red bell pepper, black olives, asparagus, tomatoes, and crusty bread cubes.

4 ounces French baguette, cut into ¹/₂-inch cubes (about 2 cups)

Vegetable oil spray (olive oil preferred)

4 Italian plum tomatoes, seeded and coarsely chopped

¹/₂ pound asparagus spears, trimmed, cut into 1-inch pieces, tips reserved separately

¹/₂ medium onion, diced

2 teaspoons olive oil

1 tablespoon fresh lemon juice

¹/₈ teaspoon pepper

4 sole fillets (about 4 ounces each)

¹/₂ medium red bell pepper, minced

8 kalamata olives, minced

Preheat the broiler.

Put the bread in a 13 × 9 × 2-inch baking pan. Lightly spray with vegetable oil spray. Toss the bread gently. Lightly spray again. Add the tomatoes, asparagus pieces (not tips), and onion. Stir to distribute evenly.

With the oven door slightly ajar, broil about 6 inches from the heat for 3 minutes, or until the bread begins to brown. Stir. Broil for 2 minutes.

Meanwhile, in a shallow dish or pie pan, stir together the olive oil, lemon juice, and pepper. Rinse the sole and pat dry with paper towels. Dip the sole in the mixture, turning to coat.

Place the sole on the broiled vegetables, overlapping as necessary. Sprinkle the bell pepper, olives, and asparagus tips over the sole.

Broil for 4 minutes. Turn off the oven and leave the pan in the oven for 3 minutes, or until the sole flakes easily when tested with a fork.

PER SERVING	
Calories 251	Cholesterol 53 mg
Total Fat 6.5 g	Sodium 384 mg
Saturated 1.0 g	Carbohydrates 24 g
Polyunsaturated 1.0 g	Fiber 4 g
Monounsaturated 3.5 g	Sugar 5 g
	Protein 24 g

sole rolls with lemon sauce and couscous

SERVES 4; 3 OUNCES FISH, 1/2 CUP VEGETABLES, AND 1/2 CUP COUSCOUS PER SERVING

Delicate sole fillets are stuffed with lightly roasted, colorful vegetables, then baked on a bed of flavored couscous. This recipe is a showstopper for entertaining or when you want to wow your family!

   Vegetable oil spray
12 baby carrots, cut into thin strips
 1 large red bell pepper, thinly sliced
 8 small sole fillets (about 2 ounces each) or 4 catfish fillets (about 4 ounces each)
 4 green onions (green and white parts), cut lengthwise into thin strips about 2 inches long
 1 cup fat-free, low-sodium chicken broth
3/4 cup uncooked tomato-basil (low-sodium) or plain couscous
1/2 teaspoon salt-free all-purpose seasoning blend
 8 ounces fat-free or low-fat plain yogurt
 2 tablespoons snipped green onions (green part only) or 2 teaspoons dried chives
 1 teaspoon grated lemon zest
 1 tablespoon fresh lemon juice

Preheat the oven to 400°F.

Lightly spray a 13 × 9 × 2-inch nonstick baking pan with vegetable oil spray. Arrange the carrots and bell peppers in a single layer in the pan.

Bake for 10 minutes, or until tender-crisp. Let cool on a cooling rack for 5 minutes. Leave the oven on.

Meanwhile, rinse the fish and pat dry with paper towels. If using catfish, cut the fillets crosswise in half. Put the fish fillets on a large, flat surface, such as a large cutting board. Place one eighth of the carrots, bell peppers, and green onions down the center of one fillet. Roll up jelly-roll style and set aside with the seam side down (no need to secure with toothpicks). Repeat with the remaining fillets and vegetables.

PER SERVING	
Calories 281	Cholesterol 56 mg
Total Fat 1.5 g	Sodium 166 mg
Saturated 0.5 g	Carbohydrates 35 g
Polyunsaturated 0.5 g	Fiber 2 g
Monounsaturated 0.5 g	Sugar 8 g
	Protein 29 g

In the baking pan, stir together the broth, couscous, and salt-free seasoning, distributing evenly in the pan.

Place the fish rolls with the seam side down on the couscous mixture. Cover the pan tightly with aluminum foil.

Bake for 18 to 20 minutes, or until the fish flakes easily when tested with a fork and the couscous is tender.

Meanwhile, in a small bowl, whisk together the remaining ingredients.

To serve, transfer the sole rolls and couscous to plates. Spoon the sauce over the fish.

caribbean tilapia

Tilapia goes tropical with rum, plantains, pineapple, and mango.

2 large plantains, peeled and cut crosswise into $1/2$-inch slices

15.25-ounce can pineapple tidbits in their own juice, undrained

1 large mango, sliced

2 tablespoons rum or $1/2$ teaspoon rum extract

1 tablespoon light brown sugar

$1/4$ teaspoon ground mace or nutmeg

$1/4$ teaspoon pepper

4 tilapia or sole fillets (about 4 ounces each)

Preheat the oven to 400°F.

In a $13 \times 9 \times 2$-inch baking pan, stir together all ingredients except the fish.

Rinse the fish and pat dry with paper towels. Arrange the fish in the pan, spooning the plantain mixture over the fish to lightly cover.

Bake for 15 minutes, or until the fish flakes easily when tested with a fork and the plantain mixture is tender.

caribbean tilapia with sweet potatoes

Substitute a 15-ounce can of sweet potatoes, drained and sliced, for the plantains.

COOK'S TIP ON PLANTAINS

A good source of beta-carotene, potassium, and vitamin C, plantains are a starchy fruit. Depending on their ripeness, plantains have two slightly different tastes; both are delicious in this recipe. Unripe plantains are green and have a mild flavor and potato-like texture. When ripe, the skin turns yellow tinged with black, much like a regular banana. The flavor is slightly sweet, like that of a banana, and the texture is starchy yet slightly creamy. Unripe plantains can be a challenge to peel and cut. The best way is to cut through the peel vertically at about 2-inch intervals. Grasp the peel with your fingers and pull to remove it.

WITH PLANTAINS

PER SERVING	
Calories 367	Cholesterol 53 mg
Total Fat 2.0 g	Sodium 100 mg
Saturated 0.5 g	Carbohydrates 69 g
Polyunsaturated 0.5 g	Fiber 5 g
Monounsaturated 0.5 g	Sugar 31 g
	Protein 21 g

WITH SWEET POTATOES

PER SERVING	
Calories 300	Cholesterol 53 mg
Total Fat 1.5 g	Sodium 151 mg
Saturated 0.5 g	Carbohydrates 49 g
Polyunsaturated 0.5 g	Fiber 4 g
Monounsaturated 0.5 g	Sugar 40 g
	Protein 21 g

grilled tuna and vegetables with balsamic dressing

Fire up the grill when you want a different kind of tuna salad. The pita triangles are great for soaking up the zippy balsamic dressing.

BALSAMIC DRESSING

$^1/_2$ cup fat-free, low-sodium chicken broth

1 tablespoon Dijon mustard

1 tablespoon olive oil

2 tablespoons balsamic vinegar

2 teaspoons brown sugar

2 medium garlic cloves, minced

$^1/_2$ teaspoon dried basil, crumbled

❖ ❖ ❖ ❖

4 tuna steaks (about 4 ounces each)

1 small eggplant (about 1 pound), unpeeled, cut lengthwise into $^1/_2$-inch slices

2 medium zucchini, cut lengthwise into $^1/_4$-inch slices

Olive oil spray

1 teaspoon dried basil, crumbled

$^1/_2$ cup halved cherry tomatoes

4 6-inch whole-wheat pita breads, quartered

In a small bowl, whisk together the dressing ingredients. Cover and refrigerate.

Preheat the grill on medium-high.

Rinse the tuna and pat dry with paper towels. Lightly spray the top of the tuna, eggplant, and zucchini with olive oil spray. Sprinkle with 1 teaspoon basil. Turn the ingredients over and lightly spray with olive oil spray.

Grill the tuna for 3 to 5 minutes on each side, or to desired doneness. Grill the eggplant slices for 2 to 3 minutes on each side, or until tender. Grill the zucchini slices for 1 to 2 minutes on each side, or until tender.

Put all the ingredients except the pita triangles in a large bowl. Toss to coat evenly. Arrange the pita triangles around the salad.

PER SERVING	
Calories 385	Cholesterol 51 mg
Total Fat 6.5 g	Sodium 471 mg
Saturated 1.0 g	Carbohydrates 49 g
Polyunsaturated 1.5 g	Fiber 9 g
Monounsaturated 3.0 g	Sugar 11 g
	Protein 35 g

greek-style tuna steaks
with roasted vegetables

SERVES 4; 3 OUNCES TUNA AND 1 CUP VEGETABLES AND COUSCOUS PER SERVING

Top tuna steaks with veggies that are quickly broiled, then tossed with fresh lemon, olive oil, oregano, and garlic to create a definite favorite.

  Vegetable oil spray
1 cup uncooked couscous
2 tablespoons olive oil (extra virgin preferred)
2 tablespoons fresh lemon juice
1 teaspoon dried oregano, crumbled
1 medium garlic clove, minced
$1/2$ teaspoon grated lemon zest
$1/2$ teaspoon salt
$1/4$ teaspoon pepper
2 8-ounce tuna steaks (about 1 inch thick)
1 medium yellow squash, diced
1 medium onion, cut into 8 wedges
1 medium green or yellow bell pepper, cut into thin strips
1 medium tomato, cut into 8 wedges
$1/4$ teaspoon paprika
1 medium lemon, cut into 4 wedges

Preheat the broiler. Lightly spray a broiler pan with vegetable oil spray.

Prepare the couscous using the package directions, omitting the salt and oil.

Meanwhile, in a small bowl, stir together the oil, lemon juice, oregano, garlic, lemon zest, salt, and pepper. Set aside.

Rinse the tuna and pat dry with paper towels. Cut the tuna in half. Place the tuna in the center of the broiler pan. Place the squash, onion, bell pepper, and tomato pieces around the tuna in a single layer. Lightly spray the tuna and vegetables with vegetable oil spray. Sprinkle the tuna with the paprika.

PER SERVING	
Calories 431	Cholesterol 51 mg
Total Fat 9.0 g	Sodium 342 mg
Saturated 1.5 g	Carbohydrates 51 g
Polyunsaturated 1.5 g	Fiber 4 g
Monounsaturated 5.5 g	Sugar 7 g
	Protein 35 g

Broil for 2 minutes. Turn the tuna over. Broil for 1 to 2 minutes, or until the tuna is the desired doneness.

Fluff the couscous with a fork. Spoon it onto the center of a serving platter. Place the tuna steaks on the couscous. Stir the lemon juice mixture; pour over the vegetables in the broiler pan. Stir. Spoon over the tuna steaks. Serve with the lemon wedges.

COOK'S TIP ON FRESH TUNA

Tuna steaks are very easy to overcook. Don't cook them until they are opaque in the center, as you would with most other fish. Tuna should still be pink or very pink in the center to avoid dryness and toughness.

grilled tuna
on panzanella salad

SERVES 4; 3 OUNCES TUNA AND 2 CUPS SALAD PER SERVING

Panzanella, an Italian bread salad, gets added flavor here from grilling the bread.

Vegetable oil spray or olive oil spray

DRESSING

> 3 tablespoons olive oil
>
> 2 tablespoons balsamic vinegar
>
> 2 teaspoons honey
>
> 1 medium garlic clove, minced
>
> $^1/_2$ teaspoon salt
>
> $^1/_2$ teaspoon dried rosemary, crushed
>
> $^1/_4$ teaspoon pepper
>
> ❖ ❖ ❖ ❖
>
> 4 tuna steaks (about 4 ounces each), about $^1/_2$ inch thick
>
> 1 loaf whole-wheat or sourdough baguette-style French bread (about 6 ounces)
>
> 6 cups packed torn romaine or mixed salad greens (about 10 ounces)
>
> 2 cups diced tomatoes or halved cherry tomatoes
>
> 1 medium red onion, thinly sliced, separated into rings
>
> 3 tablespoons thinly sliced fresh basil (optional)

Lightly spray the grill rack with vegetable oil spray. Preheat the grill on medium-high.

In a small bowl, whisk together the dressing ingredients. Spoon 1 tablespoon over the tuna.

Cut the bread in half lengthwise. Lightly spray both sides of each piece with vegetable oil spray. Arrange the tuna steaks on the center of the grill rack and the bread around the edges.

Grill, covered, for 3 minutes. Turn the tuna and bread over. Grill, covered, for 3 minutes, or until the bread is golden brown and the tuna is still red in the center, or to desired doneness.

PER SERVING	
Calories 388	Cholesterol 53 mg
Total Fat 13.0 g	Sodium 610 mg
Saturated 2.0 g	Carbohydrates 37 g
Polyunsaturated 1.5 g	Fiber 5 g
Monounsaturated 8.0 g	Sugar 10 g
	Protein 31 g

Meanwhile, in a large bowl, toss together the remaining ingredients and remaining dressing.

Cut the grilled bread into cubes. Add to the salad and toss.

To serve, arrange the salad on plates. Top with the tuna.

alternative cooking method

Pan-grill the tuna in a ridged skillet over medium-high heat for 3 minutes on each side. Broil the bread until lightly toasted on both sides.

piled-high tuna salad sandwiches

Not the typical "tuna on white," this open-face sandwich has layers of flavors.

4 3-ounce vacuum-sealed packages tuna or 2 6-ounce cans tuna in distilled or spring water, drained

1/3 cup fat-free or reduced-fat mayonnaise dressing

1 tablespoon sugar

2 medium ribs of celery, thinly sliced

4 slices of wheat berry or whole-grain bread

4 romaine leaves

4 thin slices of red onion

1 medium tomato, cut into 8 slices

1 medium red bell pepper, thinly sliced

In a medium bowl, stir together the tuna, mayonnaise, and sugar. Stir in the celery.

To assemble, place a slice of bread on each plate. Top each slice with, in order, 1 romaine leaf, 1 onion slice, 2 tomato slices, bell pepper slices, and 3/4 cup tuna mixture.

PER SERVING	Cholesterol 46 mg
Calories 211	Sodium 701 mg
Total Fat 2.0 g	Carbohydrates 23 g
Saturated 0.5 g	Fiber 3 g
Polyunsaturated 0.5 g	Sugar 9 g
Monounsaturated 0.5 g	Protein 23 g

tuna linguini
with mushrooms

Tuna is now sold in a vacuum-sealed package that saves steps—no draining, no rinsing, no can opener! Using frozen bell peppers makes this easy dish even easier.

14.5-ounce can fat-free, low-sodium chicken broth

8 ounces dried linguini, broken into thirds

8 ounces button mushrooms, sliced

2 medium green bell peppers, chopped, or 2 cups frozen chopped green bell peppers

1 teaspoon dried oregano, crumbled

4-ounce jar diced pimientos

$1/2$ cup chopped green onions (green and white parts)

$1/2$ teaspoon salt

3 3-ounce vacuum-sealed packages tuna

1 cup shredded reduced-fat medium Cheddar cheese

In a 12-inch skillet, bring the broth to a boil over high heat. Stir in the pasta, mushrooms, bell peppers, and oregano. Return to a boil. Reduce the heat and simmer, covered, for 10 minutes, or until the pasta is tender.

Remove from the heat. Stir in the pimientos, green onions, and salt. Gently fold in the tuna. Sprinkle evenly with the cheese.

Let stand, covered, for 3 minutes to allow the cheese to melt and the flavors to blend.

PER SERVING	
Calories 406	Cholesterol 49 mg
Total Fat 7.0 g	Sodium 795 mg
Saturated 3.5 g	Carbohydrates 51 g
Polyunsaturated 1.0 g	Fiber 4 g
Monounsaturated 1.0 g	Sugar 5 g
	Protein 33 g

tuna tostada
with jícama slaw

Tostadas go tropical with a colorful layered jícama slaw enhanced with mango, lime, and honey. You can mind your manners and eat them with a fork, or pick them up and dive right in—a bit messy, but worth every napkin it takes!

2 tablespoons fresh lime juice

2 teaspoons olive oil

1 teaspoon chili powder

1 teaspoon ground cumin

4 tuna steaks (about 4 ounces each)

   Vegetable oil spray

8 6-inch corn tortillas

2 cups shredded red cabbage ($^1/_2$ small)

2 cups peeled, diced jícama (1 small)

1 medium mango, diced

$^1/_4$ cup honey

1 large lime, cut into 8 wedges

1 teaspoon chili powder

In an airtight plastic bag, combine the lime juice, olive oil, 1 teaspoon chili powder, and cumin.

Rinse the tuna and pat dry with paper towels. Add to the marinade. Seal the bag and gently turn it over several times to coat the fish. Refrigerate for 15 minutes to 1 hour.

Preheat the oven to 350°F.

Lightly spray a broiler pan and rack with vegetable oil spray. Arrange the tortillas in a single layer on the rack.

Bake for 13 to 15 minutes, or until crispy. (The edges will curve slightly while baking.) Put the tortillas on plates.

PER SERVING	
Calories 316	Cholesterol 53 mg
Total Fat 2.5 g	Sodium 102 mg
Saturated 0.5 g	Carbohydrates 48 g
Polyunsaturated 1.0 g	Fiber 7 g
Monounsaturated 0.5 g	Sugar 28 g
	Protein 28 g

Put the tuna steaks on the rack.

Broil 6 inches from the heat for 4 to 6 minutes on each side, or until desired doneness. (For a smoky flavor, grill the tuna on medium-high for 3 to 5 minutes on each side, or until desired doneness.) Let the tuna cool for 5 minutes. Cut into thin slices across the grain.

To assemble, arrange the following ingredients on each tortilla: $1/4$ cup red cabbage, $1/4$ cup jícama, $1/8$ of the mango, and $1/8$ of the tuna. Drizzle each with $1/2$ tablespoon honey. Squeeze 1 lime wedge over each. Sprinkle each with $1/8$ teaspoon chili powder. Serve immediately.

tuna with orzo
and baby spinach

Stock your pantry with the essentials for this dish—tuna, orzo, chicken broth, and lemon-dill seasoning—then pick up a bag of prewashed baby spinach when you're hungry for a bowl of comforting tuna and pasta.

> 1 teaspoon olive oil
>
> 1 large onion, chopped
>
> 2 medium garlic cloves, minced
>
> ¹/₂ cup dried orzo
>
> 2¹/₂ cups fat-free, low-sodium chicken broth, divided use
>
> 12-ounce can albacore tuna packed in spring or distilled water, rinsed and drained
>
> 1 teaspoon salt-free lemon-dill seasoning blend
>
> 1 pound baby spinach leaves

Heat a large, deep skillet over medium-high heat. Pour the oil into the skillet and swirl to coat the bottom. Cook the onion and garlic for 2 to 3 minutes, or until the onion is tender, stirring occasionally.

Stir in the orzo and ¹/₂ cup broth. Cook until the liquid is absorbed, 2 to 3 minutes, stirring occasionally. Stir in another ¹/₂ cup broth. Cook until the liquid is absorbed, 2 to 3 minutes, stirring occasionally.

Stir in the remaining broth, tuna, and seasoning blend. Place the spinach on top of the mixture. (Don't stir.) Bring the mixture to a simmer. Reduce the heat and simmer, covered, for 7 minutes. Stir to incorporate the spinach into the mixture. Simmer, covered, for 8 minutes, or until the orzo is tender.

PER SERVING	
Calories 253	Cholesterol 36 mg
Total Fat 4.5 g	Sodium 211 mg
Saturated 1.0 g	Carbohydrates 25 g
Polyunsaturated 1.5 g	Fiber 5 g
Monounsaturated 1.5 g	Sugar 4 g
	Protein 28 g

creamy crab and
red pepper chowder

These steaming bowls of crab chowder are jam-packed with red bell peppers, potatoes, and corn.

Vegetable oil spray

2 medium red bell peppers, diced

1 medium rib of celery, finely chopped

8 ounces baking potatoes (russet preferred), peeled and cut into 1/2-inch cubes

3/4 cup water

2 cups fat-free milk

12 ounces crabmeat, picked over to remove any tiny shell particles

1 cup frozen whole-kernel corn, thawed

1/2 cup finely chopped green onions (green and white parts)

1 teaspoon seafood seasoning blend

1/2 cup snipped fresh parsley

3 tablespoons light tub margarine

1/2 teaspoon salt

1/4 teaspoon cayenne (optional)

Heat a Dutch oven over medium-high heat. Remove from the heat and lightly spray with vegetable oil spray (being careful not to spray near a gas flame). Cook the bell peppers and celery for 3 to 4 minutes, or until the peppers are tender-crisp, stirring frequently.

Stir in the potatoes and water. Increase the heat to high and bring to a boil. Reduce the heat and simmer, covered, for 8 minutes, or until the potatoes are tender.

Increase the heat to medium. Stir in the milk. Mash the soup lightly with a potato masher or whisk to thicken slightly.

Stir in the crabmeat, corn, green onions, and seafood seasoning. Cook, covered, for 10 minutes, or until heated thoroughly. Remove from the heat.

Stir in the remaining ingredients. Let stand, covered, for 10 minutes to absorb flavors.

PER SERVING	
Calories 259	Cholesterol 88 mg
Total Fat 5.5 g	Sodium 793 mg
Saturated 0.5 g	Carbohydrates 30 g
Polyunsaturated 1.5 g	Fiber 4 g
Monounsaturated 2.5 g	Sugar 10 g
	Protein 25 g

crab cake salad with orange-tarragon dressing

SERVES 4; 2 CRAB CAKES, 2 CROUTONS, AND 2¼ CUPS SALAD PER SERVING

The contrast of warm crab cakes on cool salad greens gives this spectacular salad its charm.

8 slices French baguette (whole wheat or regular), each ½ inch thick
Vegetable oil spray
12 ounces cooked lump crabmeat, picked over for shells and cartilage
Whites of 2 large eggs
1 cup fresh, soft whole-wheat bread crumbs
¼ cup fat-free or low-fat mayonnaise dressing
1 tablespoon fresh lemon juice
¼ teaspoon red hot-pepper sauce, or to taste

DRESSING

3 tablespoons fresh orange juice
1 tablespoon acceptable vegetable oil
1 tablespoon honey mustard, or ½ tablespoon honey and
½ tablespoon mustard
½ tablespoon chopped fresh tarragon or ½ teaspoon dried, crumbled
⅛ teaspoon pepper

❖ ❖ ❖ ❖

8 cups packed mixed salad greens or mesclun
4 thin slices small red onion, separated into rings
1½ cups cherry tomatoes or yellow pear-shaped, or teardrop, tomatoes
1 lemon, cut into 4 wedges

Lightly spray both sides of the bread slices with vegetable oil spray. Heat a 12-inch nonstick skillet over medium heat. Heat the bread for 2 minutes on each side, or until lightly toasted. Remove the bread from the skillet and set aside. (The bread also may be toasted in a toaster oven.)

PER SERVING	
Calories 287	Cholesterol 65 mg
Total Fat 6.5 g	Sodium 703 mg
Saturated 0.5 g	Carbohydrates 30 g
Polyunsaturated 2.0 g	Fiber 5 g
Monounsaturated 3.0 g	Sugar 8 g
	Protein 27 g

In a medium bowl, stir together the crabmeat and egg whites. Stir in the bread crumbs, mayonnaise, lemon juice, and hot-pepper sauce. Shape into eight 1/2-inch-thick patties about 3 inches in diameter.

Reheat the skillet over medium heat. Remove from the heat and lightly spray with vegetable oil spray (being careful not to spray near a gas flame). Cook the crab cakes for 2 to 3 minutes on each side, or until golden brown.

Meanwhile, in a large bowl, whisk together the dressing ingredients.

Add the lettuce, red onion, and tomatoes. Toss gently.

To serve, spoon the salad onto plates. Top with the crab cakes and croutons. Serve with the lemon wedges.

COOK'S TIP ON FRESH BREAD CRUMBS

To make fresh, soft bread crumbs, tear bread into about 1-inch chunks and process in a food processor to the desired texture. Freeze extra bread crumbs in an airtight plastic freezer bag for up to two months.

crab quesadillas
with avocado salsa

Instead of the usual procedure of cooking the quesadillas one at a time on the stovetop, this recipe uses the broiler and cuts the cooking time to one fourth. Fresh pineapple combined with mango or papaya sprinkled with lime juice makes a nice accompaniment to this spicy dish.

AVOCADO SALSA

2 cups chopped seeded tomatoes

$^1/_2$ cup diced ripe avocado

$^1/_3$ cup thinly sliced green onions (green and white parts)

$^1/_3$ cup snipped fresh cilantro

1 to 2 small fresh jalapeño peppers, seeded and minced, or 1 to 2 tablespoons minced drained pickled jalapeño peppers

❖ ❖ ❖ ❖

8 6-inch corn tortillas

Vegetable oil spray

4 ounces shredded fresh lump crabmeat or imitation crab (about 1 cup)

1 cup shredded light Mexican cheese blend

Preheat the broiler.

For the salsa, in a medium bowl, stir together the ingredients.

Lightly spray 4 tortillas with vegetable oil spray. Place the tortillas with the sprayed side down in a single layer on a large cookie sheet or baking sheet. Sprinkle the crabmeat evenly over the tortillas. Top with 1 cup salsa and the cheese. Place the remaining 4 tortillas over the crab mixture; lightly spray with vegetable oil spray.

Broil 6 to 8 inches from the heat source for 2 to 4 minutes, or until golden brown, watching closely after 2 minutes. Remove from the broiler. Using a large spatula, turn the quesadillas over. Broil for 2 to 4 minutes, or until golden brown.

Cut into wedges. Top with the remaining salsa.

WITH FRESH CRABMEAT

PER SERVING	
Calories 217	Cholesterol 32 mg
Total Fat 8.5 g	Sodium 365 mg
Saturated 3.5 g	Carbohydrates 20 g
Polyunsaturated 2.0 g	Fiber 4 g
Monounsaturated 3.0 g	Sugar 3 g
	Protein 17 g

WITH IMITATION CRAB

PER SERVING	
Calories 215	Cholesterol 16 mg
Total Fat 9.0 g	Sodium 496 mg
Saturated 3.5 g	Carbohydrates 23 g
Polyunsaturated 2.0 g	Fiber 4 g
Monounsaturated 3.0 g	Sugar 5 g
	Protein 14 g

angel hair pasta with mussels and tomatoes

This quick pasta dish will please the mussel lovers in your family. Fresh basil provides fabulous flavor.

$^1/_2$ tablespoon olive oil

4 medium garlic cloves, minced

1 cup fat-free, low-sodium chicken broth

9-ounce package refrigerated angel hair pasta

1 pound live mussels, scrubbed

14.5-ounce can no-salt-added diced tomatoes, undrained

$^1/_2$ teaspoon red hot-pepper sauce (optional)

2 cups packed fresh baby spinach leaves or torn spinach leaves, heavy stems discarded

$^1/_4$ cup chopped fresh basil, heavy stems discarded, or snipped Italian, or flat-leaf, parsley

Heat a large, deep skillet over medium heat. Pour the oil into the skillet and swirl to coat the bottom. Cook the garlic for 2 minutes, stirring occasionally.

Pour in the broth. Bring to a simmer.

Stir in the pasta, separating the strands with two forks.

Stir in the mussels, undrained tomatoes, and hot-pepper sauce. Simmer, covered, for 6 to 7 minutes, or until the mussels open. Discard any mussels that do not open.

Stir in the spinach. Cook, covered, for 1 minute, or until the spinach is wilted.

Remove the mussels from the mixture. Arrange around the edges of shallow bowls. Stir the pasta mixture to be sure the spinach is mixed in well.

To serve, transfer the mixture to the bowls. Sprinkle with the basil.

PER SERVING	
Calories 299	Cholesterol 24 mg
Total Fat 5.5 g	Sodium 441 mg
Saturated 0.5 g	Carbohydrates 45 g
Polyunsaturated 0.5 g	Fiber 5 g
Monounsaturated 1.5 g	Sugar 6 g
	Protein 19 g

potato-leek soup
with poached oysters

In traditional oyster stew, the oysters are poached in cream and butter. This version relies on chicken broth and pureed vegetables for its flavorful base. In addition to the healthful beta-carotene perk they provide, the carrots lend a pleasant orange glow to the soup.

2 teaspoons olive oil

2 large leeks (white and green parts), thinly sliced

2 14.5-ounce cans fat-free, low-sodium chicken broth

1 large baking potato (russet preferred) (about 12 ounces), peeled, cut into 1-inch pieces

3 medium carrots, sliced

$1/2$ teaspoon salt

$1/4$ teaspoon ground white pepper

1 pound shucked fresh small oysters, undrained

$1/4$ cup fat-free or light sour cream

$1/4$ cup chopped green onions (green part only)

Heat a large saucepan over medium heat. Pour the oil into the saucepan and swirl to coat the bottom. Cook the leeks for 5 minutes, stirring occasionally.

Stir in the broth, potato, carrots, salt, and pepper. Bring to a boil over high heat. Reduce the heat and simmer, covered, for 18 to 20 minutes, or until the vegetables are very tender.

Using an immersion blender, puree the soup, or transfer it in batches to a food processor or blender and process until pureed. Return the soup to the saucepan and bring to a simmer.

Add the oysters with their liquid. Gently poach for about 5 minutes, or until their edges curl.

To serve, ladle into soup bowls. Top with sour cream. Sprinkle with the green onions.

PER SERVING	
Calories 224	Cholesterol 31 mg
Total Fat 4.0 g	Sodium 584 mg
Saturated 1.0 g	Carbohydrates 37 g
Polyunsaturated 1.0 g	Fiber 4 g
Monounsaturated 2.0 g	Sugar 8 g
	Protein 12 g

seafood jambalaya

This Creole dish cooks in one pot in less than 20 minutes.

12 ounces bay scallops or sea scallops

6 ounces peeled large raw shrimp, thawed if frozen

1 tablespoon olive oil

1 medium green bell pepper, cut into $1/2$-inch pieces

1 cup fresh or frozen cut okra, cut into $1/2$-inch slices if fresh, thawed and drained if frozen

$1/2$ cup chopped onion

$1/2$ cup thinly sliced carrot

4 medium garlic cloves, minced

2 teaspoons seafood seasoning blend or no-salt-added Cajun seasoning

$1^3/4$ cups fat-free, no-salt-added beef broth

$1^1/2$ cups uncooked quick-cooking brown rice

14.5-ounce can no-salt-added stewed tomatoes, undrained

$1/4$ teaspoon red hot-pepper sauce

$1/4$ cup snipped fresh parsley

Rinse the scallops and shrimp. Pat dry with paper towels. If using sea scallops, cut into fourths. Set aside.

Heat a large saucepan over medium heat. Pour the oil into the saucepan and swirl to coat the bottom. Cook the bell pepper, okra, onion, carrot, and garlic for 5 minutes, stirring occasionally. Stir in the seasoning blend. Cook for 30 seconds.

Stir in the broth and rice. Bring to a boil over medium heat. Reduce the heat and simmer, covered, for 5 minutes.

Stir in the undrained tomatoes. Increase the heat to medium-high and return to a simmer.

Stir in the scallops, shrimp, and hot-pepper sauce. Cook, uncovered, for 3 to 4 minutes, or until the scallops and shrimp are opaque and the vegetables are tender, stirring occasionally.

To serve, transfer to bowls. Sprinkle with the parsley.

PER SERVING	
Calories 350	Cholesterol 93 mg
Total Fat 6.0 g	Sodium 523 mg
Saturated 0.5 g	Carbohydrates 44 g
Polyunsaturated 1.5 g	Fiber 6 g
Monounsaturated 3.0 g	Sugar 9 g
	Protein 30 g

inferno-roasted vegetable and scallop casserole

You build this casserole one layer at a time, vegetable by vegetable, until you reach the scallop pinnacle.

> ¹/₂ cup dry-packed sun-dried tomatoes, cut into matchstick-size strips
>
> 1 cup very hot water
>
> Vegetable oil spray
>
> 2 large, long baking potatoes, as flat as possible (russet preferred) (about 24 ounces)
>
> 2 teaspoons olive oil
>
> 1 tablespoon chopped fresh rosemary
>
> 2 large red bell peppers
>
> 8 medium cremini (brown) mushrooms
>
> 2 small yellow summer squash
>
> 1 small red onion
>
> 1 teaspoon olive oil
>
> ¹/₄ teaspoon salt
>
> ¹/₈ teaspoon pepper
>
> 8 large sea scallops (8 to 10 ounces)
>
> 2 tablespoons plus 2 teaspoons balsamic vinegar

Put the tomatoes in a small bowl. Pour in the water and let soak for about 30 minutes.

After the tomatoes have soaked, preheat the oven to 475°F. Lightly spray a 13 × 9 × 2-inch glass baking dish with vegetable oil spray.

Peel the potatoes. Cut a thin slice off the flattest side of each. Discard these two slices. With the potatoes sitting on the cut side, cut each potato horizontally into five slices, four about ¹/₃ inch thick plus the top one, which will be rounded. Discard the rounded slices. You'll have a total of eight slices left.

In a medium bowl, combine 2 teaspoons olive oil and the rosemary. Add the potatoes and turn to lightly coat. Place in the baking dish.

PER SERVING	
Calories 244	Cholesterol 21 mg
Total Fat 4.5 g	Sodium 260 mg
Saturated 0.5 g	Carbohydrates 39 g
Polyunsaturated 0.5 g	Fiber 7 g
Monounsaturated 2.5 g	Sugar 11 g
	Protein 17 g

Bake for 12 minutes, or until golden brown.

Meanwhile, cut off and discard a thin slice from the top and bottom of each bell pepper. Remove the ribs and seeds. Cut each pepper lengthwise into quarters. Put the peppers with the inside down on a cutting board; flatten them by pressing down until you hear a crack. Thinly slice the mushrooms and squash. Cut 8 thin crosswise slices from the onion.

When the potatoes are golden brown, top with the bell pepper slices with the skin side down, then with the onion.

Bake for 5 minutes, or until the peppers begin to soften.

Arrange a layer of squash slices over the onion. Top with the mushrooms. Lightly spray with vegetable oil spray.

Bake for 5 minutes, or until the mushrooms are softened.

Meanwhile, drain the tomatoes, reserving the liquid. In a food processor or blender, process the tomatoes (without the soaking liquid), 1 teaspoon olive oil, salt, and pepper until the tomato pieces are very fine. Depending on how dry the tomatoes are, you may need to thin the mixture with a little of the reserved soaking liquid. Pour into a small bowl.

Rinse the scallops and pat dry with paper towels. Add the scallops to the tomato mixture; turn them over. (The mixture will not coat the scallops but will help them retain some of their juiciness.) Spoon the tomato mixture onto each scallop. Place the scallops on the mushrooms.

Bake for 4 to 5 minutes, or just until the scallops firm up.

Just before serving, drizzle with the vinegar.

COOK'S TIP

For an impressive presentation, assemble the ingredients in eight stacks. Just be sure to cut the vegetables so you have perfectly flat pieces and use care as you assemble them. Bake on a baking sheet instead of in the baking dish. Once you put the scallops in place, secure each stack with a wooden toothpick. The baking times remain the same.

shrimp-and-pasta
caesar salad

SERVES 4; 2 CUPS PER SERVING

This versatile one-pan pasta salad is good warm, at room temperature, or chilled. With its variety of shapes, colors, and textures, you can't go wrong no matter how you serve it.

8 ounces dried farfalle or bow-tie pasta

10 ounces peeled raw medium shrimp

2 tablespoons fat-free or light Caesar salad dressing

8 ounces sugar snap peas, trimmed

1 cup marinated artichoke hearts, drained and coarsely chopped (6 ounces)

1 cup halved cherry tomatoes

1/3 cup fat-free or light Caesar salad dressing

Pepper to taste

Prepare the pasta using the package directions, omitting the salt and oil. Drain in a colander.

Meanwhile, rinse the shrimp and pat dry with paper towels.

In the pot used for the pasta, heat 2 tablespoons salad dressing over medium-high heat. Stir in the peas. Cook for 2 minutes, stirring once.

Stir in the shrimp. Cook for 3 to 4 minutes, or until the shrimp are opaque, stirring once.

Stir in the artichokes, tomatoes, and 1/3 cup salad dressing. Heat through, stirring once.

Stir in the pasta.

Serve warm, let the salad cool to room temperature, or transfer the salad to a large bowl, cover with plastic wrap, and refrigerate until cold. Sprinkle with pepper to taste.

COOK'S TIP ON SERVING PASTA SALAD

While chilling, the pasta will absorb the dressing. Therefore, stir in a little fat-free, low-sodium chicken broth or low-sodium vegetable broth before serving chilled.

PER SERVING	
Calories 410	Cholesterol 108 mg
Total Fat 4.5 g	Sodium 610 mg
Saturated 0.5 g	Carbohydrates 64 g
Polyunsaturated 1.0 g	Fiber 6 g
Monounsaturated 0.5 g	Sugar 8 g
	Protein 26 g

dilled shrimp salad

On hot summer nights, quickly boil, quickly cool, quickly toss, then slowly enjoy this appealing, crunchy salad.

2 quarts water

4 ounces dried rotini

^{1}/$_3$ cup fat-free or reduced-fat mayonnaise dressing

^{3}/$_4$ teaspoon seafood seasoning blend

^{1}/$_2$ teaspoon dried dillweed, crumbled

^{1}/$_2$ teaspoon salt

1 cup frozen green peas, thawed

^{1}/$_2$ medium cucumber, peeled and diced

1 medium rib of celery

10 ounces peeled raw medium shrimp

3 medium tomatoes, cut into 4 slices each

1 medium lemon, quartered

In a large saucepan, bring the water to a boil. Add the pasta; stir. Return to a boil, and boil for 4 minutes.

Meanwhile, in a large bowl, stir together the mayonnaise, seafood seasoning, dill, and salt. Stir in the peas, cucumber, and celery.

Rinse the shrimp and pat dry with paper towels. Stir the shrimp into the pasta. Return to a boil. Cook for 2 minutes, or until the shrimp is pink on the outside and opaque in the center. Drain in a colander. Run cold water over the pasta and shrimp to cool them quickly. Shake off excess water.

Gently stir the shrimp and pasta into the vegetable mixture.

Arrange the tomato slices on plates. Mound the shrimp salad on the tomatoes. Place a lemon wedge on each plate. Serve immediately for peak flavor.

COOK'S TIP ON SHRIMP

Be careful not to overcook the shrimp. It cooks very quickly, especially when peeled first.

PER SERVING	
Calories 233	Cholesterol 105 mg
Total Fat 1.5 g	Sodium 724 mg
Saturated 0.5 g	Carbohydrates 35 g
Polyunsaturated 0.5 g	Fiber 4 g
Monounsaturated 0 g	Sugar 9 g
	Protein 18 g

lemon-tarragon
shrimp vermicelli

SERVES 4; 1¹/₂ CUPS PER SERVING

Whether you're preparing for dinner by candlelight or a casual meal on the patio, you certainly won't be worn out from cooking this delicious dish. You'll be in and out of the kitchen in minutes.

 8 ounces dried vermicelli, broken into thirds
 ¹/₂ cup chopped green onions (green and white parts)
 ¹/₄ cup snipped fresh parsley
 ¹/₄ cup light tub margarine
 2 tablespoons fresh lemon juice
 2 tablespoons olive oil (extra virgin preferred)
 1¹/₂ teaspoons seafood seasoning blend
 ¹/₂ teaspoon dried tarragon, crumbled
 ¹/₂ teaspoon salt
 ¹/₄ teaspoon pepper
 10 ounces peeled raw medium shrimp
 6 ounces asparagus spears, trimmed, broken into 2-inch pieces (about 2 cups)

In a large saucepan, prepare the pasta using the package directions, omitting the salt and oil and cooking for 6 minutes. Do not drain.

Meanwhile, in a large bowl, stir together the green onions, parsley, margarine, lemon juice, oil, seafood seasoning, tarragon, salt, and pepper.

Rinse the shrimp and pat dry with paper towels. Stir the shrimp and asparagus into the pasta. Increase the heat to high; return to a boil. Stir. Boil for 2 to 3 minutes, or until the shrimp turn pink on the outside and are opaque in the center. Drain well; shake off excess water. Stir into the green onion mixture.

PER SERVING	
Calories 384	Cholesterol 105 mg
Total Fat 13.0 g	Sodium 683 mg
Saturated 1.0 g	Carbohydrates 46 g
Polyunsaturated 2.0 g	Fiber 3 g
Monounsaturated 7.5 g	Sugar 4 g
	Protein 20 g

mediterranean-style
seafood stir-fry

SERVES 4; $1^1/2$ CUPS PER SERVING

With kalamata olives, capers, and lemon zest, this stir-fry incorporates Mediterranean, rather than Asian, flavors.

8 ounces salmon fillet

6 ounces halibut steak

5 ounces medium raw shrimp in shells

1 teaspoon olive oil

2 medium garlic cloves, minced

2 medium yellow squash, sliced

15-ounce can reduced-sodium Great Northern beans, rinsed and drained

2 cups canned quartered artichokes, rinsed and drained

2 cups chopped tomatoes

$1/4$ cup sliced kalamata or black olives

1 tablespoon capers, rinsed and drained

$1/4$ cup loosely packed fresh basil, heavy stems discarded, leaves thinly sliced

1 teaspoon grated lemon zest

$1/4$ teaspoon pepper

Rinse the salmon and halibut and pat dry with paper towels. Discard the skin and bones. Cut the salmon and halibut into $3/4$-inch pieces. Rinse and peel the shrimp.

Heat a large, deep nonstick skillet or wok over medium-high heat. Pour the oil into the skillet and swirl to coat the bottom. Cook the salmon, halibut, shrimp, and garlic for 3 to 4 minutes, or until the fish is almost cooked through, stirring constantly.

Stir in the squash. Cook for 1 to 2 minutes, or until it is tender-crisp, stirring occasionally.

Stir in the beans, artichokes, tomatoes, olives, and capers. Cook for about 5 minutes, or until the mixture is warmed through, stirring occasionally.

Stir in the remaining ingredients. Cook for 1 to 2 minutes, or until the basil is wilted and the flavors are mingled, stirring occasionally.

PER SERVING	
Calories 324	Cholesterol 97 mg
Total Fat 6.5 g	Sodium 667 mg
Saturated 1.0 g	Carbohydrates 28 g
Polyunsaturated 1.5 g	Fiber 7 g
Monounsaturated 3.0 g	Sugar 7 g
	Protein 36 g

seafood paella

This colorful, traditional Spanish dish is just the thing to serve at a dinner party.

 2 teaspoons olive oil

 1 medium onion, chopped

 3 medium garlic cloves, minced

 1 cup uncooked arborio rice

 1/2 cup dry white wine (regular or nonalcoholic)

 2 cups fat-free, low-sodium chicken broth, divided use

 1/2 teaspoon saffron threads, 1/4 teaspoon ground saffron, or 1 teaspoon turmeric

 1/2 teaspoon red hot-pepper sauce

 1 medium red or orange bell pepper, coarsely chopped

 1 1/2 cups chopped Italian plum tomatoes or 14.5-ounce can no-salt-added diced
    tomatoes, drained

 1/2 cup frozen peas

 8 ounces raw peeled large shrimp, rinsed

 12 large fresh mussels, cleaned, beards removed

Heat a large, deep skillet over medium heat. Pour the oil into the skillet and swirl to coat the bottom. Cook the onions for 3 to 4 minutes, or until translucent, stirring occasionally.

Add the garlic and rice. Cook for 1 minute, stirring constantly.

Stir in the wine. Reduce the heat and simmer for 2 minutes, or until most of the wine is absorbed. Stir in 1/2 cup broth, saffron, and hot-pepper sauce. Simmer for 3 minutes, or until most of the broth is absorbed, stirring occasionally. Stir in 1/2 cup broth and the bell peppers. Simmer for 4 minutes, or until most of the broth is absorbed, stirring occasionally. Stir in 1/2 cup broth and the tomatoes. Simmer for 5 minutes, or until most of the broth is absorbed, stirring occasionally. Stir in the remaining broth and peas. Simmer for 5 minutes, stirring occasionally.

Stir in the shrimp and mussels. Simmer, covered, for 12 to 14 minutes, or until the rice is tender, shrimp are opaque, and mussels are open. Discard any mussels that don't open. Remove from the heat. Stir well. Let stand, covered, for 5 minutes before serving.

PER SERVING	
Calories 421	Cholesterol 103 mg
Total Fat 5.0 g	Sodium 319 mg
Saturated 1.0 g	Carbohydrates 60 g
Polyunsaturated 1.0 g	Fiber 4 g
Monounsaturated 2.0 g	Sugar 7 g
	Protein 26 g

shrimp and papaya
with chutney

This tropically inspired combination is delightful as a sandwich filling or served by the scoop as a salad.

        2 tablespoons mango chutney

        2 teaspoons plain rice vinegar or white wine vinegar

        $1/2$ teaspoon salt

        $1/4$ teaspoon red hot-pepper sauce

        8 ounces cooked, peeled shrimp, cut into $1/2$-inch pieces

        1 cup diced papaya

        1 small avocado, diced

        $1/4$ cup slivered almonds, dry-roasted

        4 cups packed shredded or torn romaine (about 1 small head or $1/2$ large head)

        4 6-inch whole-wheat pita bread rounds

In a medium bowl, stir together the chutney, vinegar, salt, and hot-pepper sauce. Add the shrimp, papaya, avocado, and almonds; toss. Add the romaine; toss again.

To assemble sandwiches, cut the pitas in half crosswise; open into pockets. Fill the pockets with the shrimp mixture.

COOK'S TIP ON DRY-ROASTING NUTS

Dry-roasting intensifies the flavor of nuts. You can heat them in an ungreased skillet over medium heat for 2 to 4 minutes, or until they begin to lightly brown, stirring frequently. Another method is to put the nuts in a shallow baking pan and roast them at 350°F for 10 to 15 minutes, stirring occasionally. A third way is to toast them on the tray in a toaster oven; they'll be ready in the few minutes it takes to toast a slice of bread. Whichever way you choose, watch carefully so the nuts don't burn.

PER SERVING	
Calories 360	Cholesterol 111 mg
Total Fat 11.5 g	Sodium 750 mg
Saturated 1.5 g	Carbohydrates 47 g
Polyunsaturated 2.5 g	Fiber 9 g
Monounsaturated 6.0 g	Sugar 8 g
	Protein 21 g

poultry

Sesame Seed Chicken
and Sweet Potatoes

❖

Deep-Dish Greek Chicken Pie

❖

Lemon-Pepper Chicken Layered
with Vegetables

❖

Orange Chicken Fricassee

❖

Stuffed Chicken Breasts
with Fruit Chutney Orzo

❖

Chicken, Corn, and Broccoli
Stir-Fry

❖

Greek-Style Chicken
with Lemon-Pistachio Rice

❖

Chicken with Potatoes
and Broccoli in
Creamy Mustard Sauce

❖

Biscuit-Topped Chicken Casserole

❖

Braised Chicken
with Apricots and Orzo

❖

Chicken and Double
Mushroom Stew

❖

Chicken Tetrazzini Supreme

❖

Spicy Peanut
and Chicken Noodles

❖

Poblano Chicken and Rice

❖

Chicken Piccata Stir-Fry

❖

Cajun Chicken Gumbo

❖

Pizza-Smothered Chicken
and Vegetables

❖

Homey Chicken and Vegetables

❖

Cheese-Topped Chicken
and Rice

❖

Chicken Orzo with
Mediterranean Tomatoes

❖

Chicken Rotini with Parmesan

❖

Balsamic-Glazed Rosemary
Chicken and Spinach Sandwiches

❖

Grilled Chicken and Vegetable
Sandwiches with Cilantro "Pesto"

❖

Chicken Caesar Wraps

❖

Mixed Green Salad with Seared
Chicken and Apricot-Ginger
Vinaigrette

❖

(continued on following page)

Coq au Vin

❖

Lemon-Garlic Chicken,
Asparagus, and Potatoes

❖

Spice-Roasted Chicken
and Vegetables

❖

Chicken and Mushroom
Cacciatore with Gnocchi

❖

Dijon Chicken with Stuffing
and Vegetables

❖

Open-Face Chunky Chicken Salad
Sandwiches

❖

Chicken, Brown Rice,
and Vegetable Skillet

❖

Chicken Slaw with Teriyaki
Plum Dressing

❖

Chicken Tabbouleh
with Fresh Mint

❖

Chicken and Black Bean Salad
with Salsa Dressing

❖

Old-World Sausage with Cabbage
and Noodles

❖

Chicken Ravioli Italiano

❖

Creamy Turkey
and Wild Rice Soup

❖

Glazed Turkey Supper
with Cranberry Chutney

❖

Tandoori Turkey and Pineapple
Kebabs with Brown Rice

❖

Slow-Cooker Turkey Chili

❖

Turkey Cutlets
and Vegetables Parmesan

❖

Potato-Crusted Turkey
and Vegetable Loaf

❖

Orzo Puttanesca

❖

Southwestern Turkey Lasagna

❖

Cassoulet

❖

Boiled Dinner with Smoked
Turkey Sausage and Vegetables

sesame seed chicken
and sweet potatoes

Sesame-flavored chicken nestled with pears, parsnips, and caramelized onions cooks to comfort-food perfection between layers of thinly sliced sweet potatoes.

Vegetable oil spray

2 large red onions, cut into matchstick-size strips

1 cup fat-free, low-sodium chicken broth

1 pound boneless, skinless chicken breasts, all visible fat discarded, cut into 1-inch pieces

1 teaspoon sesame oil

¹/₄ teaspoon salt

¹/₈ teaspoon pepper

2 large parsnips, peeled and grated

2 firm pears, diced

2 medium sweet potatoes (about 1¹/₄ pounds), peeled and cut into ¹/₈-inch-thick slices

1 tablespoon sesame seeds (black preferred)

Heat a Dutch oven over medium heat. Remove from the heat and lightly spray with vegetable oil spray (being careful not to spray near a gas flame). Cook the onions for 10 minutes, stirring occasionally.

Meanwhile, preheat the oven to 325°F.

Transfer half the onions to a medium bowl.

Pour the broth into the Dutch oven, stirring to loosen any browned bits. Remove from the heat.

Add the chicken, sesame oil, salt, and pepper to the onions in the bowl, stirring until the chicken is coated. Stir in the parsnips and pears.

Arrange half the sweet potatoes in the Dutch oven in an even layer. Top with an even layer of the chicken mixture, then with an even layer of the remaining sweet potatoes. Sprinkle with the sesame seeds.

Bake in the bottom third of the oven for 45 minutes to 1 hour, or until the potatoes are tender when pierced with a fork.

PER SERVING	
Calories 440	Cholesterol 66 mg
Total Fat 3.0 g	Sodium 302 mg
Saturated 0.5 g	Carbohydrates 76 g
Polyunsaturated 1.0 g	Fiber 12 g
Monounsaturated 1.0 g	Sugar 27 g
	Protein 32 g

deep-dish greek
chicken pie

Moist and tangy, this spectacular dish is in a class by itself. Add a lemon-dressed arugula salad, and you're ready to host a casually elegant dinner party.

Vegetable oil spray (olive oil spray preferred)

8 sheets frozen phyllo dough, thawed

1 tablespoon snipped fresh dillweed or $1/2$ tablespoon dried, crumbled

$1/4$ teaspoon pepper

12 ounces boneless, skinless chicken breasts, all visible fat discarded, cut into $1/2$-inch cubes

16 ounces frozen chopped spinach, thawed and squeezed dry

8 ounces fat-free or low-fat plain yogurt

1 medium red bell pepper, minced

2 small tomatoes, seeded and minced

3 medium green onions (green and white parts), thinly sliced

Egg substitute equivalent to 1 egg, or whites of 2 large eggs

2 tablespoons pine nuts

1 tablespoon snipped fresh dillweed or $1/2$ tablespoon dried, crumbled

Zest of 1 medium lemon

$1/4$ teaspoon salt

Preheat the oven to 350°F. Lightly spray a 9-inch springform pan with vegetable oil spray.

Working quickly so the phyllo won't dry out, stack the sheets and trim into 12-inch squares. Cover the squares with a barely damp dish towel. (Discard the scraps, or use them in place of bread crumbs. See Cook's Tip on Phyllo Dough, below.) Remove 1 sheet of phyllo from the stack and place it on a flat work surface. Lightly spray with vegetable oil spray. Place a second sheet so the points of the squares are about 2 inches apart and evenly spaced. (If a sheet of phyllo tears, don't worry. Just place the torn pieces on the stack.) Lightly spray with vegetable

PER SERVING	
Calories 319	Cholesterol 51 mg
Total Fat 6.0 g	Sodium 550 mg
Saturated 1.5 g	Carbohydrates 35 g
Polyunsaturated 1.5 g	Fiber 6 g
Monounsaturated 2.5 g	Sugar 8 g
	Protein 32 g

oil spray. Repeat with 2 more sheets, overlapping so the dough looks like a star with phyllo points. Sprinkle with 1 tablespoon dillweed and the pepper.

Rotating the sheets so you get a round crust with feathery edges, top with the next sheet of phyllo; spray. Continue layering and spraying until all the sheets are used, but do not spray the final sheet. Lift the phyllo stack with your fingers and carefully place it so it lines the springform pan.

In a medium bowl, stir together the remaining ingredients. Pour into the pan; smooth the top.

Bake for 45 minutes, or until the crust starts to turn golden and the center is firm to the touch. Remove from the oven. Remove the sides of the pan. Let the pie cool for 10 minutes before slicing.

COOK'S TIP ON PHYLLO DOUGH

Because it is so thin and delicate, phyllo dough dries out quickly. Cover what you aren't using with a barely damp dish towel to prevent that. When you have phyllo dough scraps, however, you can dry them out and use them as a substitute for bread crumbs. Spread the scraps of dough on a flat surface, such as your counter, and let the dough dry out. Depending on the humidity, this will take 30 to 90 minutes. Crumble the dried pieces and store them in an airtight container.

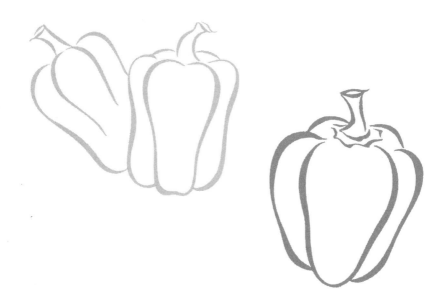

lemon-pepper chicken
layered with vegetables

SERVES 4; 1 CHICKEN BREAST HALF PLUS HEAPING 1³/₄ CUPS VEGETABLES
AND RICE PER SERVING

Chicken with a lemon-pepper crust steams on a savory bed of vegetables and jasmine rice, then is blanketed with bok choy to seal in the moisture and flavor.

Olive oil spray

1 small onion, minced

1 medium garlic clove, thinly sliced

1 medium lemon

14.5-ounce can fat-free, low-sodium chicken broth

1 large red bell pepper, cut into matchstick-size strips

1 medium carrot, grated

1 cup uncooked jasmine or long-grain white rice

¹/₃ cup water, plus more as needed

¹/₄ teaspoon pepper

¹/₈ teaspoon salt

¹/₈ to ¹/₄ teaspoon red hot-pepper sauce (optional)

4 boneless, skinless chicken breast halves (about 4 ounces each),
   all visible fat discarded

1 large bok choy (about 1¹/₂ pounds), coarsely diced

Heat a Dutch oven over medium heat. Remove from the heat and lightly spray with olive oil spray (being careful not to spray near a gas flame). Cook the onion for 4 to 5 minutes, or until it begins to brown, stirring occasionally. Add the garlic. Cook for 1 minute, stirring constantly.

Meanwhile, grate the lemon; set the zest aside. Squeeze the lemon; you should get about 2 tablespoons juice. After cooking the garlic, stir the juice into the Dutch oven, scraping any browned bits from the bottom. Cook for 2 minutes, or until the juice is nearly evaporated.

PER SERVING	
Calories 356	Cholesterol 66 mg
Total Fat 2.0 g	Sodium 291 mg
Saturated 0.5 g	Carbohydrates 50 g
Polyunsaturated 0.5 g	Fiber 5 g
Monounsaturated 0.5 g	Sugar 5 g
	Protein 34 g

Stir in the broth, bell pepper, carrot, rice, and water. Bring to a boil. Reduce the heat and simmer, covered, for 6 to 7 minutes, or until the rice begins to plump and the vegetables begin to soften, adding more water if needed.

Meanwhile, on a plate, stir together the lemon zest, pepper, salt, and hot-pepper sauce. Add the chicken, turning to coat evenly. When the broth mixture is thick enough that the chicken won't sink into it, stir the mixture. Place the chicken on top, trying to avoid overlapping. Increase the heat to medium-low. Cook, covered, for 12 minutes.

Distribute the bok choy evenly over the chicken. Cook for 6 to 8 minutes, or until the chicken is no longer pink in the center.

orange chicken fricassee

SERVES 4; 3 OUNCES CHICKEN AND 1^1/$_2$ CUPS FRUIT
AND VEGETABLE MIXTURE PER SERVING

Combining just the right amount of orange juice with leeks is the secret to this excellent dish. Yukon gold potatoes thicken the sauce as they simmer.

3 medium oranges

^{1}/$_2$ cup all-purpose flour

1 tablespoon paprika

^{1}/$_2$ teaspoon pepper

^{1}/$_4$ teaspoon salt

4 boneless, skinless chicken breast halves (about 4 ounces each),
all visible fat discarded

Vegetable oil spray

2 large leeks (white parts only), split lengthwise and thinly sliced

2 large Yukon gold potatoes, peeled, each cut into 8 wedges

1 cup fat-free, low-sodium chicken broth

3 large carrots, grated

Remove the zest from the oranges. Peel and section 2 oranges; cut the sections into 1-inch pieces. Squeeze the juice from the remaining orange. Set the zest, pieces, and juice aside separately.

Heat a 12-inch skillet over medium-high heat.

Meanwhile, on a plate, stir together the flour, paprika, pepper, and salt. Dust the chicken breasts with the seasoned flour; shake off the excess.

Remove the skillet from the heat and lightly spray with vegetable oil spray (being careful not to spray near a gas flame). Cook the chicken for 3 minutes on each side, or until golden brown. Transfer to a plate; cover with aluminum foil. Set aside.

Reduce the heat to medium. Stir the orange juice and leeks into the skillet. Cook for 3 to 4 minutes, or until most of the liquid evaporates, stirring occasionally.

Stir in the potatoes and broth. Cook, covered, for 10 minutes.

PER SERVING	
Calories 345	Cholesterol 66 mg
Total Fat 2.0 g	Sodium 264 mg
Saturated 0.5 g	Carbohydrates 51 g
Polyunsaturated 0.5 g	Fiber 9 g
Monounsaturated 0.5 g	Sugar 15 g
	Protein 32 g

Stir in the carrots and half the orange zest. Add the chicken; spoon some liquid over each piece. Reduce the heat and simmer, covered, for 10 minutes.

Sprinkle with the orange pieces. Simmer, covered, for 5 minutes, or until the chicken is no longer pink in the center. With a slotted spoon, transfer the chicken and vegetables to plates.

Stir the remaining zest into the skillet. Increase the heat to high. Cook for 3 minutes, or until the pan juices reduce to about $1/2$ cup. Spoon the sauce over the chicken.

stuffed chicken breasts
with fruit chutney orzo

SERVES 4; 1 CHICKEN BREAST HALF AND 1¹/₂ CUPS CHUTNEY AND ORZO PER SERVING

Simmering fruit chutney fills your kitchen with a wonderful aroma. One of the nicest parts of this recipe is that none of the fruit must be peeled, and you can use the varieties you prefer or that are the freshest.

FRUIT CHUTNEY

   1 teaspoon acceptable vegetable oil

   1 large onion, diced

   1 medium apple, minced

   1 medium pear, minced

   1 large peach, minced

   1 medium plum, minced

   Zest of 1 medium orange

   1 teaspoon ground cumin

¹/₈ teaspoon ground cloves

   ❖ ❖ ❖ ❖

   4 ounces fat-free or reduced-fat cream cheese, softened to room temperature

¹/₄ cup raisins

¹/₄ teaspoon salt

¹/₈ teaspoon pepper

   4 boneless, skinless chicken breast halves (about 4 ounces each), all visible fat discarded

3¹/₄ cups water

1¹/₃ cups uncooked orzo

   2 tablespoons cider vinegar

Heat the oil in a Dutch oven over medium heat. Swirl the oil to coat the bottom. Cook the onion for 5 minutes, stirring occasionally.

   Stir in the remaining chutney ingredients. Reduce the heat and simmer, covered, for 20 minutes. Uncover and simmer for 20 minutes, stirring occasionally.

PER SERVING	
Calories 501	Cholesterol 71 mg
Total Fat 4.0 g	Sodium 373 mg
Saturated 0.5 g	Carbohydrates 77 g
Polyunsaturated 1.0 g	Fiber 6 g
Monounsaturated 1.0 g	Sugar 26 g
	Protein 39 g

Meanwhile, in a small bowl, stir together the cream cheese, raisins, salt, and pepper to thoroughly combine.

Butterfly a chicken breast by placing it flat on a cutting board and slicing it lengthwise down the center *almost* in half; don't cut completely through. (You should be able to open it like a book.) Repeat with the remaining breasts.

Open a chicken breast. Spread a quarter of the raisin mixture on one half; close. Repeat with the remaining breasts and raisin mixture.

Stir the water and orzo into the chutney. Increase the heat to high. Bring to a boil, stirring occasionally. Stir in the vinegar.

Place the chicken breasts in a single layer in the liquid. Reduce the heat and simmer, covered, for 20 to 25 minutes, or until all the liquid is absorbed and the chicken is no longer pink in the center.

COOK'S TIP ON PITTING PEACHES AND PLUMS

Cut through to the peach or plum pit in a circle, following the natural crevice. To separate, use your hands to twist the two halves in opposite directions. Use a melon baller to easily remove the pit.

chicken, corn, and broccoli stir-fry

SERVES 4; 2 CUPS PER SERVING

You don't need to own a wok to make this attractive stir-fry. Finish the meal with mandarin oranges or tangerines.

1¹/₂ cups fat-free, low-sodium chicken broth

¹/₂ cup pineapple juice

3 tablespoons bottled stir-fry sauce

1 tablespoon light brown sugar

1 tablespoon cornstarch

1 teaspoon toasted sesame oil

¹/₄ to ¹/₂ teaspoon crushed red pepper flakes

1 pound boneless, skinless chicken breasts, all visible fat discarded

1 teaspoon acceptable vegetable oil

2 medium carrots, thinly sliced

1 medium onion, chopped

8 ounces broccoli florets

15-ounce can cut baby corn packed in water, rinsed and drained

¹/₂ cup sliced water chestnuts, rinsed and drained

4 ounces uncooked rice noodles

In a small bowl, whisk together the broth, pineapple juice, stir-fry sauce, brown sugar, cornstarch, sesame oil, and red pepper flakes until the cornstarch dissolves. Set aside.

Cut the chicken into bite-size pieces.

Heat a large, deep nonstick skillet over medium-high heat. Pour the vegetable oil into the skillet and swirl to coat the bottom. Cook the chicken for 3 to 4 minutes, or until no longer pink in the center, stirring occasionally.

Stir in the carrots and onion. Cook for 1 to 2 minutes, or until the onion is tender-crisp, stirring occasionally.

Stir in the broccoli and corn. Cook for 1 to 2 minutes, or until the broccoli is barely tender-crisp, stirring occasionally.

PER SERVING	Cholesterol 66 mg
Calories 386	Sodium 727 mg
Total Fat 4.0 g	Carbohydrates 53 g
Saturated 0.5 g	Fiber 9 g
Polyunsaturated 1.5 g	Sugar 14 g
Monounsaturated 1.5 g	Protein 34 g

Stir the reserved chicken broth mixture. Stir it into the chicken mixture. Bring to a simmer. Stir in the rice noodles. Simmer, covered, for 5 minutes, or until the vegetables and noodles are tender.

COOK'S TIP ON CANNED BABY CORN

Look for canned baby corn in the Asian section of the grocery. Avoid brands that contain vinegar or are labeled "pickled." Those tart-flavored products are not suitable for savory dishes such as this.

greek-style chicken with lemon-pistachio rice

SERVES 4; 3 OUNCES CHICKEN AND ABOUT 1 CUP RICE AND VEGETABLES PER SERVING

When you remove this meal from the oven, you'll think you're in a kitchen in Greece. The aroma is a delightful portent of good things to come. (See photograph on cover.)

1^1/$_2$ cups fat-free, low-sodium chicken broth

1 cup uncooked instant brown rice

10 ounces frozen chopped spinach, thawed and squeezed dry

2 large tomatoes, chopped

2 teaspoons lemon zest

2 tablespoons fresh lemon juice

2 tablespoons chopped pistachio nuts

1 tablespoon finely chopped fresh oregano or 1 teaspoon dried, crumbled

1 tablespoon snipped fresh dillweed or 1 teaspoon dried, crumbled

^{1}/$_2$ teaspoon ground cinnamon

^{1}/$_4$ teaspoon pepper

4 boneless, skinless chicken breast halves (about 4 ounces each), all visible fat discarded

8 ounces fat-free or low-fat plain yogurt

2 teaspoons fresh lemon juice

2 tablespoons chopped pistachio nuts

Fresh oregano, dillweed, and lemon zest (optional)

Preheat the oven to 375°F.

In an 8-inch glass or metal baking dish, stir together the broth, rice, spinach, tomatoes, lemon zest, 2 tablespoons lemon juice, 2 tablespoons pistachios, 1 tablespoon oregano, 1 tablespoon dillweed, cinnamon, and pepper. Push the mixture to the side.

Add the chicken breasts. Spoon a small amount of the rice mixture over them. Cover with aluminum foil.

PER SERVING	
Calories 333	Cholesterol 67 mg
Total Fat 6.5 g	Sodium 207 mg
Saturated 1.0 g	Carbohydrates 32 g
Polyunsaturated 2.0 g	Fiber 6 g
Monounsaturated 2.5 g	Sugar 8 g
	Protein 37 g

Bake for 50 to 60 minutes, or until the chicken is no longer pink in the center and the rice is tender.

Meanwhile, stir together the yogurt and 2 teaspoons lemon juice.

To serve, spoon the yogurt mixture over the chicken, rice, and vegetables. Sprinkle with the remaining pistachios. Garnish with oregano, dillweed, and lemon zest.

COOK'S TIP

If you're freezing this dish, delay making the yogurt sauce. Prepare it shortly before serving the reheated dish.

chicken with potatoes and broccoli in creamy mustard sauce

SERVES 4; 1¹/₂ CUPS PER SERVING

A guilt-free, creamy sauce envelops plump chicken tenders, chunks of potatoes, and vitamin-rich broccoli. The Dijon mustard adds just a touch of the exotic to this homey dish.

1 teaspoon olive oil

1 pound chicken breast tenders, all visible fat discarded

4 medium red potatoes (about 4 ounces each), unpeeled, quartered

1 cup fat-free, low-sodium chicken broth

16 ounces frozen chopped broccoli

10.75-ounce can reduced-fat, reduced-sodium condensed cream of chicken soup

2 tablespoons Dijon mustard

1 tablespoon dried minced onion

¹/₄ teaspoon salt

¹/₈ teaspoon pepper

Heat a large, deep skillet over medium-high heat. Pour the oil into the skillet and swirl to coat the bottom. Cook the chicken for 5 to 6 minutes, or until brown and almost cooked through, stirring occasionally.

Stir in the potatoes and broth. Bring to a simmer. Reduce the heat and simmer, covered, for 10 to 15 minutes, or until the potatoes are tender when pierced with a knife.

Stir in the broccoli. Simmer, covered, for 5 minutes, or until the broccoli is tender-crisp.

Stir in the remaining ingredients. Increase the heat to medium. Cook until the chicken is no longer pink in the center and the mixture is warmed through, 3 to 4 minutes, stirring occasionally.

PER SERVING	
Calories 303	Cholesterol 72 mg
Total Fat 4.0 g	Sodium 736 mg
Saturated 1.0 g	Carbohydrates 34 g
Polyunsaturated 0.5 g	Fiber 6 g
Monounsaturated 1.0 g	Sugar 6 g
	Protein 34 g

biscuit-topped chicken casserole

SERVES 5; 1¹/₂ CUPS PER SERVING

What could be more tempting than chicken and vegetables cooked until tender in a bubbling, creamy sauce topped with golden brown biscuits? Stock your freezer and pantry with the necessary ingredients, and you'll be ready to prepare this casserole anytime.

10.75-ounce can reduced-fat, reduced-sodium condensed cream of chicken soup

1 cup fat-free, low-sodium chicken broth

1 pound boneless, skinless chicken breasts, all visible fat discarded, cut into bite-size pieces

3 cups frozen green beans, thawed

1 1/2 cups frozen pearl onions, thawed

1 1/2 cups frozen sliced carrots, thawed

1 teaspoon salt-free all-purpose seasoning blend

7.5-ounce can (10 count) refrigerated low-fat buttermilk biscuits

Preheat the oven to 400°F.

In an 8-inch square nonstick baking pan, stir together the soup and broth. Stir in the remaining ingredients except the biscuits. Cover the pan with aluminum foil.

Bake for 50 to 60 minutes, or until the chicken is no longer pink in the center. Place the biscuits on the chicken mixture.

Bake, uncovered, for 12 to 13 minutes, or until the biscuits are golden brown and cooked through.

PER SERVING	
Calories 323	Cholesterol 58 mg
Total Fat 3.5 g	Sodium 702 mg
Saturated 1.0 g	Carbohydrates 44 g
Polyunsaturated 0.5 g	Fiber 4 g
Monounsaturated 0.5 g	Sugar 7 g
	Protein 28 g

braised chicken
with apricots and orzo

For a different twist, braise chicken breasts, red onion slices, dried apricots, and fresh ginger, then add orzo to soak up the braising liquid.

- 1 teaspoon acceptable vegetable oil
- 1 pound boneless, skinless chicken breast halves (about 4 ounces each), all visible fat discarded
- 1 large red onion, sliced (about 2 cups)
- 1 large green bell pepper, sliced (optional)
- 2 cups fat-free, low-sodium chicken broth
- 6-ounce package dried apricots, sliced if desired
- ¹/₂ cup fresh orange juice
- 1 tablespoon grated peeled gingerroot
- ¹/₄ teaspoon salt
- ¹/₈ teaspoon pepper
- ³/₄ cup dried orzo

Heat a large, deep skillet over medium-high heat. Pour in the oil and swirl to coat the bottom. Cook the chicken for 3 to 4 minutes on each side, or until golden brown.

Add the onion and bell pepper. Cook for 2 to 4 minutes, or until the vegetables are slightly tender, stirring occasionally.

Stir in the remaining ingredients except the orzo. Bring to a simmer over medium-high heat, stirring occasionally. Reduce the heat and simmer, covered, for 10 minutes, or until the chicken is no longer pink in the center and the apricots are soft.

Stir in the orzo. Simmer, covered, for 15 minutes, or until the pasta is tender, stirring occasionally.

PER SERVING	
Calories 440	Cholesterol 66 mg
Total Fat 3.5 g	Sodium 260 mg
Saturated 0.5 g	Carbohydrates 70 g
Polyunsaturated 1.0 g	Fiber 8 g
Monounsaturated 1.0 g	Sugar 39 g
	Protein 35 g

chicken and double
mushroom stew

When you reveal that this beefy-tasting stew is made with chicken and meaty-textured mushrooms, your family and friends may be surprised.

2 teaspoons olive oil

1 pound boneless, skinless chicken breasts, all visible fat discarded, cut into 1-inch pieces

2 cups fat-free, low-sodium chicken broth

2 cups fat-free, no-salt-added beef broth

1/2 cup dry red wine (regular or nonalcoholic) or fat-free, low-sodium chicken broth

6 ounces mini portobello mushrooms, stems trimmed, halved, or 2 large portobello mushrooms, stems removed, caps cut into 1-inch cubes

8 dried shiitake mushrooms, cut into bite-size pieces, or 8 fresh shiitake mushrooms, stems discarded, caps quartered

8 dry-packed sun-dried tomato halves, quartered

8 medium garlic cloves

2 tablespoons imitation bacon bits

2 teaspoons salt-free all-purpose or onion seasoning blend

1 1/2 cups dried whole-wheat spiral noodles, such as rotini

Heat a Dutch oven over medium-high heat. Pour the oil into the Dutch oven and swirl to coat the bottom. Cook the chicken for 3 to 4 minutes, or until golden brown, stirring occasionally.

Stir in the remaining ingredients except the noodles. Bring to a boil over high heat, stirring occasionally. Reduce the heat and simmer, covered, for 30 minutes, or until the chicken is no longer pink in the center and the mushrooms are tender (no stirring needed). Increase the heat to medium-high and bring the mixture to a boil. Stir in the noodles. Boil, uncovered, for 10 minutes, or until the noodles are tender, stirring occasionally.

PER SERVING	
Calories 349	Cholesterol 66 mg
Total Fat 5.0 g	Sodium 190 mg
Saturated 1.0 g	Carbohydrates 36 g
Polyunsaturated 1.0 g	Fiber 5 g
Monounsaturated 2.5 g	Sugar 3 g
	Protein 38 g

chicken tetrazzini
supreme

A creamy vegetable-studded sauce envelops chicken strips and whole-wheat pasta spirals in this family favorite. Fresh basil and tomatoes add a burst of extra flavor.

1 teaspoon olive oil

1 pound boneless, skinless chicken breasts, all visible fat discarded, cut into 1-inch strips

1 small carrot, thinly sliced

1/2 cup chopped onion

8 ounces medium button mushrooms, quartered

1 1/2 cups fat-free, low-sodium chicken broth

1/2 cup dry white wine (regular or nonalcoholic) or fat-free, low-sodium chicken broth

1/2 teaspoon dried oregano, crumbled

1/4 teaspoon pepper

1 1/2 cups dried whole-wheat spiral pasta

1/2 cup fat-free or light sour cream

1 cup diced tomatoes

1/4 cup shredded or grated Parmesan cheese

1/4 cup loosely packed fresh basil, heavy stems discarded, leaves thinly sliced (optional)

Heat a large, deep nonstick skillet over medium-high heat. Pour in the olive oil and swirl to coat the bottom. Cook the chicken for 3 to 4 minutes, or until browned, stirring occasionally.

Stir in the carrot and onion. Cook over medium heat for 2 to 3 minutes, or until the vegetables are tender-crisp, stirring occasionally.

Stir in the mushrooms. Cook for 2 to 3 minutes, or until the mushrooms are tender, stirring occasionally.

Stir in the chicken broth, wine, oregano, and pepper. Increase the heat to medium-high and bring to a simmer, stirring occasionally.

PER SERVING	
Calories 351	Cholesterol 74 mg
Total Fat 4.5 g	Sodium 222 mg
Saturated 1.5 g	Carbohydrates 35 g
Polyunsaturated 1.0 g	Fiber 4 g
Monounsaturated 1.5 g	Sugar 7 g
	Protein 37 g

Stir in the pasta. Reduce the heat and simmer, covered, for 10 minutes, or until the pasta is tender and the chicken is no longer pink in the center.

With the heat on low, let the mixture cool slightly, uncovered, for 3 to 4 minutes, or until it stops bubbling and most of the steam subsides, stirring occasionally. (If the mixture is too hot, the sour cream may curdle when added.)

Meanwhile, in a small bowl, stir together the remaining ingredients. Stir into the chicken mixture. Cook over low heat for 2 to 3 minutes, or until warmed through, stirring occasionally.

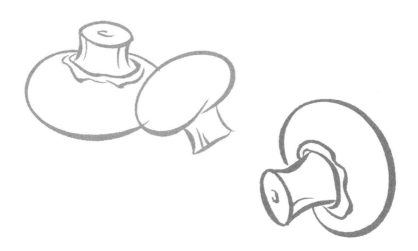

spicy peanut
and chicken noodles

SERVES 4; 1 CUP NOODLES PLUS 1 HEAPING CUP CHICKEN MIXTURE PER SERVING

Light coconut milk helps make a velvety sauce for this dish.

8-ounce package dried bean threads (cellophane or glass noodles)

4 cups warm water

2 tablespoons low-salt soy sauce

3 teaspoons toasted sesame oil, divided use

1 pound chicken tenders or boneless, skinless chicken breasts, all visible fat discarded, cut into 1 × 1/4-inch strips

2 medium garlic cloves, minced

1 teaspoon minced peeled gingerroot

1/4 to 3/4 teaspoon crushed red pepper flakes

1 1/2 cups chopped mixed bell peppers or 1 large red or yellow bell pepper, chopped

8 ounces fresh snow peas, trimmed, diagonally halved if large

1 tablespoon low-salt soy sauce

1/2 cup canned light unsweetened coconut milk

1 tablespoon cornstarch

1 tablespoon cold water

1/4 cup chopped dry-roasted peanuts

1/4 cup snipped fresh cilantro or thinly sliced green onions

In a large bowl, soak the bean threads in the warm water for 12 minutes, or until softened. Drain well. Cut into 2-inch pieces and return to the bowl. Stir in 2 tablespoons soy sauce and 1 teaspoon sesame oil. Set aside.

Heat a large skillet over medium heat. Pour the remaining sesame oil into the skillet and swirl to coat the bottom. Cook the chicken, garlic, gingerroot, and red pepper flakes for 2 minutes, stirring frequently. Add the bell peppers and snow peas. Cook for 2 minutes, stirring frequently. Add 1 tablespoon soy sauce. Cook for 1 minute, stirring frequently. Add the coconut milk. Cook for about 2 minutes, or until the chicken is no longer pink in the center and the vegetables are

PER SERVING	
Calories 484	Cholesterol 66 mg
Total Fat 11.0 g	Sodium 383 mg
Saturated 2.5 g	Carbohydrates 63 g
Polyunsaturated 3.5 g	Fiber 4 g
Monounsaturated 4.0 g	Sugar 5 g
	Protein 31 g

tender-crisp, stirring frequently. (Using two wooden paddles and tossing the ingredients frequently works well for these steps.)

Put the cornstarch in a cup. Add the water, stirring to dissolve. Stir into the chicken mixture. Cook for about 1 minute, or until the sauce thickens, stirring frequently.

Arrange the noodles on plates. Top with the chicken mixture. Sprinkle with the peanuts and cilantro.

COOK'S TIP ON BEAN THREADS

Almost transparent when cooked, these noodles—also known as cellophane noodles or glass noodles—are made from mung bean flour. They must be softened in warm water before they can be cooked unless they are being deep-fried.

TIME-SAVER

Look for packaged chicken that is cut for stir-frying. The size will be just right for this recipe.

poblano chicken and rice

Intensely flavored poblano peppers add Mexican flair to this simple chicken and rice dish.

2 poblano peppers

Vegetable oil spray

2 medium onions, chopped

2 medium ribs of celery, thinly sliced

2 cups fat-free, low-sodium chicken broth

3/4 cup uncooked rice

1/2 teaspoon ground turmeric

12 ounces boneless, skinless chicken breasts, all visible fat discarded, cut into bite-size pieces

3/4 cup shredded reduced-fat sharp Cheddar cheese

1/2 teaspoon ground cumin

1/2 teaspoon salt

1/8 to 1/4 teaspoon crushed red pepper flakes (optional)

Remove the stems from the peppers. Cut the peppers in half lengthwise. Holding the peppers under running water, remove the seeds and ribs. Shake off excess water. Cut the peppers into thin strips.

Heat a large skillet over medium-high heat. Remove from the heat and lightly spray with vegetable oil spray (being careful not to spray near a gas flame). Cook the peppers, onions, and celery for 8 minutes, or until the edges of the peppers begin to brown, stirring occasionally.

Stir in the broth, rice, and turmeric. Increase the heat to high. Bring the mixture to a boil. Reduce the heat and simmer, covered, for 15 minutes.

Stir in the chicken. Simmer, covered, for 10 minutes, or until the chicken is no longer pink in the center, the rice is cooked, and most of the liquid is absorbed. Remove from the heat. Stir in the remaining ingredients.

PER SERVING	
Calories 337	Cholesterol 61 mg
Total Fat 5.0 g	Sodium 536 mg
Saturated 3.0 g	Carbohydrates 40 g
Polyunsaturated 0.5 g	Fiber 3 g
Monounsaturated 1.0 g	Sugar 7 g
	Protein 31 g

chicken piccata stir-fry

If you've limited stir-fry techniques to Asian foods, you have a world of possibilities to explore. Here, stir-fried chicken, vegetables, and noodles take on a tasty Italian twist with the lemon, garlic, and capers of a traditional piccata sauce.

1/2 tablespoon olive oil

Juice of 1 medium lemon

1 tablespoon capers, rinsed and drained

3 medium garlic cloves, minced

1 pound boneless, skinless chicken breasts, all visible fat discarded, cut across the grain into 1/8-inch slices

Vegetable oil spray

6 to 8 ounces oyster mushrooms, cut into 1-inch strips

2 cups fat-free, low-sodium chicken broth

9 ounces refrigerated angel hair pasta

3/4 pound asparagus spears, trimmed, cut into 1-inch pieces

Juice of 1/2 medium lemon

In a medium bowl, stir together the olive oil, juice of 1 lemon, capers, and garlic. Stir in the chicken to coat. Set aside.

Heat a deep 12-inch skillet over high heat. Remove from the heat and lightly spray with vegetable oil spray (being careful not to spray near a gas flame). Cook the mushrooms for 5 minutes, or until very soft and beginning to brown, stirring occasionally. Transfer to a large bowl.

In the same skillet, bring the broth to a boil. Stir in the pasta, asparagus, and juice of 1/2 lemon. Using tongs or two long-handled spoons, toss gently. Cook for 3 minutes, or until the pasta absorbs most of the broth, tossing gently four or five times. Using the tongs, transfer the pasta and asparagus to the bowl with the mushrooms. (A small amount of liquid will remain in the skillet.)

Add the chicken to the skillet. Cook for 4 to 5 minutes, or until the liquid evaporates and the chicken is no longer pink in the center, tossing frequently.

Return the pasta mixture to the skillet. Cook for 1 minute, tossing constantly.

PER SERVING	
Calories 356	Cholesterol 66 mg
Total Fat 3.5 g	Sodium 292 mg
Saturated 0.5 g	Carbohydrates 43 g
Polyunsaturated 0.5 g	Fiber 5 g
Monounsaturated 1.0 g	Sugar 4 g
	Protein 37 g

cajun chicken gumbo

SERVES 6; 1¹/₂ CUPS GUMBO PLUS ¹/₂ CUP COOKED RICE PER SERVING

Gumbo can be made with seafood, poultry, or simply vegetables. It's one of the South's most beloved comfort foods, jam-packed with slow-simmered flavors. Like so many other soups and stews, this gumbo tastes even better if made a day early.

3 tablespoons all-purpose flour

3 tablespoons olive oil

3 medium onions, chopped

2 medium green bell peppers, finely chopped

2 medium ribs of celery, chopped

14.5-ounce can no-salt-added diced tomatoes seasoned with bell peppers and onions, undrained

14.5-ounce can fat-free, low-sodium chicken broth

8 ounces frozen cut okra, thawed

1 cup water

4 bay leaves

1 cup uncooked rice

1¹/₂ pounds boneless, skinless chicken breasts, all visible fat discarded, cut into bite-size pieces

¹/₂ teaspoon red hot-pepper sauce, or to taste

1 teaspoon salt

Heat a Dutch oven over medium-high heat. Put the flour and oil in the pot. Cook for 2 minutes, stirring constantly (a flat spatula works well) until richly golden brown. Reduce the heat to medium.

Stir in the onions, bell peppers, and celery. Cook for 8 minutes, or until the vegetables begin to brown, stirring frequently.

Stir in the undrained tomatoes, broth, okra, water, and bay leaves. Increase the heat to high and bring to a boil. Reduce the heat and simmer, covered, for 30 minutes, or until the vegetables are very tender.

Meanwhile, prepare the rice using the package directions, omitting the salt and margarine.

PER SERVING	
Calories 382	Cholesterol 66 mg
Total Fat 8.5 g	Sodium 527 mg
Saturated 1.5 g	Carbohydrates 43 g
Polyunsaturated 1.0 g	Fiber 5 g
Monounsaturated 5.5 g	Sugar 9 g
	Protein 32 g

Stir the chicken into the vegetable mixture. Cook for 5 minutes, or until the chicken is no longer pink in the center. Remove from the heat. Stir in the hot-pepper sauce and salt. Let stand for a few minutes to absorb flavors. Remove the bay leaves.

To serve, put $1/2$ cup rice in each bowl. Ladle about $1^1/_2$ cups gumbo over each serving.

pizza-smothered chicken and vegetables

Pizza flavors transfer delightfully into a skillet casserole.

14.5-ounce can fat-free, low-sodium chicken broth

4 ounces dried vermicelli or other very thin pasta, broken into thirds

6 ounces green beans, trimmed

4 ounces button mushrooms, sliced

4 boneless, skinless chicken breast halves (about 3 ounces each),
all visible fat discarded

1/2 teaspoon dried basil, crumbled

1 cup pizza sauce

1/8 to 1/4 teaspoon crushed red pepper flakes

1/2 cup shredded nonfat or part-skim mozzarella cheese

2 tablespoons shredded or grated Parmesan cheese

In a large skillet, bring the broth to a boil over high heat.

Stir in the pasta, green beans, and mushrooms. Top with the chicken. Sprinkle with the basil. Spoon the pizza sauce over the chicken. Sprinkle with red pepper flakes. Return to a boil. Reduce the heat and simmer, covered, for 10 minutes, or until the chicken is no longer pink in the center. Cook, uncovered, for 5 minutes, or until the liquid is absorbed.

Sprinkle the mozzarella over the chicken. Sprinkle the Parmesan over all.

PER SERVING	Cholesterol 54 mg
Calories 276	Sodium 466 mg
Total Fat 2.5 g	Carbohydrates 30 g
Saturated 1.0 g	Fiber 4 g
Polyunsaturated 0.5 g	Sugar 5 g
Monounsaturated 0.5 g	Protein 32 g

homey chicken and vegetables

SERVES 4; 3 OUNCES CHICKEN
PLUS 1 1/2 CUPS VEGETABLE MIXTURE PER SERVING

Cook chicken breasts on a bed of corn, green beans, and pimientos, then top with a creamy sauce for a super-simple, family-pleasing dinner.

> Vegetable oil spray
>
> 4 boneless, skinless chicken breast halves (about 4 ounces each),
> all visible fat discarded
>
> 10.75-ounce can reduced-fat, reduced-sodium condensed cream of chicken soup
>
> 16 ounces frozen green beans, thawed
>
> 16 ounces frozen whole-kernel corn, thawed
>
> 4-ounce jar sliced pimientos, drained if desired
>
> 1 tablespoon light tub margarine
>
> 1/8 teaspoon salt
>
> 1/4 teaspoon pepper (plus more if desired)

Heat a 12-inch skillet over high heat. Remove from the heat and lightly spray with vegetable oil spray (being careful not to spray near a gas flame). Cook the chicken with the smooth side down for 2 minutes. Turn the chicken over and move the pieces to one side of the skillet.

Stir in the soup, beans, corn, and pimientos. Place the chicken with the browned side up on the vegetables. Reduce the heat to medium-high and bring to a boil. Reduce the heat and simmer, covered, for 15 to 20 minutes, or until the chicken is no longer pink in the center.

Remove the skillet from the heat. Transfer the chicken to a platter. Stir the margarine, salt, and 1/4 teaspoon pepper into the vegetable mixture. Spoon it around the chicken. Sprinkle with additional pepper.

COOK'S TIP ON BROWNING CHICKEN

Be sure the chicken pieces are dry before trying to brown them. If the chicken has moisture on it, it will not achieve a rich brown color.

PER SERVING	
Calories 328	Cholesterol 72 mg
Total Fat 5.0 g	Sodium 475 mg
Saturated 1.0 g	Carbohydrates 41 g
Polyunsaturated 1.0 g	Fiber 7 g
Monounsaturated 1.0 g	Sugar 5 g
	Protein 33 g

cheese-topped chicken and rice

You'll want this oh-so-easy recipe in your repertoire of busy-day standbys.

Vegetable oil spray

3 medium onions, chopped

14.5-ounce can fat-free, low-sodium chicken broth

^{3}/$_4$ cup uncooked rice

1 pound boneless, skinless chicken breasts, all visible fat discarded, cut into bite-size pieces

2 medium yellow squash, sliced

1 medium garlic clove, minced

^{1}/$_2$ teaspoon dried thyme, crumbled

^{1}/$_2$ teaspoon ground turmeric (optional)

4-ounce jar diced pimientos, drained if desired

^{1}/$_4$ teaspoon salt

1 cup shredded fat-free or reduced-fat sharp Cheddar cheese

Heat a 12-inch nonstick skillet over medium-high heat. Remove from the heat and lightly spray with vegetable oil spray (being careful not to spray near a gas flame). Cook the onions for 3 to 4 minutes, or until translucent, stirring occasionally.

Stir in the broth, rice, chicken, squash, garlic, thyme, and turmeric. Increase the heat to high. Bring to a boil. Reduce the heat and simmer, covered, for 30 minutes, or until the rice is tender.

Remove from the heat. Stir in the pimientos and salt. Sprinkle with the cheese. Let stand, covered, for 3 minutes to allow the cheese to melt.

PER SERVING	
Calories 373	Cholesterol 68 mg
Total Fat 2.0 g	Sodium 476 mg
Saturated 0.5 g	Carbohydrates 45 g
Polyunsaturated 0.5 g	Fiber 5 g
Monounsaturated 0.5 g	Sugar 9 g
	Protein 43 g

chicken orzo with
mediterranean tomatoes

SERVES 4; 3 OUNCES CHICKEN, $3/4$ CUP ORZO MIXTURE,
AND $1/2$ CUP TOMATO MIXTURE PER SERVING

A piquant tomato-caper mixture complements basil-flavored chicken breasts.

MEDITERRANEAN TOMATOES

10 ounces grape tomatoes or cherry tomatoes, quartered (about 2 cups)

12 kalamata olives, coarsely chopped

$1/4$ cup snipped fresh parsley

2 tablespoons capers, rinsed and drained

2 tablespoons red wine vinegar

2 teaspoons olive oil (extra virgin preferred)

1 teaspoon dried basil, crumbled

❖ ❖ ❖ ❖

Vegetable oil spray

1 pound boneless, skinless chicken breasts, all visible fat discarded

14.5-ounce can fat-free, low-sodium chicken broth

1 cup dried orzo

$1/2$ teaspoon dried basil, crumbled

2 ounces feta cheese with sun-dried tomatoes and basil, crumbled

For the tomato mixture, in a medium bowl, gently toss all the ingredients. Set aside.

Heat a 12-inch nonstick skillet over medium-high heat. Remove from the heat and lightly spray with vegetable oil spray (being careful not to spray near a gas flame). Cook the chicken with the smooth side down for 2 minutes. Remove the chicken.

Put the broth and orzo in the same skillet. Increase the heat to high. Bring to a boil, scraping the browned bits from the bottom of the skillet. Place the chicken with the browned side up on the orzo. Sprinkle with $1/2$ teaspoon basil. Reduce the heat and simmer, covered, for 12 minutes, or until the chicken is no longer pink in the center and the orzo mixture is thickened slightly, stirring occasionally.

To serve, spoon the orzo mixture onto each plate. Top with the chicken, tomato mixture, and feta.

PER SERVING	Cholesterol 76 mg
Calories 399	Sodium 523 mg
Total Fat 10.5 g	Carbohydrates 38 g
Saturated 3.0 g	Fiber 2 g
Polyunsaturated 1.0 g	Sugar 4 g
Monounsaturated 4.5 g	Protein 36 g

chicken rotini
with parmesan

This extra-easy dish offers a variety of shapes, textures, colors, and flavors—something to please everyone.

Vegetable oil spray
8 ounces button mushrooms, sliced
1 medium zucchini, thinly sliced
1 medium onion, chopped
1 medium yellow squash, thinly sliced
1/2 tablespoon dried oregano, crumbled
1/4 teaspoon crushed red pepper flakes (optional)
14.5-ounce can fat-free, low-sodium chicken broth
1 pound boneless, skinless chicken breasts, all visible fat discarded, cut into bite-size pieces
6 ounces dried rotini
1/4 cup snipped fresh parsley
1/4 teaspoon salt
1/4 cup shredded or grated Parmesan cheese

Heat a 12-inch nonstick skillet over medium-high heat. Remove from the heat and lightly spray with vegetable oil spray (being careful not to spray near a gas flame). Put the mushrooms, zucchini, onion, yellow squash, oregano, and red pepper flakes in the skillet; stir. Lightly spray with vegetable oil spray. Cook for 4 minutes, or until the onion is translucent, stirring occasionally.

Increase the heat to high. Stir in the broth, chicken, and pasta. Bring to a boil. Reduce the heat and simmer, covered, for 15 minutes, or until the liquid is absorbed, stirring occasionally.

Remove the skillet from the heat. Stir in the parsley and salt. Sprinkle with the Parmesan.

PER SERVING	Cholesterol 69 mg
Calories 357	Sodium 339 mg
Total Fat 4.0 g	Carbohydrates 42 g
Saturated 1.5 g	Fiber 4 g
Polyunsaturated 0.5 g	Sugar 7 g
Monounsaturated 1.0 g	Protein 38 g

balsamic-glazed rosemary chicken and spinach sandwiches

SERVES 4; 1 OPEN-FACE SANDWICH PER SERVING

Serve this hearty open-face sandwich with crunchy baby carrots.

Olive oil spray

2 teaspoons olive oil (rosemary flavored preferred)

4 boneless, skinless chicken breast halves (about 4 ounces each),
all visible fat discarded

2 medium garlic cloves, minced

3/4 teaspoon dried rosemary, crushed

1/4 teaspoon salt

1/4 teaspoon pepper

2 tablespoons balsamic vinegar

1 tablespoon honey

7 ounces baby spinach (about 4 cups packed)

4 slices sourdough bread

4 large pieces of bottled roasted red bell peppers, rinsed and drained

Heat a large skillet over medium heat. Remove from the heat and lightly spray with olive oil spray (being careful not to spray near a gas flame). Pour in the oil and swirl to coat the bottom. Put the chicken in the skillet. Sprinkle with the garlic, rosemary, salt, and pepper. Cook for 4 minutes. Turn the chicken over. Add the vinegar and honey. Cook for 4 to 5 minutes, or until the chicken is no longer pink in the center and is glazed, turning over once more. Transfer the chicken to a plate. Cover with aluminum foil to keep warm.

Put the spinach in the skillet, pressing down (the skillet will be full). Cook, covered, for 1 minute, or until the spinach wilts. Cook, uncovered, for 3 minutes, turning often. Tongs work well for this.

Meanwhile, toast the bread.

To assemble, put the toast on four plates. Place 1 breast half on each piece of toast. Top with the spinach and peppers.

PER SERVING	Cholesterol 66 mg
Calories 421	Sodium 716 mg
Total Fat 15.0 g	Carbohydrates 38 g
Saturated 2.0 g	Fiber 5 g
Polyunsaturated 5.0 g	Sugar 4 g
Monounsaturated 7.0 g	Protein 34 g

grilled chicken and vegetable sandwiches with cilantro "pesto"

An easy pestolike mixture spread on chicken and vegetables before they're grilled makes this main-dish sandwich special.

Vegetable oil spray

1 large or 2 medium garlic cloves

1 cup packed fresh cilantro, heavy stems discarded

$1/4$ cup chopped walnuts

2 tablespoons olive oil

$1/2$ teaspoon salt

$1/4$ teaspoon cayenne or black pepper

4 boneless, skinless chicken breast halves (about 4 ounces each), all visible fat discarded

2 medium red or yellow bell peppers, or a combination

2 medium zucchini

8 slices sourdough bread

2 tablespoons fat-free or reduced-fat mayonnaise dressing (optional)

Spray the grill rack with vegetable oil spray. Preheat the grill on medium.

With the motor running, drop the garlic through the feed tube of a food processor. Process until the garlic is minced. Add the cilantro and walnuts. Process until finely chopped. Add the oil. Process to a paste consistency.

Sprinkle the salt and cayenne over the chicken. Cut the bell peppers in half lengthwise. Discard the stems and seeds. Cut the zucchini lengthwise into $1/4$-inch slices. Lightly spray the chicken, bell peppers, zucchini, and bread with vegetable oil spray.

Put the chicken, bell peppers, and zucchini on the grill. Grill, covered, for 5 minutes. Turn the pieces over. Spread evenly with the cilantro mixture. Place

PER SERVING		WITH MAYONNAISE DRESSING	
		PER SERVING	
Calories 421	Cholesterol 66 mg	Calories 429	Cholesterol 66 mg
Total Fat 15.0 g	Sodium 716 mg	Total Fat 15.0 g	Sodium 779 mg
Saturated 2.0 g	Carbohydrates 38 g	Saturated 2.0 g	Carbohydrates 39 g
Polyunsaturated 5.0 g	Fiber 5 g	Polyunsaturated 5.0 g	Fiber 5 g
Monounsaturated 6.5 g	Sugar 4 g	Monounsaturated 6.5 g	Sugar 5 g
	Protein 4 g		Protein 34 g

the bread around the edges of the grill. Grill, covered, for 3 minutes. Turn the bread over. Grill, covered, for 3 to 4 minutes, or until the chicken is no longer pink in the center, the vegetables are tender, and the bread is lightly toasted. Remove everything from the grill.

Spread the mayonnaise over the bread and assemble the sandwiches. Serve warm or at room temperature.

broiled chicken and vegetable sandwiches with cilantro "pesto"

Broil the chicken and vegetables 4 to 5 inches from the heat source, following the directions for grilling. Toast the bread lightly while the chicken and vegetables are broiling.

chicken caesar wraps

Typical Caesar ingredients aren't just for salad anymore. Try them in this crunchy wrap to see what we mean.

Vegetable oil spray

4 boneless, skinless chicken breast halves (about 4 ounces each), all visible fat discarded

1 teaspoon salt-free grilling blend for poultry or other salt-free seasoning blend

1/3 cup fat-free or low-fat buttermilk

2 tablespoons fat-free or light mayonnaise dressing

1 medium garlic clove, minced

1/2 teaspoon anchovy paste

1/4 teaspoon pepper

1/8 teaspoon salt

1/2 medium cucumber, peeled and diced

4 thin slices red onion

1/4 cup shredded or grated Parmesan cheese

4 outer leaves of iceberg lettuce

Heat a large skillet over medium heat. Remove the skillet from the heat and lightly spray with vegetable oil spray (being careful not to spray near a gas flame). Sprinkle the smooth side of the chicken with the grilling blend. Cook the chicken with the seasoned side down for 5 minutes. Turn and cook for 4 to 5 minutes, or until no longer pink in the center. Thinly slice the chicken.

Meanwhile, in a large bowl, whisk together the buttermilk, mayonnaise, garlic, anchovy paste, pepper, and salt until smooth.

Add the cucumber and onions. Toss until completely coated. Add the Parmesan. Toss gently, just to slightly incorporate.

Spoon the mixture down the center of each lettuce leaf. Top with the chicken. Roll up. Secure with wooden toothpicks, if desired.

PER SERVING	
Calories 178	Cholesterol 71 mg
Total Fat 3.5 g	Sodium 422 mg
Saturated 1.5 g	Carbohydrates 5 g
Polyunsaturated 0.5 g	Fiber 1 g
Monounsaturated 1.0 g	Sugar 4 g
	Protein 30 g

mixed green salad with seared chicken and apricot-ginger vinaigrette

SERVES 6; 2 CUPS PER SERVING

A sweetly tangy vinaigrette dresses—and dresses up—this quick-to-fix salad.

Vegetable oil spray

6 boneless, skinless chicken breast halves (about 4 ounces each), all visible fat discarded

1 tablespoon low-salt soy sauce

1/3 cup all-fruit apricot spread

3 tablespoons low-salt soy sauce

3 tablespoons honey

2 tablespoons cider vinegar

1 tablespoon grated peeled gingerroot

1/4 teaspoon crushed red pepper flakes

5-ounce package mixed baby salad greens

3 ounces fresh snow peas, trimmed

1 medium red bell pepper, thinly sliced

2 medium green onions, chopped (green and white parts)

3-ounce package ramen noodles, broken into small pieces, seasoning packet discarded

1/2 cup snipped fresh cilantro (optional)

Heat a 12-inch skillet over medium-high heat. Remove from the heat and lightly spray with vegetable oil spray (being careful not to spray near a gas flame). Put the chicken in the skillet. Spoon 1 tablespoon soy sauce over the chicken. Cook for 4 minutes. Turn the chicken and cook for 4 minutes, or until no longer pink in the center. Remove the chicken and cut into thin slices.

Put the apricot spread, 3 tablespoons soy sauce, honey, vinegar, gingerroot, and red pepper flakes in the skillet and whisk together until well blended.

Stir in the remaining ingredients except the chicken. Toss gently to coat. Add the chicken and toss gently.

PER SERVING	
Calories 267	Cholesterol 66 mg
Total Fat 4.0 g	Sodium 399 mg
Saturated 1.5 g	Carbohydrates 27 g
Polyunsaturated 0.5 g	Fiber 2 g
Monounsaturated 0.5 g	Sugar 15 g
	Protein 30 g

coq au vin

The intensely flavored red wine sauce that anchors this classic chicken dish is a
little bit of heaven.

2 cups robust red wine, such as cabernet sauvignon

1 cup fat-free, low-sodium chicken broth

1 ounce low-fat, lower-sodium ham, minced

2 tablespoons no-salt-added tomato paste

1 bay leaf

1 medium garlic clove, minced

½ teaspoon dried thyme, crumbled

⅛ teaspoon pepper

3 large red potatoes (about 1 pound), cut into 1-inch cubes

6 ounces button mushrooms, sliced

3 large carrots, cut into ¼-inch slices

4 skinless chicken breast halves with bone (about 6 ounces each),
all visible fat discarded

Vegetable oil spray

¼ teaspoon salt

In a Dutch oven, combine the wine, broth, ham, tomato paste, bay leaf, garlic,
thyme, and pepper, stirring to dissolve the tomato paste. Bring to a boil over high
heat. Boil for 10 to 15 minutes, or until reduced to about 1 cup.

Stir in the potatoes, mushrooms, and carrots. Reduce the heat to medium.
Cook, covered, for 5 minutes.

Preheat the broiler.

Meanwhile, stir the vegetable mixture. Place the chicken with the bone side
down on the vegetables. Lightly spray the chicken with vegetable oil spray.

Broil about 6 inches from the heat for about 5 minutes, or until lightly brown.

PER SERVING	
Calories 321	Cholesterol 82 mg
Total Fat 2.0 g	Sodium 339 mg
Saturated 0.5 g	Carbohydrates 30 g
Polyunsaturated 0.5 g	Fiber 5 g
Monounsaturated 0.5 g	Sugar 7 g
	Protein 38 g

Return the Dutch oven to the stove. Spoon some of the sauce and a few mushrooms over the chicken. Cook, covered, over low heat for 15 minutes. Turn over the chicken. Sprinkle with the salt. Cook, covered, for 15 minutes, or until the chicken is no longer pink in the center and the potatoes are tender. Using a slotted spoon, transfer the chicken and vegetables to plates.

Increase the heat to high. Cook the sauce for 4 to 5 minutes, or until thick and reduced to about $1/2$ cup. Spoon 2 tablespoons sauce over each piece of chicken.

lemon-garlic chicken, asparagus, and potatoes

SERVES 4; 3 OUNCES CHICKEN, 3 POTATO WEDGES,
AND $^2/_3$ CUP ASPARAGUS PER SERVING

Garlic and lemon create a dynamic flavor duo in this easy-to-assemble and hearty roasted supper. Cutting the asparagus on the diagonal makes it look attractive.

Vegetable oil spray (olive oil spray preferred)

2 large baking potatoes (russet preferred) (about 24 ounces)

2 teaspoons olive oil

1 medium lemon

$^1/_2$ cup fat-free, low-sodium chicken broth

1 teaspoon olive oil

4 medium garlic cloves, minced

4 skinless chicken breast halves with bone (about 6 ounces each), all visible fat discarded

1 teaspoon salt

$^1/_2$ teaspoon pepper

$^1/_2$ cup fresh, soft whole-wheat bread crumbs

1 pound asparagus spears, cut diagonally into $1^1/_2$-inch pieces

2 tablespoons snipped fresh parsley

Preheat the oven to 375°F. Lightly spray a $15 \times 10 \times 1$-inch rimmed baking sheet or the bottom of a large broiler pan with vegetable oil spray.

Cut each potato lengthwise into 6 wedges. Place on the baking sheet with the skin side down. Brush the wedges with 2 teaspoons oil.

Bake for 10 minutes.

Meanwhile, grate 1 teaspoon lemon zest. Set aside. Squeeze 2 tablespoons lemon juice into a small bowl. Stir in the broth, remaining 1 teaspoon oil, and garlic.

Remove the pan from the oven. Add the chicken. Brush the chicken and potatoes with the broth mixture. Sprinkle with the salt and pepper, then with the bread crumbs.

PER SERVING	
Calories 311	Cholesterol 79 mg
Total Fat 5.5 g	Sodium 716 mg
Saturated 1.0 g	Carbohydrates 30 g
Polyunsaturated 0.5 g	Fiber 5 g
Monounsaturated 3.0 g	Sugar 5 g
	Protein 38 g

Bake for 30 minutes. Remove the pan from the oven. Brush the potatoes with the pan juices. Add the asparagus.

Bake for 10 minutes, or until the chicken is no longer pink in the center and the potatoes and asparagus are tender.

To serve, sprinkle with the parsley and lemon zest.

COOK'S TIP ON LEMON ZEST

Use a food rasp or the fine shredding side of a box grater to grate the lemon zest before cutting and squeezing the lemon to get the juice. Be careful to avoid getting the white pith, which is bitter.

spice-roasted chicken and vegetables

SERVES 4; 1 CHICKEN BREAST HALF, $^1/_2$ CUP VEGETABLES, AND $^3/_4$ CUP RICE PER SERVING

The heady aroma of the curry and cumin gives your family the first clue—this isn't the same old chicken-and-vegetable dish they've had before.

$^1/_2$ teaspoon curry powder

$^1/_2$ teaspoon ground cumin

$^1/_2$ teaspoon paprika

$^1/_4$ teaspoon garlic powder

$^1/_4$ teaspoon cayenne (optional)

$^1/_4$ teaspoon salt

  Vegetable oil spray

4 skinless chicken breast halves with bone (about 6 ounces each), all visible fat discarded

4 medium carrots, diced

2 medium onions, chopped

6 ounces uncooked quick-cooking white and wild rice mix, $^1/_2$ seasoning packet discarded

Preheat the oven to 425°F.

In a small bowl, stir together the curry, cumin, paprika, garlic powder, cayenne, and salt.

Lightly spray a nonstick baking sheet with vegetable oil spray. Place the chicken breasts with bone side down, carrots, and onions on the baking sheet. Sprinkle the chicken with the curry mixture. Lightly spray the chicken and vegetables with vegetable oil spray.

Bake for 22 to 25 minutes, or until the chicken is no longer pink in the center.

Meanwhile, prepare the rice using the package directions but with only half the seasoning packet.

To serve, spoon the rice onto the center of a serving platter. Spoon the vegetables over the rice. Arrange the chicken around the rice.

PER SERVING	
Calories 355	Cholesterol 76 mg
Total Fat 4.0 g	Sodium 532 mg
Saturated 1.0 g	Carbohydrates 47 g
Polyunsaturated 1.0 g	Fiber 5 g
Monounsaturated 1.0 g	Sugar 10 g
	Protein 33 g

chicken and mushroom
cacciatore with gnocchi

SERVES 4; 1 CHICKEN THIGH, $^3/_4$ CUP VEGETABLES AND SAUCE,
AND $^1/_2$ CUP GNOCCHI PER SERVING

Chicken thighs become tender and succulent in a tasty cacciatore sauce. For variety, you can substitute your favorite pasta or polenta for the gnocchi.

 Vegetable oil spray (olive oil spray preferred)

4 boneless, skinless chicken thighs (about 4 ounces each), all visible fat discarded

2 medium garlic cloves, minced

1 teaspoon salt-free Italian seasoning, crumbled

4 ounces exotic, cremini (brown), or button mushrooms, sliced

1 large green bell pepper, diced

$1^1/_2$ cups fat-free, low-sodium spaghetti sauce, such as tomato-basil

12 ounces potato gnocchi

$^1/_4$ cup sliced or chopped fresh basil, heavy stems removed, or snipped Italian or flat-leaf parsley

Heat a large nonstick skillet over medium heat. Remove from the heat and lightly spray with vegetable oil spray (being careful not to spray near a gas flame). Add the chicken. Sprinkle with the garlic and Italian seasoning. Cook for 3 minutes on each side, or until nicely browned.

Stir in the mushrooms and bell peppers. Cook for 3 minutes.

Stir in the spaghetti sauce. Reduce the heat and simmer for 15 minutes, or until the chicken is no longer pink in the center, stirring frequently.

Meanwhile, prepare the gnocchi using the package directions, omitting the salt and oil.

To serve, transfer the gnocchi to plates. Place the chicken next to the gnocchi. Spoon the vegetables and sauce over both. Sprinkle with the basil.

COOK'S TIP ON POTATO GNOCCHI

Pasta made from potatoes? That's what potato gnocchi, sort of Italian potato dumplings, are. Look for packages of shelf-stable gnocchi by the pasta in the supermarket, or check the freezer section.

PER SERVING	
Calories 328	Cholesterol 94 mg
Total Fat 5.0 g	Sodium 401 mg
Saturated 1.0 g	Carbohydrates 39 g
Polyunsaturated 1.0 g	Fiber 2 g
Monounsaturated 1.5 g	Sugar 7 g
	Protein 31 g

dijon chicken with
stuffing and vegetables

SERVES 4; 3 OUNCES CHICKEN, $^1/_2$ CUP STUFFING,
AND $^3/_4$ CUP VEGETABLES PER SERVING

A coating of herb-seasoned Dijon mustard works magic to turn everyday roast chicken into something special.

1 tablespoon Dijon mustard

$^1/_2$ teaspoon dried sage

$^1/_2$ teaspoon dried basil, crumbled

$^1/_2$ teaspoon dried tarragon, crumbled

$^1/_2$ teaspoon dried thyme, crumbled

$^1/_4$ teaspoon pepper

$2^1/_2$-pound whole chicken

$^2/_3$ cup fat-free, low-sodium chicken broth

$2^1/_2$ cups herb-seasoned stuffing mix

1 large fennel bulb or 2 medium turnips

8 small beets, about 1 inch in diameter

8 cipolline onions or medium shallots, peeled

$^1/_3$ cup fat-free, low-sodium chicken broth

2 tablespoons chopped mixed fresh herbs or snipped fresh parsley

Preheat the oven to 375°F.

In a small bowl, stir together the mustard, sage, basil, tarragon, thyme, and pepper. Starting at the neck cavity, loosen the skin from the breast of the chicken by gently pushing with your fingers between the skin and the meat. Rub the mustard mixture under the loosened skin.

In a microwave-safe medium bowl, microwave $^2/_3$ cup broth at high power for 1 to 2 minutes, or until simmering. Stir in the stuffing. Spoon the stuffing into the chicken cavity. Place the chicken with the breast side up in a large, shallow roasting pan. Put the remaining stuffing in a small casserole dish. Set the casserole dish aside.

PER SERVING	
Calories 353	Cholesterol 99 mg
Total Fat 8.0 g	Sodium 653 mg
Saturated 2.0 g	Carbohydrates 34 g
Polyunsaturated 1.0 g	Fiber 7 g
Monounsaturated 1.0 g	Sugar 9 g
	Protein 37 g

Trim the fennel (or peel the turnip); cut into ¼-inch slices. Trim the beets. Put the fennel, beets, and onions in the roasting pan. Drizzle ⅓ cup broth over the vegetables.

Bake, uncovered, for 40 minutes. Stir the vegetables.

Bake for 10 minutes. Put the casserole of stuffing in the oven with the chicken and vegetables. Bake for 20 minutes, or until the internal temperature of the chicken reaches 170°F on an instant-read thermometer.

Transfer the chicken to a carving board. Cover loosely with aluminum foil; let stand for 10 minutes before carving.

Meanwhile, stir the herbs into the vegetables in the roasting pan. Continue to bake until the vegetables are tender, if needed, or turn off the oven and keep them warm.

Carve the chicken, discarding the skin. Serve with the stuffing and vegetables.

COOK'S TIP ON CIPOLLINE ONIONS

Also known as *wild onions* and *Italian pearl onions,* these small, slightly flattened onions are sweet and crunchy.

open-face chunky chicken
salad sandwiches

SERVES 4; 1 CUP CHICKEN SALAD AND 1 SLICE OF BREAD PER SERVING

Toasted pecans, juicy red grapes, and chunks of chicken tossed in a sweet and creamy dressing mounded on wheat berry bread—a perfect cool-weather, warm-weather, whatever-the-weather open-face sandwich.

1/4 cup chopped pecans

1/4 cup fat-free or light mayonnaise dressing

2 teaspoons sugar (increase to 1 tablespoon sugar if using light mayonnaise dressing)

1/2 teaspoon ground cumin

12 ounces frozen cooked boneless, skinless chicken breasts, thawed and diced

3/4 cup thinly sliced celery

2 medium green onions, chopped (green and white parts)

3/4 cup halved seedless red grapes

4 slices wheat berry or pumpernickel bread

4 leaves of leafy lettuce, such as red-leaf

4 small clusters of seedless red grapes (about 1/4 cup each)

Heat a small skillet over medium-high heat. Dry-roast the pecans for 2 to 3 minutes, or until they begin to lightly brown and are fragrant, stirring occasionally. Watch carefully so they don't burn. Remove from the heat.

In a medium bowl, stir together the mayonnaise, sugar, and cumin.

Stir in the chicken, celery, green onions, and halved grapes, coating completely.

To assemble, put each slice of bread on a plate. Place the lettuce on the bread. Spoon the salad over the lettuce. Place a cluster of grapes on each plate.

PER SERVING	
Calories 285	Cholesterol 46 mg
Total Fat 7.5 g	Sodium 524 mg
Saturated 0.5 g	Carbohydrates 31 g
Polyunsaturated 2.0 g	Fiber 3 g
Monounsaturated 3.5 g	Sugar 18 g
	Protein 24 g

chicken, brown rice, *Delicious*
and vegetable skillet

SERVES 4; ABOUT 1²/₃ CUPS PER SERVING

Dried porcini mushrooms give this quick-cooking skillet dish a rich, slow-cooked flavor. Use kitchen shears to snip the mushrooms into small pieces.

  2 teaspoons olive oil
  1/2 cup chopped onion
  1/2 cup coarsely chopped celery
  14.5-ounce can fat-free, low-sodium chicken broth
  3 to 4 tablespoons snipped dried porcini mushrooms
  1 1/2 cups uncooked quick-cooking brown rice
  13.75-ounce can artichoke hearts, rinsed, drained, and coarsely chopped   *Hearts of palm*
  2 cups matchstick-size strips of carrot
  2 cups chopped grilled skinless chicken breasts, cooked without salt
  1/2 teaspoon dried sage
  1/4 teaspoon pepper   *w/garlic*
  1/4 teaspoon salt

Heat a 12-inch skillet or Dutch oven over medium heat. Pour in the oil and swirl to coat the bottom. Cook the onion and celery for 4 minutes, stirring occasionally.

Stir in the broth and mushrooms. Bring to a boil. Stir in the rice. Reduce the heat and simmer, covered, for 5 minutes.

Stir in the artichoke hearts and carrots. Simmer, covered, for 5 minutes.

Stir in the chicken, sage, and pepper. Simmer, uncovered, until most of the liquid is absorbed and the chicken is hot. Stir in the salt.

COOK'S TIP

Refrigerate any leftovers and toss with a light vinaigrette dressing to make a flavorful salad for another meal.

PER SERVING	
Calories 354	Cholesterol 60 mg
Total Fat 6.5 g	Sodium 430 mg
Saturated 1.0 g	Carbohydrates 42 g
Polyunsaturated 1.5 g	Fiber 6 g
Monounsaturated 3.0 g	Sugar 6 g
	Protein 31 g

chicken slaw with teriyaki plum dressing

Turn chicken leftovers into this light yet filling slaw. It's perfect for a picnic.

4 ounces uncooked rice noodles

3 tablespoons plum preserves

2 tablespoons light teriyaki sauce

2 tablespoons plain rice vinegar

1 tablespoon acceptable vegetable oil

$1/2$ teaspoon toasted sesame oil

12 ounces boneless, skinless cooked chicken breasts, cooked without salt, shredded

2 cups shredded cabbage

$1/2$ cup green onions (green and white parts), thinly sliced

Prepare the rice noodles using the package directions, omitting the salt and oil. Transfer to a colander and rinse with cold water to cool the noodles. Drain well, leaving the noodles in the colander.

In a large bowl, whisk together the plum preserves, teriyaki sauce, rice vinegar, vegetable oil, and sesame oil.

Just before serving, add the remaining ingredients, including the noodles. Using two spoons or a pair of tongs, toss to combine.

COOK'S TIP

If you can't find rice noodles, you can substitute dried angel hair pasta.

COOK'S TIP ON COOKED CHICKEN BREASTS

For moist cooked chicken with easy cleanup, preheat the oven to 450°F. Put 4 boneless, skinless chicken breast halves in the center of a large piece of aluminum foil. Using 1 teaspoon salt-free all-purpose seasoning blend, season the chicken on both sides. Fold the foil to cover the chicken; crimp the edges to seal. Put the foil-wrapped chicken on a baking sheet. Bake for 30 to 40 minutes, or until the chicken is no longer pink in the center.

PER SERVING	
Calories 335	Cholesterol 72 mg
Total Fat 7.0 g	Sodium 206 mg
Saturated 1.0 g	Carbohydrates 37 g
Polyunsaturated 2.0 g	Fiber 1 g
Monounsaturated 3.5 g	Sugar 11 g
	Protein 28 g

chicken tabbouleh
with fresh mint

Tabbouleh (tuh-BOO-luh) is a Middle Eastern dish that includes bulgur wheat, tomatoes, fresh herbs, and lemon. This variation takes a new direction, using chicken, cucumber, and feta cheese and becoming an entrée. Just omit the chicken for a great side dish.

   1^1/$_2$ cups water

   5.25-ounce package tabbouleh wheat salad

      9-ounce package frozen diced cooked skinless chicken breasts, thawed

      1 large tomato, seeded if desired and diced

   ^{1}/$_2$ medium cucumber, peeled, seeded, and diced

   ^{1}/$_2$ small onion, finely chopped

   ^{1}/$_2$ cup snipped fresh parsley

   ^{1}/$_2$ cup chopped fresh mint

      1 ounce feta cheese with sun-dried tomatoes and basil, crumbled

   ^{1}/$_4$ cup cider vinegar

      2 tablespoons olive oil (extra virgin preferred)

   ^{1}/$_2$ tablespoon dried oregano, crumbled

      1 medium garlic clove, minced

      4 cups mixed baby salad greens

In a large bowl, stir together the water and wheat salad mix. Let stand for 30 to 40 minutes, or until all the water is absorbed.

   Add the remaining ingredients except the salad greens. Toss gently.

   To serve, arrange the salad greens on each plate. Spoon about 1^1/$_2$ cups wheat mixture on each serving.

COOK'S TIP ON TABBOULEH

   You can reconstitute the wheat salad mix up to 24 hours in advance. For peak flavors, however, don't add the remaining ingredients until serving time.

PER SERVING	
Calories 313	Cholesterol 39 mg
Total Fat 10.0 g	Sodium 735 mg
Saturated 2.0 g	Carbohydrates 36 g
Polyunsaturated 1.0 g	Fiber 9 g
Monounsaturated 5.5 g	Sugar 5 g
	Protein 23 g

chicken and black bean
salad with salsa dressing

SERVES 4; ABOUT 2 CUPS PER SERVING

Jícama, salsa, and cilantro add a south-of-the-border touch to this salad. Serve it with a fresh fruit compote for a refreshing meal.

> 6 cups packed torn mixed salad greens
>
> 15-ounce can no-salt-added black beans, rinsed and drained
>
> 10-ounce package cooked chicken breast strips
>
> 1 large tomato, chopped
>
> 1 cup matchstick-size strips of jícama

DRESSING

> 1/4 cup salsa or picante sauce
>
> 2 tablespoons snipped fresh cilantro
>
> 2 tablespoons fresh lime juice
>
> 1 tablespoon acceptable vegetable oil
>
> 1 tablespoon honey
>
> ❖ ❖ ❖ ❖
>
> 1/2 cup coarsely crushed baked tortilla chips (optional)
>
> 1/4 cup snipped fresh cilantro (optional)

In a large bowl, toss the salad greens, beans, chicken, tomato, and jícama.

For the dressing, in a small bowl, stir together all ingredients. Pour over the salad. Toss well.

To serve, transfer the salad to plates. Sprinkle with tortilla chips and cilantro.

COOK'S TIP

If you want to lower the amount of sodium in this dish, replace the packaged chicken strips with chicken cooked at home without salt.

COOK'S TIP ON JÍCAMA

Jícama is a root vegetable with a thin light brown skin and slightly sweet, crunchy white flesh. Refrigerate leftover jícama in plastic wrap for up to one week.

WITH CHIPS

PER SERVING		PER SERVING	
Calories 259	Cholesterol 38 mg	Calories 286	Cholesterol 38 mg
Total Fat 4.5 g	Sodium 299 mg	Total Fat 5.0 g	Sodium 349 mg
Saturated 0.5 g	Carbohydrates 30 g	Saturated 0.5 g	Carbohydrates 36 g
Polyunsaturated 1.5 g	Fiber 8 g	Polyunsaturated 1.5 g	Fiber 9 g
Monounsaturated 2.5 g	Sugar 11 g	Monounsaturated 2.5 g	Sugar 11 g
	Protein 25 g		Protein 25 g

old-world sausage
with cabbage and noodles

Very earthy and very welcoming on even the coldest of nights, this dish features chicken sausages flavored with bits of apple.

  6 ounces dried yolk-free noodles

  2 teaspoons olive oil

  4 4-ounce chicken link sausages with apples

  3 cups green cabbage, coarsely chopped, not shredded

  2 medium onions, chopped

  1 medium green bell pepper, chopped

  2 medium carrots, thinly sliced

  1 medium garlic clove, minced

  $^1/_2$ teaspoon dried thyme, crumbled

  $^1/_4$ teaspoon salt

   Pepper to taste

In a large saucepan, prepare the noodles using the package directions, omitting the salt and margarine.

Meanwhile, heat a Dutch oven over medium-high heat. Pour in the oil and swirl to coat the bottom. Cook the sausages for 2 to 3 minutes, or until richly browned, turning frequently. Transfer the sausages to a plate. Cover with aluminum foil to keep warm, if desired.

In the Dutch oven, cook the cabbage, onions, bell pepper, carrots, garlic, and thyme for 4 to 5 minutes, or until the edges of the vegetables begin to brown, stirring frequently. Stir in the salt and pepper.

Add the sausages and any accumulated juices. Remove from the heat. Let stand, covered, for 3 minutes so the flavors mingle and the sausages heat slightly.

To serve, spoon the noodles onto plates. Spoon the sausage mixture over the noodles.

PER SERVING	
Calories 412	Cholesterol 83 mg
Total Fat 13.5 g	Sodium 751 mg
Saturated 3.5 g	Carbohydrates 54 g
Polyunsaturated 0.5 g	Fiber 9 g
Monounsaturated 1.5 g	Sugar 12 g
	Protein 21 g

chicken ravioli
italiano

Assorted fresh vegetables and basil transform convenience foods into a delightful meal-in-one.

2 9-ounce packages refrigerated chicken-filled ravioli

6-ounce package baby spinach leaves or 4 cups packed torn spinach leaves

1 tablespoon olive oil

2 medium yellow summer squash or golden zucchini, cut into 1/4-inch slices, or 2 1/2 cups halved yellow or green baby pattypan squash

4 medium garlic cloves, minced

2 cups fat-free, low-sodium spaghetti sauce, such as tomato-basil

1/4 cup chopped fresh basil, heavy stems removed, or snipped Italian or flat-leaf parsley

Prepare the ravioli using the package directions, omitting the salt and oil. Stir in the spinach during the last 1 minute of cooking. Drain in a colander.

Heat the same saucepan over medium heat. Pour the oil into the pan and swirl to coat the bottom. Cook the squash and garlic for 6 minutes, stirring occasionally.

Stir in the spaghetti sauce. Bring to a simmer. Reduce the heat and simmer for 6 minutes, or until the squash is tender. Return the ravioli and spinach to the pan; heat through.

To serve, ladle the mixture into bowls. Sprinkle with the basil.

PER SERVING	
Calories 244	Cholesterol 0 mg
Total Fat 9.5 g	Sodium 539 mg
Saturated 4.0 g	Carbohydrates 69 g
Polyunsaturated 0.5 g	Fiber 6 g
Monounsaturated 2.5 g	Sugar 11 g
	Protein 21 g

creamy turkey
and wild rice soup

Tarragon gives this elegant soup a delicate flavor. Whole-wheat rolls and fresh fruit make nice accompaniments.

> 1 tablespoon acceptable vegetable oil
>
> 8 ounces turkey tenderloin, turkey breast cutlets, or boneless, skinless chicken breasts, all visible fat discarded, cut into bite-size pieces
>
> 1 teaspoon dried tarragon, crumbled
>
> ¹/₄ teaspoon salt
>
> ¹/₄ teaspoon pepper
>
> 3 cups water or fat-free, low-sodium chicken broth
>
> 6-ounce package long-grain and wild rice mix
>
> 1 cup ³/₄-inch pieces of fresh green beans or frozen green beans, thawed (about 4 ounces)
>
> 1 cup matchstick-size carrot slices
>
> ¹/₄ cup fat-free milk
>
> 2 tablespoons all-purpose flour
>
> 1¹/₂ cups fat-free milk

In a large saucepan, heat the oil over medium-high heat. Cook the turkey, tarragon, salt, and pepper for 3 minutes, or until the turkey is no longer pink in the center. Transfer to a bowl. Set aside.

In the same saucepan, stir together the water, rice, and contents of the rice seasoning packet. Bring to a boil. Reduce the heat and simmer, covered, for 10 minutes.

Stir in the green beans and carrots. Simmer, covered, for 12 minutes, or until the rice and vegetables are tender.

In a small bowl, whisk together ¹/₄ cup milk and the flour until smooth. Stir into the soup. Simmer for 1 minute, or until thickened.

Stir in the reserved turkey mixture and the remaining milk. Bring to a simmer.

PER SERVING	
Calories 313	Cholesterol 41 mg
Total Fat 4.5 g	Sodium 683 mg
Saturated 0.5 g	Carbohydrates 46 g
Polyunsaturated 1.5 g	Fiber 3 g
Monounsaturated 2.5 g	Sugar 8 g
	Protein 22 g

glazed turkey supper
with cranberry chutney

SERVES 6; 3 OUNCES TURKEY, 1 CUP VEGETABLES,
AND HEAPING $1/8$ CUP CHUTNEY PER SERVING

A boneless turkey breast takes less time to roast than a bone-in breast and is easier to carve. The apricot-Dijon glaze on the skinless breast holds in the turkey's natural juices.

Vegetable oil spray

$1^{1}/_{2}$- to $1^{3}/_{4}$-pound boneless turkey breast, skin and all visible fat discarded

2 teaspoons fines herbes or herbes de Provence

1 teaspoon paprika

1 teaspoon salt

$^{1}/_{2}$ teaspoon pepper

$^{1}/_{4}$ teaspoon garlic powder

2 tablespoons all-fruit apricot spread

2 tablespoons Dijon mustard

$1^{1}/_{2}$ pounds red or Yukon gold potatoes, cut into $1^{1}/_{2}$- to 2-inch cubes

1 tablespoon olive oil

3 medium zucchini, cut crosswise into $^{3}/_{4}$-inch slices

1 cup cranberry chutney or cranberry sauce

Preheat the oven to 375°F.

Lightly spray a roasting pan or heavy rimmed baking sheet with vegetable oil spray. Place the turkey breast in the center of the pan.

In a medium bowl, stir together the fines herbes, paprika, salt, pepper, and garlic powder. Sprinkle 1 teaspoon of the mixture over the turkey.

In a small bowl, stir together the apricot spread and mustard. Spread over the turkey.

Stir the potatoes and oil into the remaining herb mixture. Place the potatoes around the turkey. Sprinkle the potatoes with any remaining herb mixture.

PER SERVING	
Calories 334	Cholesterol 84 mg
Total Fat 4.5 g	Sodium 585 mg
Saturated 0.5 g	Carbohydrates 41 g
Polyunsaturated 0.5 g	Fiber 5 g
Monounsaturated 2.0 g	Sugar 20 g
	Protein 34 g

Bake for 40 minutes. Stir the zucchini into the potato mixture. Bake for 15 to 20 minutes, or until the vegetables are tender and the internal temperature of the turkey breast registers 165°F on an instant-read thermometer. Remove from the oven and cover with aluminum foil. Let rest for 5 minutes.

Cut the turkey crosswise into thin slices. Serve the turkey and vegetables with the chutney.

COOK'S TIP ON HERBES DE PROVENCE AND FINES HERBES

Both herbes de Provence (herbs from France's Provence region) and fines herbes (finely chopped herbs) are combinations of dried herbs used to flavor foods from omelets to vegetables to meats. Herbes de Provence often contains basil, marjoram, rosemary, thyme, sage, fennel or aniseed, lavender, and summer savory. Fines herbes might be a mixture of parsley, tarragon, chervil, and chives, plus, perhaps, oregano and/or bay leaf.

tandoori turkey and pineapple kebabs with brown rice

SERVES 4; 2 TURKEY KEBABS AND $^1/_2$ CUP RICE PER SERVING

No rainy day can spoil your plans for kebabs, since this recipe is cooked indoors in a large skillet.

 8 ounces fat-free or low-fat plain yogurt

 1 tablespoon acceptable vegetable oil

 2 teaspoons salt-free tandoori seasoning

 2 medium garlic cloves, minced

 2 to 3 drops red food coloring (optional)

 2 to 3 drops yellow food coloring (optional)

 1 pound boneless, skinless turkey breast or tenderloins, all visible fat discarded, cut into $^3/_4$-inch pieces

20-ounce can pineapple chunks in their own juice

 1 large green bell pepper

 Vegetable oil spray

$^3/_4$ cup fat-free, low-sodium chicken broth

 1 cup uncooked instant brown rice

In a large airtight plastic bag, combine the yogurt, oil, tandoori seasoning, garlic, and food coloring. Seal the bag and knead gently to combine the ingredients. Add the turkey. Seal the bag and knead gently to coat the turkey with the marinade. Refrigerate for 30 minutes to 24 hours.

Meanwhile, drain the pineapple, reserving $^1/_2$ cup juice. Cut the bell pepper into $^3/_4$-inch squares.

Open the bag wide so you can easily access the turkey pieces. Thread the turkey, pineapple, and bell peppers alternately on eight 9-inch wooden or metal skewers. Discard any remaining marinade.

Heat a large, deep nonstick skillet (at least 12 inches wide) over medium-high heat. Remove from the heat and lightly spray with vegetable oil spray (being care-

PER SERVING	
Calories 305	Cholesterol 77 mg
Total Fat 2.0 g	Sodium 79 mg
Saturated 0.5 g	Carbohydrates 39 g
Polyunsaturated 0.5 g	Fiber 3 g
Monounsaturated 0.5 g	Sugar 19 g
	Protein 30 g

ful not to spray near a gas flame). Cook the kebabs for 2 minutes on each side, or until golden brown. Remove the skillet from the heat and let it cool slightly, 3 to 4 minutes (so the liquid won't evaporate too quickly when you add it).

Pour the broth and reserved pineapple juice into the skillet. Add the rice. Bring to a simmer over medium-high heat, stirring occasionally. Reduce the heat and simmer, covered, for 10 minutes, or until the rice is tender.

GRILLED KEBABS

For a slightly smoky, grilled flavor, thread the kebabs on metal skewers and cook them on an outdoor grill on medium-high heat for 2 minutes on each side. Combine the pineapple juice and broth with the rice in a large skillet, place the kebabs on top, and cook as directed.

COOK'S TIP ON TANDOORI SEASONING

Make your own salt-free tandoori seasoning blend by combining 2 teaspoons each of ground coriander, ginger, and cumin with $1/2$ teaspoon each of ground cloves, cinnamon, turmeric, nutmeg, and paprika in a small bowl. You may also add $1/2$ teaspoon of ground cardamom and a pinch of cayenne if you wish. This seasoning will keep in an airtight container for up to six months.

slow-cooker turkey chili

SERVES 4; 1¹/₂ CUPS PER SERVING

Boasting big flavors from the variety of spices in its tomato base, this slow-cooker chili stands out from the crowd.

1 pound turkey tenderloins, all visible fat discarded, or 1 pound lean ground turkey breast, skin discarded before grinding (tenderloins preferred)

15-ounce can no-salt-added pinto beans, rinsed if desired and drained

14.5-ounce can no-salt-added diced tomatoes, undrained

1 cup water

8-ounce can no-salt-added tomato sauce

1 medium red bell pepper, diced

1 medium onion, diced

2 teaspoons whole coriander seeds

2 teaspoons celery seeds

1 tablespoon chili powder

1 teaspoon paprika

1 teaspoon ground cumin

1/2 teaspoon dried oregano, crumbled

1/2 teaspoon salt

If using the tenderloins, cut them into 3/4-inch cubes. Put the tenderloins or ground turkey in a slow cooker.

Stir in the pinto beans, undrained tomatoes, water, tomato sauce, bell pepper, and onion.

Using a mortar and pestle, crush the coriander and celery seeds together (or put the seeds in an airtight plastic bag and crush them with a rolling pin). Stir into the slow cooker with the remaining ingredients.

Cook on high for 3 to 5 hours or on low for 7 to 10 hours, or until the turkey is no longer pink in the center and the vegetables are tender.

PER SERVING	
Calories 294	Cholesterol 77 mg
Total Fat 2.0 g	Sodium 427 mg
Saturated 0.5 g	Carbohydrates 33 g
Polyunsaturated 0.5 g	Fiber 9 g
Monounsaturated 0.5 g	Sugar 13 g
	Protein 35 g

COOK'S TIP

The chili will be ready after the minimum times called for. If dinner is delayed or a longer cooking time just fits your schedule better, continuing to cook for up to the maximum times will work as well.

COOK'S TIP ON MORTAR AND PESTLE

This useful kitchen tool releases the flavors of dried herbs and seeds, such as the coriander and celery seeds in this recipe. The bowl-like mortar holds the items to be ground; the pestle is used to grind the items. A mixture of 1 to 2 tablespoons dried seeds—for example, caraway, dill, mustard, and cumin—ground with a mortar and pestle makes an aromatic dry rub for a lean 1- to 2-pound eye-of-round roast or pork tenderloin.

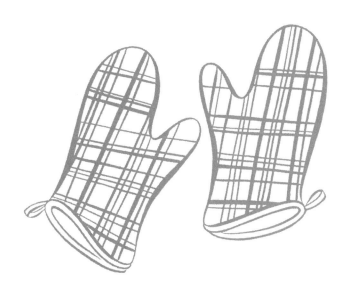

turkey cutlets and vegetables parmesan

SERVES 4; 4 OUNCES TURKEY, ABOUT $^2/_3$ CUP ZUCCHINI, 2 SLICES POLENTA, AND $^1/_4$ CUP SAUCE PER SERVING

In this version of an Italian favorite, turkey cutlets replace veal and polenta is a nice change from the usual pasta accompaniment.

Whites of 2 large eggs

1 tablespoon water

$^1/_2$ cup plain dried bread crumbs

$^1/_4$ cup finely grated Parmesan cheese

1 teaspoon salt-free Italian seasoning or dried basil, crumbled

$^1/_4$ teaspoon salt

$^1/_4$ teaspoon pepper

Vegetable oil spray

1 pound turkey breast cutlets, cut $^1/_4$ inch thick

2 medium zucchini or yellow squash, or a combination, cut diagonally into $^1/_3$-inch slices

16-ounce tube flavored or plain fat-free polenta, cut crosswise into 8 slices

$^1/_2$ cup fat-free, low-sodium spaghetti sauce

Preheat the oven to 400°F.

In a shallow bowl, beat together the egg whites and water. In another shallow bowl, placed beside the first bowl, stir together the bread crumbs, Parmesan, Italian seasoning, salt, and pepper. Lightly spray two large baking sheets with vegetable oil spray. Set them next to the bowls.

Dip each cutlet in the egg white mixture, letting any excess drip off. Lightly coat with the bread crumb mixture. Place the turkey in a single layer on one baking sheet. Repeat with each slice of squash, placing the squash with the turkey.

Place the polenta slices on the second sheet. Put the turkey and squash on the center oven rack and the polenta on the lower oven rack.

PER SERVING	
Calories 317	Cholesterol 81 mg
Total Fat 3.5 g	Sodium 773 mg
Saturated 1.5 g	Carbohydrates 31 g
Polyunsaturated 0.5 g	Fiber 3 g
Monounsaturated 1.0 g	Sugar 6 g
	Protein 37 g

Bake for 12 minutes, or until the cutlets are no longer pink in the center, the squash is tender, and the polenta is hot. Remove the baking sheets from the oven.

Set the oven on broil. Broil the turkey and squash 5 to 6 inches from the heat for 2 minutes, or until golden brown.

Meanwhile, microwave the spaghetti sauce in a microwave-safe measuring cup or bowl on 100 percent power (high) for 1 to 2 minutes, or until hot. If you prefer, heat the sauce in a small pan over medium-high heat for 3 to 4 minutes.

Transfer the cutlets, squash, and polenta to plates. Spoon 2 tablespoons sauce over each serving.

potato-crusted turkey and vegetable loaf

SERVES 4; 1 1/2 CUPS PER SERVING

A simple layered entrée, this dish starts with a savory turkey and sage base, then hides a layer of aromatic vegetables under more turkey and a crisp potato crust.

Olive oil spray

1 medium onion, diced

3 medium carrots, grated

2 medium ribs of celery, finely diced

1/4 cup loosely packed fresh sage, large stems discarded

12 ounces lean ground turkey breast, skin discarded before grinding

Egg substitute equivalent to 1 egg, or whites of 2 large eggs

1/4 cup no-salt-added tomato paste

1/4 teaspoon salt

1/4 teaspoon pepper

1 slice white bread

2 medium baking potatoes (russet preferred) (about 8 ounces)

Pepper to taste

1 tablespoon egg substitute, or white of 1 large egg

Preheat the oven to 425°F.

Lightly spray a nonstick rimmed baking sheet with olive oil spray. Spread the onion, carrots, and celery in a single layer.

Bake for 10 minutes. Remove the pan from the oven. Reduce the temperature to 350°F. Push the vegetables to one side of the pan.

Meanwhile, chop the sage. In a large bowl, stir together three fourths of the sage (reserving the rest), the turkey, egg substitute, tomato paste, salt, and 1/4 teaspoon pepper.

Hold the bread under running water just long enough to wet it thoroughly; squeeze out excess water. Stir the bread into the turkey mixture until no white shows.

PER SERVING	
Calories 216	Cholesterol 58 mg
Total Fat 1.5 g	Sodium 308 mg
Saturated 0.5 g	Carbohydrates 27 g
Polyunsaturated 0.5 g	Fiber 5 g
Monounsaturated 0 g	Sugar 8 g
	Protein 26 g

Peel and grate the potatoes (makes about 2 cups lightly packed).

In the center of the pan, form the turkey mixture into an $8 \times 4 \times 1$-inch rectangle; smooth evenly. Arrange the cooked vegetables on the turkey mixture. (The top can be flat or somewhat rounded.) Press gently to make compact.

Spread the potatoes on a flat surface, such as a cutting board. Season the potatoes to taste with pepper. Sprinkle with the reserved sage. Add 1 tablespoon egg substitute. Using your fingers, toss just to combine. Spread over the top and sides of the turkey loaf, pressing gently (don't pack firmly) so most of the mixture adheres. (A small amount of potato may fall off.)

Bake for 45 minutes, or until the internal temperature reaches 175°F when tested with an instant-read meat thermometer. Using a fork, pry open a small crack in the potatoes and remove a piece of potato closest to the meat. If the potato is not tender, continue baking for 5 to 10 minutes.

If the top is not golden-brown, place under the broiler 5 to 6 inches from the heat for 2 to 3 minutes. Let stand at room temperature for 10 minutes before slicing.

COOK'S TIP ON LEFTOVER TOMATO PASTE

If you have a recipe that calls for less than a can of tomato paste, don't waste the paste! Freeze what's left over in handy portions for future use. Spread a sheet of plastic wrap on a flat surface, such as a counter. Spoon 1 tablespoon tomato paste onto the plastic wrap at one end in the center. Three inches above that, spoon out another tablespoon. Continue until all the tomato paste is on the plastic wrap. Gently roll the plastic wrap jelly-roll style; fold the edges over. Place the plastic wrap in an airtight plastic bag; put it in the freezer. Once the tomato paste is frozen, you can easily peel off individual portions as you need them.

orzo puttanesca

The trademark of puttanesca sauce is the boldness of its ingredients—garlic, capers, Greek olives, and if you wish, a little anchovy paste.

Vegetable oil spray
1 small onion, minced
4 medium garlic cloves, minced
1 pound lean ground turkey breast, skin discarded before grinding
6 Italian plum tomatoes, coarsely chopped
12 kalamata olives, minced
3 tablespoons capers, rinsed and drained
¹/2 teaspoon anchovy paste (optional)
¹/4 teaspoon salt
2 cups hot water
1¹/2 cups dried orzo
2 small zucchini, grated (about 2 cups firmly packed)
2 tablespoons chopped fresh sage
Pepper to taste
1¹/2 tablespoons fresh lemon juice

Heat a large saucepan over medium heat. Remove from the heat and lightly spray with vegetable oil spray (being careful not to spray near a gas flame). Cook the onion for 3 to 4 minutes, or until translucent, stirring occasionally.

Add the garlic. Cook for 1¹/2 minutes, stirring constantly.

Stir in the turkey. Cook for 3 minutes, or until most of the pink is gone, stirring constantly to break up the turkey.

Stir in the tomatoes, olives, capers, anchovy paste, and salt. Cook, covered, for 2 minutes.

Stir in the water and orzo. Cook, covered, for 5 minutes.

Stir in the zucchini and sage. Cook, covered, for 5 to 6 minutes, or until the orzo is tender.

Season to taste with pepper. Stir in the lemon juice.

WITH ANCHOVY PASTE

PER SERVING		PER SERVING	
Calories 438	Cholesterol 77 mg	Calories 443	Cholesterol 78 mg
Total Fat 5.5 g	Sodium 574 mg	Total Fat 6.0 g	Sodium 679 mg
Saturated 1.0 g	Carbohydrates 59 g	Saturated 1.0 g	Carbohydrates 59 g
Polyunsaturated 1.0 g	Fiber 4 g	Polyunsaturated 1.0 g	Fiber 4 g
Monounsaturated 2.5 g	Sugar 8 g	Monounsaturated 2.5 g	Sugar 8 g
	Protein 38 g		Protein 38 g

southwestern turkey lasagna

SERVES 6; 1¹/₂ CUPS PER SERVING

You will love how simple it is to prepare this south-of-the-border spin on an Italian favorite.

Vegetable oil spray

8 ounces lean ground turkey breast, skin discarded before grinding

12 6-inch corn tortillas, halved

14.5-ounce can no-salt-added diced tomatoes, drained

4 medium zucchini, shredded

2 teaspoons chili powder

4 ounces fat-free or low-fat ricotta cheese

2.25-ounce can sliced black olives, rinsed and drained

10-ounce can green chile enchilada sauce

1¹/₂ cups shredded reduced-fat Monterey Jack cheese

Heat a Dutch oven over medium-high heat. Remove from the heat and lightly spray with vegetable oil spray (being careful not to spray near a gas flame). Cook the turkey for 7 to 8 minutes, or until browned on the outside and no longer pink in the center, stirring occasionally to turn and break up the turkey. Pour into a colander and rinse under hot water to remove excess fat. Drain well. Wipe the Dutch oven with a paper towel.

Preheat the oven to 350°F.

To assemble, arrange 8 tortilla halves in the Dutch oven, overlapping the tortillas so they cover the bottom evenly. Put half the tomatoes and half the zucchini on the tortillas. Spoon half the turkey over the vegetables. Sprinkle with 1 teaspoon chili powder. Spoon half the ricotta cheese over the vegetables; spread evenly. Sprinkle with half the olives. Pour one third of the enchilada sauce over all. Sprinkle with ¹/₂ cup Monterey Jack cheese. Repeat the layers, including tortillas. Top with the remaining tortillas, enchilada sauce, and Monterey Jack cheese.

Bake, covered, for 30 minutes, or until warmed through.

PER SERVING	
Calories 269	Cholesterol 43 mg
Total Fat 9.0 g	Sodium 657 mg
Saturated 3.5 g	Carbohydrates 24 g
Polyunsaturated 1.0 g	Fiber 5 g
Monounsaturated 2.0 g	Sugar 6 g
	Protein 24 g

cassoulet

Simmered to mouthwatering perfection in a savory tomato-based sauce, white beans and turkey sausage partner in this quicker version of a true classic.

Vegetable oil spray

1 medium onion, diced

2 medium garlic cloves, minced

8 ounces low-fat turkey breakfast sausage links, cut into 1-inch pieces

2 large portobello mushrooms, gills and stems discarded, caps coarsely diced

3 large tomatoes, seeded if desired and diced

2 15-ounce cans no-salt-added navy beans or no-salt-added kidney beans, rinsed if desired and drained

$1/2$ cup fat-free, no-salt-added beef broth

2 strips turkey bacon, minced

2 sprigs of fresh rosemary

1 bay leaf

$3/4$ teaspoon dried thyme, crumbled

$3/4$ teaspoon dried sage

$1/2$ teaspoon pepper

$1/2$ cup snipped fresh parsley

$1/4$ cup plain dried bread crumbs

Heat a stockpot or Dutch oven over medium heat. Remove from the heat and lightly spray with vegetable oil spray (being careful not to spray near a gas flame). Cook the onion for 3 to 4 minutes, or until translucent, stirring occasionally.

Add the garlic. Cook for 1 minute, stirring constantly. Add the sausage. Cook for 2 to 3 minutes, or until the casings are lightly browned, stirring frequently. Stir in the mushrooms. Cook, covered, for 3 to 4 minutes, or until the mushrooms start to release their liquid and begin to soften.

Stir in the tomatoes, beans, broth, bacon, rosemary, bay leaf, thyme, sage, and pepper. Reduce the heat and simmer, covered, for 15 minutes.

Stir in the parsley and bread crumbs. Increase the heat to medium and cook, uncovered, for 5 minutes, stirring occasionally.

PER SERVING	
Calories 415	Cholesterol 52 mg
Total Fat 12.0 g	Sodium 556 mg
Saturated 3.5 g	Carbohydrates 50 g
Polyunsaturated 3.0 g	Fiber 12 g
Monounsaturated 4.5 g	Sugar 13 g
	Protein 29 g

boiled dinner with
smoked turkey sausage
and vegetables

SERVES 6; ABOUT 1^1/$_2$ CUPS PER SERVING

Boiled dinners are usually made with corned beef, but our heart-healthy version uses smoked turkey sausage and the whole nine yards of seasonings and vegetables.

    4 cups water

    2 cups fat-free, low-sodium chicken broth

    1 tablespoon whole coriander seeds, crushed

    1 tablespoon whole allspice

    1 tablespoon whole mustard seeds

    1 teaspoon caraway seeds

    ^{1}/$_4$ teaspoon pepper

    12 small red potatoes (about 1^1/$_2$ pounds), unpeeled

    12 ounces reduced-fat smoked turkey sausage, cut into 2-inch pieces

    2 medium kohlrabi or 2 medium turnips, peeled and quartered

    6 boiling onions, peeled

    2 cups fresh or frozen green beans, trimmed if fresh

    12 medium fresh or frozen brussels sprouts, trimmed if fresh

    6 frozen half ears of corn

In a large, deep pot, such as a Dutch oven or stockpot, bring the water, broth, coriander, allspice, mustard seeds, caraway seeds, and pepper to a simmer over medium-high heat. Reduce the heat and simmer, covered, for 5 minutes.

Stir in the potatoes, sausage, kohlrabi, and onions. Increase the heat to medium-high; bring to a simmer, stirring occasionally. Reduce the heat and simmer, covered, for 25 minutes, or until the vegetables are just tender.

Stir in the green beans, brussels sprouts, and corn. Increase the heat to medium-high; return to a simmer. Reduce the heat and simmer, covered, for 8 to 10 minutes, or until the vegetables are tender.

To serve, using a slotted spoon, transfer the sausage and vegetables to plates.

PER SERVING	Cholesterol 24 mg
Calories 283	Sodium 711 mg
Total Fat 0.5 g	Carbohydrates 59 g
Saturated 0 g	Fiber 10 g
Polyunsaturated 0.5 g	Sugar 15 g
Monounsaturated 0 g	Protein 19 g

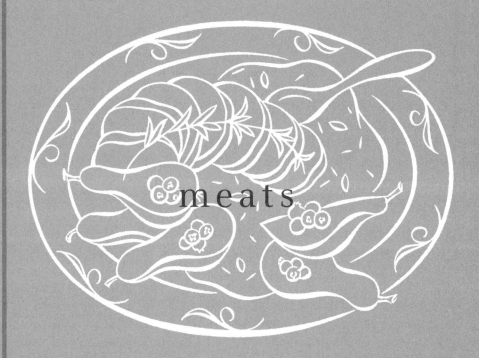

meats

(continued on following page)

Creamy Corn and Ham Chowder

❖

Ham and Potato Skillet Pie

❖

Scalloped Potatoes with Ham
and Asparagus

❖

Salad of Pork, Corn, and Brussels
Sprouts with Honey-Mustard
Dressing

❖

Braised Pork Loin
with Apple Ratatouille

❖

Herbed Pork Tenderloin
and Root Vegetables

❖

Thai Coconut and Curry Soup

❖

Korean-Style Grilled Pork
and Potato Salad

❖

Grilled Pork-and-Vegetable Pitas

❖

Jerked Pork with Sweet Potatoes
and Pineapple

❖

Stuffed Pork Tenderloin
and Pesto Couscous

❖

Horseradish Pork
with Blue Cheese Tomatoes

❖

Rosemary Pork and Pears
with Dried Berries

❖

Dijon Pork with Potatoes
and Carrots

❖

Chipotle Pork Posole

❖

Pork and Toasted Peanut
Fusion Wrap

❖

Thai Pork and Noodles

❖

Cajun Pork Chop Skillet

❖

Pork Chops and Potatoes
in Creamy Gravy

❖

Pork with Bell Peppers and Orzo

❖

Sweet-and-Sour Pork
with Brown Rice and Bok Choy

❖

Sausage and Barley
with Pine Nuts and
Golden Raisins

❖

Sausage and Potato Frittata

❖

Mushroom-Stuffed Veal Marsala

❖

Curried Lamb and Couscous
Skillet

pot roast cacciatore

SERVES 4; 3 OUNCES MEAT, 1 POTATO, AND $^2/_3$ CUP VEGETABLES PER SERVING
(PLUS ABOUT 12 OUNCES MEAT RESERVED)

Slow-cooked tomatoes, onion, garlic, and mushrooms make a heavenly sauce. Add a roast and some potatoes to the simmering pot, and you have a rustic Italian feast. You'll even have enough roast left for a second meal.

Vegetable oil spray

2 pounds boneless chuck roast, all visible fat discarded

2 14.5-ounce cans no-salt-added diced tomatoes, drained

1 large onion, chopped

6 ounces button mushrooms, sliced

4 medium garlic cloves, coarsely chopped

1 tablespoon fresh oregano, coarsely chopped

$^1/_2$ teaspoon salt

Pepper to taste

4 medium red potatoes, halved (about 6 ounces each)

Heat a Dutch oven over medium-high heat. Remove from the heat and lightly spray with vegetable oil spray (being careful not to spray near a gas flame). Brown the roast on all sides, about 3 minutes on each.

Add the remaining ingredients except the potatoes. Distribute evenly around the roast. Reduce the heat to low. Cook, covered, for 1 hour 30 minutes.

Arrange the potatoes around the meat, submerging them as much as possible in the cooking liquid. Cook, covered, for 1 hour 30 minutes to 1 hour 45 minutes, or until the meat is tender enough to break apart with a fork.

Remove the meat from the Dutch oven. Slice the meat against the grain. Set aside half the meat (about 12 ounces) for another use. Place the remaining meat on plates. Transfer the vegetables to the plates. Spoon the sauce over all.

PER SERVING	
Calories 328	Cholesterol 66 mg
Total Fat 5.0 g	Sodium 419 mg
Saturated 2.0 g	Carbohydrates 47 g
Polyunsaturated 0.5 g	Fiber 8 g
Monounsaturated 2.0 g	Sugar 14 g
	Protein 30 g

east meets west
pot roast

SERVES 8; 3 OUNCES MEAT AND 1 CUP VEGETABLES PER SERVING

If you are tempted to experiment with Asian-style vegetables, this user-friendly recipe is a good place to begin. Be sure to check the Cook's Tip on Taro Root, Daikon Radish, and Lotus Root for pointers.

Vegetable oil spray

2 pounds eye-of-round roast, all visible fat discarded

8 medium shallots, peeled and left whole

4 cups fat-free, no-salt-added beef broth

2 tablespoons hoisin sauce

1 tablespoon low-salt soy sauce

1 teaspoon toasted sesame oil

1/4 teaspoon pepper (white preferred)

1 medium taro root, peeled and cut into 1-inch cubes (about 1 pound)

1/2 medium daikon radish, peeled and cut into 1-inch cubes (about 8 ounces)

1 cup baby carrots

1 cup peeled, sliced fresh lotus root (about 4 ounces) or 1 cup canned cut baby corn packed in water, rinsed and drained

1 tablespoon cornstarch

1/4 cup water

Preheat the oven to 350°F.

Heat a Dutch oven over high heat. Remove from the heat and lightly spray with vegetable oil spray (being careful not to spray near a gas flame). Sear the beef for 2 to 3 minutes on each side, being careful not to let the meat burn. Add the shallots during the last 2 to 3 minutes of browning to cook them slightly, stirring occasionally so they don't burn.

Stir in the broth, hoisin sauce, soy sauce, sesame oil, and pepper. Reduce the heat to medium-high and bring the mixture to a simmer.

Bake, covered, for 1 1/2 hours (no stirring needed).

Stir in the taro root, daikon radish, baby carrots, and lotus root.

PER SERVING	
Calories 257	Cholesterol 58 mg
Total Fat 5.0 g	Sodium 183 mg
Saturated 1.5 g	Carbohydrates 24 g
Polyunsaturated 0.5 g	Fiber 4 g
Monounsaturated 2.0 g	Sugar 4 g
	Protein 29 g

Put the cornstarch in a cup. Add the water, stirring to dissolve. Stir into the meat mixture.

Bake, covered, for 30 minutes, or until the vegetables and meat are tender. Remove from the oven. Transfer the meat to a cutting board, cover lightly with aluminum foil, and let rest for 10 to 15 minutes for easier cutting. Cut the meat into thin slices. Serve with the vegetables and sauce.

COOK'S TIP ON TARO ROOT, DAIKON RADISH, AND LOTUS ROOT

Potato enthusiasts will love the tuber known as *taro root*. It is starchy like a potato and, when cooked, has a nutty flavor. Use a knife to peel the thick, brown, and slightly fuzzy skin. Daikon radish looks like a large, round white cylinder and has a sweet and slightly peppery flavor and crisp texture. It is easy to peel with a vegetable peeler and is delicious raw in salads (shredded or cut into small dice) and cooked in soups or stews. The lotus water lily is prized in Asian cooking, which uses the roots, seeds, and leaves. The lotus root is tan and cylindrical. Peel it with a vegetable peeler and cut it into crosswise slices (the slices will resemble a honeycomb). Good in stir-fries, soups, and stews, lotus root has a crispy texture like that of a water chestnut and has a slight coconut flavor. Some grocery stores carry lotus root or can order it, or look in Asian grocery stores, which also carry canned small young lotus roots. (Don't buy the pickled variety for this recipe.)

brisket with
sweet-and-sour vegetables

SERVES 8; 2³/4 OUNCES MEAT, 2¹/2 CUPS VEGETABLES,
AND ABOUT 3¹/2 TABLESPOONS SAUCE PER SERVING

Spend time with your family on a leisurely Sunday while this tasty dinner roasts unwatched. If you have leftovers, reheat them for a second dinner to serve on a hectic weeknight.

> 1 large onion, sliced
>
> 2¹/4-pound flat-cut beef brisket, all visible fat discarded
>
> 3 medium garlic cloves, minced
>
> ¹/2 teaspoon pepper
>
> 1 cup chili sauce
>
> ¹/4 cup packed light brown sugar
>
> ¹/4 cup cider vinegar
>
> 1¹/2 pounds red potatoes, cut into 1¹/2-inch pieces
>
> 16-ounce package baby carrots
>
> 1 very small head or ¹/2 medium head red or green cabbage (about 1 pound), cut through the core into 1-inch wedges
>
> ¹/2 teaspoon salt
>
> 2 tablespoons all-purpose flour
>
> 2 tablespoons cold water

Preheat the oven to 350°F.

Arrange the onion slices in a large roasting pan. Put the brisket on the onions. Sprinkle with the garlic and pepper.

In a small bowl, stir together the chili sauce, brown sugar, and vinegar. Pour over the brisket.

Bake, covered, for 1 hour.

Add the potatoes and carrots to the pan, stirring to coat with the pan juices. Put the cabbage on the brisket and vegetables. Spoon some of the pan juices over the cabbage. Sprinkle the salt over the vegetables.

PER SERVING	
Calories 320	Cholesterol 75 mg
Total Fat 5.5 g	Sodium 689 mg
Saturated 1.5 g	Carbohydrates 42 g
Polyunsaturated 0.5 g	Fiber 5 g
Monounsaturated 2.0 g	Sugar 21 g
	Protein 29 g

Bake, covered, for 1 hour 15 minutes, or until the brisket and vegetables are fork-tender.

Transfer the brisket to a carving board. Cover loosely with aluminum foil. Using a slotted spoon, transfer the vegetables to a serving dish and keep warm. Put the roasting pan over a stovetop burner, or pour the pan juices into a small saucepan.

In a cup or small bowl, whisk together the flour and water. Stir into the pan juices. Bring to a boil over medium-high heat. Boil for 1 minute, or until slightly thickened, stirring frequently.

Carve the brisket against the grain into thin slices. Arrange the brisket and vegetables on plates. Spoon the juices over all.

COOK'S TIP ON BRISKET

The flat cut of the brisket is the leaner part, making it a better choice. If your roasting pan doesn't have a lid, cover it tightly with a sheet of heavy-duty aluminum foil.

beef and barley stew

Minimal effort is needed for preparing this tasty combination of lean beef, vegetables, and barley. The oven method gives a nice roasted flavor, and the slow-cooker method is handy if you want to start fixing dinner in the morning. Like many other stews, this one is even better if made ahead and reheated.

> 1 pound eye-of-round roast, all visible fat discarded, cut into ³/₄-inch cubes
>
> 2 cups fat-free, no-salt-added beef broth
>
> ¹/₂ cup water, plus more as needed
>
> 14.5-ounce can no-salt-added diced tomatoes, undrained
>
> 1 cup baby carrots
>
> 1 large onion, chopped
>
> 2 medium ribs of celery, cut into ¹/₂-inch slices
>
> 1 tablespoon very low sodium or low-sodium Worcestershire sauce
>
> 2 teaspoons salt-free garlic-herb seasoning
>
> ¹/₂ teaspoon salt
>
> ¹/₄ teaspoon pepper
>
> ¹/₂ cup uncooked pearl barley

Preheat the oven to 350°F.

In a Dutch oven or ovenproof 3- to 4-quart casserole dish, stir together all the ingredients except the barley.

Bake, covered, for 1 hour (no stirring needed). Stir in the barley. Bake, covered, for 1 hour, or until the barley and meat are tender (no stirring needed).

slow-cooker method

Put all the ingredients except the barley in a 3¹/₂- to 4-quart slow cooker. Cook on high for 2 hours or on low for 6 hours; stir in the barley. Cook on high for 2 to 3 hours or on low for 2 to 4 hours, or until the barley and beef are tender.

PER SERVING	
Calories 308	Cholesterol 61 mg
Total Fat 5.5 g	Sodium 469 mg
Saturated 2.0 g	Carbohydrates 34 g
Polyunsaturated 0.5 g	Fiber 8 g
Monounsaturated 2.0 g	Sugar 9 g
	Protein 32 g

beef and chunky vegetables
with bloody mary sauce

SERVES 6; 3 OUNCES BEEF, 1^1/$_3$ CUPS VEGETABLES, AND ^{1}/$_3$ CUP SAUCE PER SERVING

The Bloody Mary mix and the cloves give this dish a subtle, distinctive sweet-spice flavor.

1^1/$_2$ pounds boneless eye of round, all visible fat discarded

2 cups Bloody Mary mix

1 tablespoon very low sodium or low-sodium Worcestershire sauce

1 teaspoon dried oregano, crumbled

6 whole cloves

1^1/$_2$ pounds medium red potatoes, quartered

2 cups baby carrots

2 medium onions, each cut into eighths

1 medium green bell pepper, cut into thin strips

2 to 3 teaspoons sugar

^{1}/$_4$ teaspoon salt

Heat a Dutch oven over medium-high heat. Brown the beef for 1 minute on each side. Remove the beef.

Put the Bloody Mary mix, Worcestershire sauce, oregano, and cloves in the Dutch oven. Increase the heat to high and bring to a boil. Stir in the potatoes, carrots, onions, and bell pepper. Return to a boil.

Place the beef on the vegetables. Reduce the heat and simmer, covered, for 35 minutes, or until the potatoes are tender. The beef should still be pink in the center; it toughens if cooked too long.

Transfer the beef to a cutting board. Let stand for 5 minutes before thinly slicing against the grain.

Meanwhile, stir the sugar and salt into the vegetable mixture.

To serve, place the roast on a platter. Arrange the vegetable mixture around the roast.

PER SERVING	
Calories 296	Cholesterol 61 mg
Total Fat 5.0 g	Sodium 546 mg
Saturated 1.5 g	Carbohydrates 36 g
Polyunsaturated 0.5 g	Fiber 5 g
Monounsaturated 2.0 g	Sugar 12 g
	Protein 30 g

sirloin and asparagus stir-fry with hoisin-coriander sauce

This dish looks scrumptious, with bright colors from the asparagus and carrots—and it tastes as good as it looks!

Vegetable oil spray
1 pound boneless top sirloin, all visible fat discarded, cut into thin strips
1/2 medium onion, cut into thin strips
2 medium garlic cloves, minced
2 large carrots, thinly sliced
1 1/2 cups fat-free, no-salt-added beef broth
2 tablespoons hoisin sauce
1 teaspoon coriander seeds, crushed
1 teaspoon toasted sesame oil
4 ounces whole-wheat angel hair pasta, broken into 2-inch pieces
8 to 10 medium asparagus spears, trimmed, cut into 1-inch pieces

Heat a large, deep nonstick skillet or wok over medium-high heat. Remove from the heat and lightly spray with vegetable oil spray (being careful not to spray near a gas flame). Cook the beef for 1 minute, or until it just starts to brown, stirring constantly.

Add the onion and garlic. Cook for 2 to 3 minutes, or until the onion is tender-crisp, stirring constantly.

Add the carrots. Cook for 1 minute, stirring occasionally.

Stir in the broth, hoisin sauce, coriander seeds, and sesame oil. Bring to a simmer, stirring occasionally.

Stir in the pasta. Reduce the heat and simmer, covered, for 5 minutes, or until the pasta is tender and the beef is cooked through.

Stir in the asparagus. Simmer, covered, for 1 to 2 minutes, or until the asparagus is tender-crisp.

PER SERVING	
Calories 311	Cholesterol 69 mg
Total Fat 6.5 g	Sodium 149 mg
Saturated 2.0 g	Carbohydrates 32 g
Polyunsaturated 1.0 g	Fiber 6 g
Monounsaturated 2.5 g	Sugar 8 g
	Protein 32 g

orange beef and chinese
noodle stir-fry

SERVES 4; 1^1/$_2$ CUPS PER SERVING

There's no need for high-fat takeout when you can make this delicious, healthful dish so quickly.

8-ounce can sliced water chestnuts

2 cups water

3-ounce package ramen noodles (beef flavor preferred), broken into small pieces, seasoning packet reserved

Vegetable oil spray

1 pound boneless top sirloin steak, all visible fat discarded, thinly sliced

2 medium onions, thinly sliced

2 medium carrots, cut into matchstick-size strips

3 ounces fresh snow peas, trimmed

^{1}/$_2$ cup fresh orange juice

2 tablespoons sugar

2 tablespoons low-salt soy sauce

Put the water chestnuts in a colander. Drain. Set aside in the colander.

In a large skillet or wok, bring the water to a boil over high heat. Stir in the noodles. Reduce the heat and simmer for 3 minutes. Drain the noodles over the water chestnuts in the colander; leave both in the colander.

Heat the skillet over high heat. Remove from the heat and lightly spray with vegetable oil spray (being careful not to spray near a gas flame). Cook the beef for 2 minutes, or until barely pink, stirring constantly. Put the beef on the noodle mixture.

Reduce the heat to medium-high. Respray the skillet with vegetable oil spray (being careful not to spray near a gas flame). Cook the onions and carrots for 4 minutes, stirring frequently.

Stir in the snow peas. Cook for 2 minutes, stirring frequently.

Add the noodle mixture and the remaining ingredients, including the seasoning packet. Cook for 1 minute, stirring constantly.

PER SERVING	
Calories 348	Cholesterol 69 mg
Total Fat 8.5 g	Sodium 658 mg
Saturated 4.0 g	Carbohydrates 40 g
Polyunsaturated 0.5 g	Fiber 5 g
Monounsaturated 2.0 g	Sugar 18 g
	Protein 29 g

sichuan beef and broccoli

Crushed red pepper flakes provide a bit of heat and teriyaki sauce adds a little sweetness to this easy stir-fry. Serve it with sliced cucumbers marinated in a little rice vinegar and a pinch of sugar.

> 1 pound boneless sirloin steak, all visible fat discarded
>
> 8 ounces wide lo mein noodles, rice noodles, or udon noodles
>
> Vegetable oil spray
>
> 3 medium garlic cloves, minced
>
> 1 teaspoon minced peeled gingerroot
>
> 1/4 teaspoon crushed red pepper flakes
>
> 7 to 8 ounces small broccoli florets
>
> 1 medium red bell pepper, cut into short, thin strips
>
> 3 tablespoons water
>
> 1 1/2 tablespoons cornstarch
>
> 1/4 cup low-salt soy sauce
>
> 1/2 cup sliced green onions (green and white parts)

Cut the steak into very thin strips about 1 1/2 inches long.

Cook the noodles using the package directions, omitting the salt and oil.

Meanwhile, heat a large nonstick skillet over medium-high heat. Remove from the heat and lightly spray with vegetable oil spray (being careful not to spray near a gas flame). Cook the steak, garlic, gingerroot, and red pepper flakes for about 3 minutes, or until the steak is barely pink in the center, stirring constantly. Transfer to a bowl. Set aside.

Reduce the heat to medium. In the same skillet, stir together the broccoli, bell pepper, and water. Cook, covered, for 2 minutes.

Put the cornstarch in a cup. Add the soy sauce, stirring to dissolve. Pour into the broccoli mixture. Cook for 1 to 2 minutes, or until the sauce thickens and the vegetables are tender-crisp, stirring constantly.

Stir in the steak mixture. Cook for 1 minute, stirring constantly. (Don't overcook, or the beef may become tough.) Stir in the green onions.

To serve, spoon the noodles onto plates. Top with the steak mixture.

PER SERVING	
Calories 408	Cholesterol 69 mg
Total Fat 5.5 g	Sodium 466 mg
Saturated 2.0 g	Carbohydrates 57 g
Polyunsaturated 0.5 g	Fiber 4 g
Monounsaturated 2.0 g	Sugar 3 g
	Protein 32 g

steak-and-potatoes soup

SERVES 4; 1³/4 CUPS PER SERVING

Caramelized onion adds the flavor of French onion soup to this dish of steak and potatoes in a bowl.

- 1 teaspoon olive oil
- 1 large onion, thinly sliced
- 2 portobello mushrooms, stems discarded, caps cut into 1-inch cubes
- 4 cups fat-free, no-salt-added beef broth
- 4 medium red potatoes (about 1 pound), unpeeled, cut into 1-inch cubes
- ¹/4 cup steak sauce
- ¹/4 teaspoon pepper
- 1 pound boneless top sirloin steak, all visible fat discarded, cut into thin strips
- 2 ounces crumbled blue cheese (optional)

Heat a large saucepan over medium heat. Pour the oil into the saucepan and swirl to coat the bottom. Cook the onion for 2 to 3 minutes, or until tender, stirring occasionally. Increase the heat to medium-high. Cook for 8 to 10 minutes, or until slightly caramelized, stirring constantly.

Stir in the mushrooms. Reduce the heat to medium. Cook for 3 to 4 minutes, or until the mushrooms are tender, stirring occasionally.

Stir in the broth, potatoes, steak sauce, and pepper. Increase the heat to medium-high and bring to a simmer. Simmer, covered, for 10 minutes, or until the potatoes are tender when pierced with a knife.

Add the steak. Simmer, covered, for 3 to 4 minutes, or until the steak is just cooked through, stirring occasionally.

Stir in the cheese.

WITH BLUE CHEESE

PER SERVING		PER SERVING	
Calories 292	Cholesterol 69 mg	Calories 342	Cholesterol 80 mg
Total Fat 6.0 g	Sodium 232 mg	Total Fat 10.5 g	Sodium 430 mg
Saturated 2.0 g	Carbohydrates 29 g	Saturated 4.5 g	Carbohydrates 29 g
Polyunsaturated 0.5 g	Fiber 4 g	Polyunsaturated 0.5 g	Fiber 4 g
Monounsaturated 3.0 g	Sugar 9 g	Monounsaturated 4.0 g	Sugar 9 g
	Protein 33 g		Protein 36 g

peppery beef tips
with noodles

SERVES 5; 1¹/₄ CUPS BEEF AND VEGETABLE MIXTURE
AND ²/₃ CUP NOODLES PER SERVING

A tomato-based sauce perked up with a poblano pepper complements beef tips and noodles.

6 ounces dried yolk-free noodles

4 bacon slices

1 pound boneless sirloin steak, all visible fat discarded

2 medium onions

2 large or 3 medium tomatoes (about 12 ounces)

1 poblano pepper, or 1 medium green bell pepper plus ¹/₄ teaspoon cayenne

10 to 12 ounces button mushrooms

Vegetable oil spray

2 teaspoons dried oregano, crumbled

1 tablespoon sugar

1 teaspoon salt

In a Dutch oven, prepare the noodles using the package directions, omitting the salt and oil. Drain in a colander. Set aside (still in the colander).

Meanwhile, cut the bacon slices in half. Cut the sirloin into 1-inch cubes. Chop the onions, tomatoes, and pepper. Thickly slice the mushrooms.

Heat the Dutch oven over medium-high heat. Cook the bacon for 4 minutes, or until crisp, turning constantly. Drain on paper towels; pat off any remaining grease. Discard the grease in the pot. Wipe any remaining grease from the pot, being careful not to burn yourself.

Lightly spray the pot with vegetable oil spray. Return the Dutch oven to the stovetop. Cook the beef for 1 minute, stirring constantly. Remove the beef.

Reduce the heat to medium. Cook the onions and pepper for 4 minutes, or until translucent, stirring frequently.

Add the tomatoes, mushrooms, and oregano. Cook, covered, for 10 minutes.

PER SERVING	
Calories 342	Cholesterol 55 mg
Total Fat 8.0 g	Sodium 612 mg
Saturated 2.5 g	Carbohydrates 41 g
Polyunsaturated 0.5 g	Fiber 5 g
Monounsaturated 3.0 g	Sugar 11 g
	Protein 26 g

Stir in the beef and any accumulated juices. Cook, covered, for 5 minutes. Don't cook any longer, or the meat will become tough. Remove from the heat.

Crumble the bacon. Add the bacon, sugar, and salt to the beef mixture. Stir well. Let stand, covered, for about 10 minutes.

To reheat the noodles, leave them in the colander and run them under hot water for 20 to 25 seconds. Shake off excess water.

To serve, spoon the noodles onto plates. Top with the beef mixture.

teriyaki beef stir-fry

SERVES 4; SCANT 1 CUP BEEF MIXTURE AND 3/4 CUP RICE PER SERVING

Using a convenient mix of frozen vegetables allows you to have this dish on the table in near-record time. You may want to add a bit of fire with crushed red pepper flakes to contrast with the slightly sweet teriyaki sauce.

1 cup uncooked brown or white rice

2 teaspoons toasted sesame oil

1 pound boneless top sirloin steak, all visible fat discarded, cut into very thin strips

4 medium garlic cloves, minced

1/2 teaspoon crushed red pepper flakes (optional)

16-ounce package frozen Chinese stir-fry vegetables, thawed and well drained

1/3 cup light teriyaki sauce

1 tablespoon cornstarch

1 tablespoon water

1/4 teaspoon salt

1/4 cup snipped fresh cilantro

Prepare the rice using the package directions, omitting the salt and margarine.

After 10 minutes of cooking the white rice or 40 minutes of cooking the brown rice, heat a large skillet over medium-high heat. Pour in the oil and swirl to coat the bottom.

Cook the steak, garlic, and red pepper flakes for 3 to 5 minutes, or until the steak is still pink just in the center, stirring constantly. Transfer to a plate. Set aside.

In the skillet, cook the vegetables and teriyaki sauce for 2 minutes, or until the vegetables are tender-crisp, stirring constantly.

Put the cornstarch in a cup. Add the water, stirring to dissolve. Stir the cornstarch mixture into the vegetables. Cook for 1 minute, or until the sauce thickens, stirring constantly.

Stir in the steak with any accumulated juices. Cook for 1 minute, or until the steak is hot, stirring constantly.

Spoon the rice onto plates. Sprinkle with the salt. Spoon the beef mixture over the rice. Sprinkle with the cilantro.

PER SERVING	Cholesterol 69 mg
Calories 332	Sodium 591 mg
Total Fat 8.0 g	Carbohydrates 32 g
Saturated 2.0 g	Fiber 4 g
Polyunsaturated 1.5 g	Sugar 5 g
Monounsaturated 3.0 g	Protein 29 g

cowboy beef and beans

Hickory-flavored barbecue sauce imparts an extra dimension to this beef-and-beans dish.

Vegetable oil spray

1 pound top sirloin or top round steak, all visible fat removed, cut into 1/8-inch strips

1 teaspoon meat seasoning blend

1/4 teaspoon pepper

1/4 teaspoon garlic powder

2 medium green bell peppers, chopped in 1/2-inch pieces, or 2 cups chopped mixed bell peppers

1 large onion, coarsely chopped

16-ounce can butter beans, rinsed and drained

15- or 16-ounce can no-salt-added pinto beans, rinsed if desired and drained

1/2 cup hickory barbecue sauce

Heat a large nonstick skillet over high heat. Remove from the heat and lightly spray with vegetable oil spray (being careful not to spray near a gas flame). Cook the steak, meat seasoning, pepper, and garlic powder for 2 to 3 minutes, or until the steak is browned on the outside but still pink in the center, stirring constantly. Transfer to a medium bowl. Set aside.

Lightly spray the skillet with vegetable oil spray. Cook the bell peppers and onion for 5 minutes, stirring constantly.

Reduce the heat to medium. Stir in the butter beans, pinto beans, and barbecue sauce. Reduce the heat and simmer for 3 minutes, or until the peppers are tender. Stir in the beef with any accumulated juices. Heat through.

COOK'S TIP

To keep the beef strips from becoming tough, cook them only until they are still pink in the center.

PER SERVING	
Calories 402	Cholesterol 69 mg
Total Fat 5.0 g	Sodium 794 mg
Saturated 2.0 g	Carbohydrates 55 g
Polyunsaturated 0.5 g	Fiber 11 g
Monounsaturated 2.0 g	Sugar 21 g
	Protein 37 g

sirloin and vegetable
skewers

SERVES 4; 3 OUNCES STEAK, 1/2 EAR CORN, AND 1 CUP VEGETABLES PER SERVING

Tea in the marinade and brussels sprouts on the skewers make this grilled dinner deliciously out of the ordinary.

> 1/3 cup strong tea
>
> 2 tablespoons light or dark brown sugar
>
> 2 tablespoons fresh lemon juice
>
> 1/4 teaspoon salt
>
> 1/4 teaspoon red hot-pepper sauce
>
> 16 small cremini (brown) mushrooms, stems discarded
>
> 1 pound sirloin steak, all visible fat discarded, cut into 1-inch cubes
>
> 1 large red bell pepper, cut into 1-inch squares
>
> 16 medium brussels sprouts, trimmed
>
> 2 medium ears of fresh corn, husks and silk discarded, cut in half crosswise
>
> Vegetable oil spray (if using metal skewers)

In a large bowl, stir together the tea, brown sugar, lemon juice, salt, and hot-pepper sauce. Stir in the remaining ingredients except the vegetable oil spray. Cover and let marinate for 1 to 3 hours in the refrigerator.

If using bamboo skewers, soak six skewers for at least 10 minutes in cold water to keep them from charring. For metal skewers, lightly spray with vegetable oil spray. (If you use metal skewers, the food will cook a little faster because metal is a good conductor of heat.)

Heat a grill pan over medium-high heat, or preheat the grill on medium-high.

Alternating ingredients, thread the mushrooms, steak, and bell pepper on four skewers. Thread the brussels sprouts on two skewers, leaving about 1/8 inch between the sprouts.

Put the corn and the skewers in the pan or on the grill. Cook the corn and the brussels sprouts for about 3 minutes on each side, or until a few kernels of corn on each side turn golden and the sprouts give when squeezed and have some grill

PER SERVING	
Calories 234	Cholesterol 64 mg
Total Fat 6.0 g	Sodium 224 mg
Saturated 2.0 g	Carbohydrates 20 g
Polyunsaturated 0.5 g	Fiber 5 g
Monounsaturated 2.5 g	Sugar 6 g
	Protein 28 g

marks, turning occasionally. Cook the steak skewers for about 2 minutes on each side, turning after each side browns, for between medium-rare and medium. For medium, add an extra minute on each side, an extra 1^1/$_2$ minutes on each side for medium-well.

To serve, slide all the ingredients from one mixed skewer and half the brussels sprouts from a sprouts skewer onto each plate.

COOK'S TIP

Try to buy all your mushrooms and brussels sprouts about the same size for uniform cooking.

flank steak and
green bean stir-fry

SERVES 4; 3 OUNCES STEAK, 1 CUP BEANS,
AND 3/4 CUP NOODLES PER SERVING

The flavors of a broth-based vinaigrette permeate crunchy green beans, strips of flank steak, and pasta.

14.5-ounce can fat-free, low-sodium chicken broth

1/4 cup red wine vinegar

3 medium garlic cloves, minced

1 teaspoon sugar

1 teaspoon Dijon mustard

1/4 teaspoon pepper

9-ounce package refrigerated fettuccine

1 pound fresh green beans, strings discarded

1 pound flank steak, all visible fat and silver skin discarded, cut across the grain into very thin slices (1/8 to 1/4 inch thick)

Heat a deep 12- to 14-inch skillet over high heat. Stir together the broth, vinegar, garlic, sugar, mustard, and pepper. Bring to a boil.

Add the fettuccine. Cook for 3 to 4 minutes, stirring gently and constantly. Using tongs, transfer the noodles to a medium bowl. Pour half the remaining liquid (about 1/4 cup) into a measuring cup or small bowl.

Cook the beans in the liquid remaining in the skillet for 5 to 7 minutes, or until tender but still bright green and slightly crunchy, stirring constantly. Add the beans to the fettuccine.

Cook the steak and the reserved cooking liquid for 4 minutes, or until nearly all the pink is gone, stirring constantly.

Return the beans and fettuccine to the skillet. Heat for 1 minute, stirring constantly.

PER SERVING	
Calories 399	Cholesterol 54 mg
Total Fat 9.5 g	Sodium 249 mg
Saturated 3.5 g	Carbohydrates 44 g
Polyunsaturated 0.5 g	Fiber 6 g
Monounsaturated 3.5 g	Sugar 5 g
	Protein 32 g

beef and eggplant
skillet casserole

This aromatic dish is similar to its cousins, moussaka and pastitsio.

8 ounces lean ground beef

8 ounces unpeeled eggplant, diced

2 medium onions, chopped

8-ounce can no-salt-added tomato sauce with Italian seasoning

1 cup water

1 tablespoon sugar

1 teaspoon ground cinnamon

$^1/_2$ teaspoon ground cumin

$^1/_4$ teaspoon ground nutmeg

$^3/_4$ cup nonfat or low-fat plain yogurt

3 ounces light cream cheese

Egg substitute equivalent to 1 egg

4 ounces dried elbow macaroni

$^3/_4$ teaspoon salt

In a 12-inch skillet, cook the beef over medium-high heat for 3 minutes, or until browned on the outside and no longer pink in the center, stirring occasionally to turn and break up the beef. Pour into a colander and rinse under hot water to remove excess fat. Drain well. Set aside. Wipe the skillet with a paper towel.

Put the eggplant and onions in the skillet. Reduce the heat to medium. Cook for 4 minutes, or until the onions are translucent, stirring occasionally.

Return the beef to the skillet. Stir in the tomato sauce, water, sugar, cinnamon, cumin, and nutmeg. Increase the heat to high. Bring to a boil. Reduce the heat and simmer, covered, for 10 minutes, or until the eggplant is tender.

Meanwhile, in a food processor or blender, process the yogurt, cream cheese, and egg substitute until smooth.

When the eggplant is tender, stir in the macaroni and salt. Pour the yogurt mixture over all. Simmer, covered, for 15 minutes, or until the macaroni is tender.

Remove from the heat. Let stand for 5 minutes. Cut into 4 wedges.

PER SERVING	
Calories 335	Cholesterol 43 mg
Total Fat 7.5 g	Sodium 637 mg
Saturated 4.0 g	Carbohydrates 44 g
Polyunsaturated 0.5 g	Fiber 4 g
Monounsaturated 2.5 g	Sugar 18 g
	Protein 22 g

cantonese beef
lettuce wraps

Beef and rice, full of ginger and garlic and wrapped in lettuce leaves, become the Chinese version of the burrito—fun-to-eat finger food!

12 ounces lean ground beef

1 tablespoon minced peeled gingerroot

4 medium garlic cloves, minced

2^1/$_2$ cups water

2 cups uncooked quick-cooking brown rice

1 tablespoon low-salt soy sauce

2 cups matchstick-size carrot strips

2 cups sliced baby bok choy or bok choy (^{1}/$_4$-inch strips)

^{1}/$_2$ cup hoisin sauce

12 large lettuce leaves, such as romaine

In a large saucepan, cook the beef, ginger, and garlic over medium heat for 5 minutes, or until the beef is browned and no longer pink in the center, stirring occasionally to turn and break up the beef. Pour off and discard the drippings.

Stir in the water, rice, and soy sauce. Increase the heat to high and bring to a boil. Reduce the heat and simmer, covered, for 5 minutes.

Stir in the carrots and bok choy. Simmer, covered, for 5 minutes, or until the liquid is absorbed. Stir in the hoisin sauce. Simmer until heated through.

To assemble, spoon the mixture down the center of each lettuce leaf. Fold the edges over the filling and roll up lengthwise.

COOK'S TIP ON HOISIN SAUCE

Sweet, spicy, and thick, hoisin sauce is made of soybeans, vinegar, garlic, sugar, chiles, and spices. It is used as a condiment as well as a sauce. If refrigerated in a tightly closed jar, hoisin sauce, also called Peking sauce, will keep well for months.

PER SERVING	
Calories 397	Cholesterol 31 mg
Total Fat 9.5 g	Sodium 381 mg
Saturated 3.0 g	Carbohydrates 53 g
Polyunsaturated 1.0 g	Fiber 5 g
Monounsaturated 4.0 g	Sugar 13 g
	Protein 24 g

beef and broccoli
with savory wine sauce

Ground beef becomes a gourmet delight in this saucy dish.

1 pound lean ground beef

4 ounces button mushrooms, stems discarded, caps sliced

2 medium garlic cloves, minced

1 cup frozen pearl onions, thawed

1$^1/_2$ cups fat-free, no-salt-added beef broth

$^1/_2$ cup dry red wine (regular or nonalcoholic) or fat-free, no-salt-added beef broth

2 teaspoons very low sodium or low-sodium Worcestershire sauce

1 bay leaf

$^1/_4$ teaspoon pepper

1 pound broccoli florets

4 ounces dried pasta, such as gemelli, penne, farfalle, or rotelle

$^1/_2$ cup fat-free or light sour cream

2 tablespoons sliced almonds, dry-roasted if desired

In a large, deep skillet, cook the beef over medium-high heat for 7 to 8 minutes, or until browned on the outside and no longer pink in the center, stirring occasionally to turn and break up the beef. Pour into a colander and rinse under hot water to remove excess fat. Drain well. Wipe the skillet with a paper towel.

Cook the beef, mushrooms, and garlic over medium-high heat for 2 to 3 minutes, or until the mushrooms are tender, stirring occasionally.

Stir in the onions, broth, wine, Worcestershire sauce, bay leaf, and pepper. Bring to a simmer.

Stir in the broccoli and pasta. Reduce the heat and simmer, covered, for 10 minutes, or until the pasta and broccoli are tender. Remove from the heat; stir constantly to cool the mixture slightly.

Stir in the sour cream and almonds. Cook over low heat for 1 to 2 minutes, or until the mixture is warmed through, stirring occasionally. Don't let the mixture come to a boil; the sour cream might curdle.

PER SERVING	
Calories 386	Cholesterol 56 mg
Total Fat 6.5 g	Sodium 142 mg
Saturated 1.5 g	Carbohydrates 44 g
Polyunsaturated 1.0 g	Fiber 5 g
Monounsaturated 2.5 g	Sugar 8 g
	Protein 34 g

southwestern beef
and vegetable quiche

SERVES 4; 1¹/₂ CUPS PER SERVING

Do real cowboys eat quiche? They do when it has a meaty filling and south-western seasoning in a hash brown potato crust.

1 pound lean ground beef

3 cups frozen nonfat hash brown potatoes, thawed

White of 1 large egg

¹/₂ teaspoon chili powder

Vegetable oil spray

1 teaspoon ground cumin

¹/₄ teaspoon pepper

2 cups chopped tomatoes (about 2 large)

4.5-ounce can green chiles, rinsed and drained

¹/₂ cup sliced black olives

³/₄ cup shredded reduced-fat sharp Cheddar cheese

1 cup fat-free half-and-half

Egg substitute equivalent to 2 eggs, or whites of 4 large eggs

¹/₂ teaspoon chili powder

Preheat the oven to 375°F.

In a 10-inch ovenproof nonstick skillet, cook the beef over medium-high heat for 7 to 8 minutes, or until browned on the outside and no longer pink in the center, stirring occasionally to turn and break up the beef. Pour into a colander and rinse under hot water to remove excess fat. Drain well; set the meat aside in the colander. Wipe the skillet with a paper towel and let cool for 5 minutes.

In the skillet, stir together the hash browns, 1 egg white, and ¹/₂ teaspoon chili powder. With a spoon or your fingers, press the mixture evenly over the bottom and up the side of the skillet to form a crust. Lightly spray the top of the mixture with vegetable oil spray.

PER SERVING	
Calories 413	Cholesterol 62 mg
Total Fat 10.0 g	Sodium 621 mg
Saturated 4.5 g	Carbohydrates 43 g
Polyunsaturated 0.5 g	Fiber 5 g
Monounsaturated 4.0 g	Sugar 8 g
	Protein 39 g

Bake for 10 minutes, or until the potatoes are light golden brown around the edges. Put the skillet on a cooling rack. Reduce the oven temperature to 350°F.

Spread the beef over the potato crust. Sprinkle with cumin and pepper. In this order, cover the beef with the tomatoes, chiles, olives, and cheese.

In a small bowl, whisk together the half-and-half, egg substitute, and $1/2$ teaspoon chili powder. Pour evenly over the beef mixture.

Bake for 35 to 40 minutes, or until the mixture is completely warmed through and the cheese is melted. Let cool on a cooling rack for 10 minutes before cutting.

hearty chili con carne

This "bowl of red" will be ready in under 30 minutes. Chipotle salsa gives the dish a slightly smoky flavor, but if it is not available, you can use regular salsa or picante sauce.

1 pound lean ground beef

1 medium onion, chopped

1 medium green or red bell pepper, coarsely chopped

3 medium garlic cloves, minced

2 teaspoons chili powder

2 teaspoons ground cumin

15-ounce can chili beans in spicy sauce, undrained

14.5-ounce can no-salt-added diced tomatoes, undrained

1/2 cup chipotle salsa

1/8 teaspoon salt

1/4 cup nonfat or light sour cream (optional)

1/4 cup snipped fresh cilantro or thinly sliced green onions

In a large saucepan, cook the beef and onion over medium heat for 5 minutes, or until the beef is browned on the outside and no longer pink in the center, stirring occasionally to turn and break up the beef. Pour into a colander and rinse under hot water to remove excess fat. Drain well. Wipe the saucepan with a paper towel. Return the beef mixture to the pan.

Stir in the bell pepper, garlic, chili powder, and cumin. Cook for 2 minutes, stirring occasionally.

Stir in the chili beans, tomatoes, salsa, and salt. Bring to a boil over high heat. Reduce the heat and simmer, covered, for 15 minutes, or until the vegetables are tender.

To serve, ladle into bowls. Top with dollops of sour cream, then sprinkle with cilantro.

PER SERVING	Cholesterol 51 mg
Calories 282	Sodium 728 mg
Total Fat 5.5 g	Carbohydrates 30 g
Saturated 1.5 g	Fiber 8 g
Polyunsaturated 0.5 g	Sugar 8 g
Monounsaturated 2.0 g	Protein 28 g

WITH SOUR CREAM

PER SERVING	Cholesterol 54 mg
Calories 300	Sodium 740 mg
Total Fat 5.5 g	Carbohydrates 33 g
Saturated 1.5 g	Fiber 8 g
Polyunsaturated 0.5 g	Sugar 9 g
Monounsaturated 2.0 g	Protein 29 g

beef and blue cheese

SERVES 4; 1¹/2 CUPS PER SERVING

Blue cheese gives a subtle kick to this stovetop casserole.

Vegetable oil spray
12 ounces lean ground beef
3 medium onions, chopped
1¹/4 pounds red potatoes, diced
8 ounces button mushrooms, sliced
1 cup water
2 teaspoons very low sodium beef bouillon granules
1 teaspoon dried oregano, crumbled
1/2 teaspoon pepper
1/8 teaspoon salt
1/2 cup crumbled blue cheese
1/4 to 1/2 cup snipped fresh parsley

Heat a Dutch oven over medium-high heat. Remove from the heat and lightly spray with vegetable oil spray (being careful not to spray near a gas flame). Cook the beef for 2 minutes, or until browned on the outside and no longer pink in the center, stirring occasionally to turn and break up the beef. Pour into a colander and rinse under hot water to remove excess fat. Drain well. Set aside.

Wipe the Dutch oven with a paper towel. Lightly spray with vegetable oil spray. Cook the onions for 3 to 4 minutes, or until translucent, stirring occasionally.

Stir in the potatoes, mushrooms, water, beef granules, oregano, and pepper. Increase the heat to high. Bring to a boil. Reduce the heat and simmer, covered, for 10 minutes, or until the potatoes are tender. Remove from the heat.

Stir in the beef and the remaining ingredients. Let stand for 2 minutes to absorb flavors.

PER SERVING	
Calories 317	Cholesterol 51 mg
Total Fat 8.0 g	Sodium 356 mg
Saturated 4.5 g	Carbohydrates 40 g
Polyunsaturated 0.5 g	Fiber 6 g
Monounsaturated 2.5 g	Sugar 11 g
	Protein 26 g

beefy macaroni

If you want to serve something kid-pleasing for dinner, this hamburger casserole is just what you need.

Vegetable oil spray
1 pound lean ground beef
2 medium red bell peppers, chopped
2 medium onions, chopped
1 medium zucchini, sliced
2 cups water
6 ounces dried elbow macaroni
1 cup frozen whole-kernel corn
¹/₂ tablespoon dried oregano, crumbled
¹/₄ cup no-salt-added ketchup
¹/₂ to 1 tablespoon balsamic vinegar (optional)
1 teaspoon ground cumin
³/₄ teaspoon salt
¹/₈ to ¹/₄ teaspoon crushed red pepper flakes

Heat a Dutch oven over medium-high heat. Remove from the heat and lightly spray with vegetable oil spray (being careful not to spray near a gas flame). Cook the beef for 8 to 10 minutes, or until browned, stirring occasionally. Pour into a colander and rinse under hot water to remove excess fat. Drain well. Set aside.

Wipe the Dutch oven with a paper towel. Lightly spray with vegetable oil spray. Cook the peppers, onions, and zucchini for 3 to 4 minutes, or until the onions are translucent, stirring occasionally.

Stir in the water, macaroni, corn, and oregano. Increase the heat to high. Bring to a boil. Reduce the heat and simmer, covered, for 10 minutes, or until the pasta is tender. Remove from the heat.

Stir in the beef and the remaining ingredients. Let stand for 5 minutes to absorb flavors.

PER SERVING	
Calories 391	Cholesterol 51 mg
Total Fat 5.5 g	Sodium 498 mg
Saturated 1.5 g	Carbohydrates 57 g
Polyunsaturated 1.0 g	Fiber 6 g
Monounsaturated 2.0 g	Sugar 11 g
	Protein 30 g

cajun dirty rice

SERVES 4; 1¹/₂ CUPS PER SERVING

One of Louisiana's best-known dishes, dirty rice, gets a heart-healthy makeover. Lean ground beef replaces high-cholesterol chicken gizzards or livers, and whole-grain brown rice substitutes for white. Vitamin-rich turnip greens and the spicy seasoning add lots of delicious flavor.

> 1 **pound lean ground beef**
>
> 1 **cup frozen chopped onion, bell pepper, and celery blend or** ¹/₃ **cup of each**
>
> 4 **cups frozen chopped turnip greens**
>
> 1¹/₂ **cups fat-free, no-salt-added beef broth**
>
> 1 **cup uncooked instant brown rice**
>
> 2 **tablespoons imitation bacon bits**
>
> 1 **tablespoon salt-free Cajun or Creole seasoning blend**

In a large, deep skillet, cook the beef over medium-high heat for 7 to 8 minutes, or until browned on the outside and no longer pink in the center, stirring occasionally to turn and break up the beef. Pour into a colander and rinse under hot water to remove excess fat. Drain well. Wipe the skillet with a paper towel. Return the beef to the skillet.

Add the onion, bell pepper, and celery blend. Cook over medium-high heat for 3 to 4 minutes, or until the vegetables are tender, stirring occasionally.

Stir in the remaining ingredients. Bring to a simmer, stirring occasionally. Reduce the heat and simmer, covered, for 10 minutes, or until the rice is tender and the liquid is absorbed.

PER SERVING	
Calories 274	Cholesterol 51 mg
Total Fat 6.0 g	Sodium 139 mg
Saturated 1.5 g	Carbohydrates 26 g
Polyunsaturated 1.0 g	Fiber 6 g
Monounsaturated 2.0 g	Sugar 2 g
	Protein 30 g

upside-down
stuffed peppers

Don't want to take the time to preheat the oven, stuff the peppers, and then wait for them to bake? Cooking quickly on top of their stuffing, these Mexican-flavored peppers are a cinch to make on the stovetop.

12 ounces lean ground beef

$1/2$ of a 14.5- or 15-ounce can no-salt-added pinto beans, rinsed if desired and drained

1 cup frozen whole-kernel corn

$3/4$ cup picante sauce

$3/4$ cup water

1 tablespoon sugar

1 teaspoon ground cumin

2 large green or red bell peppers, halved, stems, seeds, and ribs discarded

$1/4$ cup yellow cornmeal

$1/2$ teaspoon salt

$3/4$ cup shredded reduced-fat sharp Cheddar cheese

In a large skillet, cook the beef over medium-high heat for 3 minutes, or until browned on the outside and no longer pink in the center, stirring occasionally to turn and break up the beef. Pour into a colander and rinse under hot water to remove excess fat. Drain well. Wipe the skillet with a paper towel. Return the beef to the skillet.

Stir in the beans, corn, picante sauce, water, sugar, and cumin. Top with the bell pepper halves with the cut side down. Increase the heat to high. Bring to a boil. Reduce the heat and simmer, covered, for 15 minutes, or until the bell peppers are tender. Remove the peppers and place with the cut side up on a serving platter.

Stir the cornmeal and salt into the beef mixture. Cook for 2 minutes, or until thickened. Mound 1 cup of the mixture on each pepper half. Sprinkle 2 tablespoons cheese over each serving.

PER SERVING	Cholesterol 50 mg
Calories 317	Sodium 675 mg
Total Fat 7.5 g	Carbohydrates 35 g
Saturated 4.0 g	Fiber 5 g
Polyunsaturated 0.5 g	Sugar 9 g
Monounsaturated 2.0 g	Protein 27 g

beef and lentils
in tomato-wine sauce

For a speedy dinner that requires little effort, try this savory blend of ground beef, carrots, and lentils. Unlike dried beans, lentils don't require any soaking time and cook quickly.

Vegetable oil spray
1 pound lean ground beef
14.5-ounce can fat-free, low-sodium chicken broth
1 cup water
1 cup dried lentils, sorted for stones and shriveled lentils and rinsed
2 large carrots, thinly sliced
8-ounce can no-salt-added tomato sauce
1/2 cup dry red or white wine (regular or nonalcoholic) or fat-free, low-sodium chicken broth
2¹/2 teaspoons salt-free garlic-herb seasoning blend
1/2 tablespoon dried oregano, crumbled
1 teaspoon celery seeds
1 teaspoon paprika
1/4 teaspoon pepper
1/4 teaspoon salt

Lightly spray a Dutch oven with vegetable oil spray. Cook the beef over medium-high heat for 7 to 8 minutes, or until browned on the outside and no longer pink in the center, stirring occasionally to turn and break up the beef. Pour into a colander and rinse under hot water to remove excess fat. Drain well. Wipe the Dutch oven with a paper towel. Return the beef to the Dutch oven.

Stir in the remaining ingredients. Bring to a simmer over medium-high heat. Reduce the heat and simmer, covered, for 25 to 30 minutes, or until the carrots and lentils are tender, stirring occasionally.

PER SERVING	
Calories 351	Cholesterol 51 mg
Total Fat 4.5 g	Sodium 256 mg
Saturated 1.5 g	Carbohydrates 36 g
Polyunsaturated 0.5 g	Fiber 17 g
Monounsaturated 2.0 g	Sugar 8 g
	Protein 35 g

best-ever chili mac

Macaroni simmers in broth for this hearty one-dish chili that's sure to please the whole family. Chiliheads may want a bottle of hot sauce on the table.

1 pound lean ground beef

1 small onion, chopped

3 medium garlic cloves, minced

14.5-ounce can fat-free, no-salt-added beef broth

1 cup dried elbow macaroni or small shell pasta

¹/₂ teaspoon salt

14.5-ounce can no-salt-added diced tomatoes, undrained

1 medium green bell pepper, diced

1¹/₂ tablespoons chili powder

2 teaspoons ground cumin

1 teaspoon dried oregano, crumbled

¹/₄ teaspoon cayenne or red hot-pepper sauce, or to taste

¹/₄ cup snipped fresh cilantro or thinly sliced green onions

¹/₄ cup shredded fat-free or reduced-fat Cheddar cheese (optional)

In a large saucepan, cook the beef, onion, and garlic over medium heat for 5 minutes, or until browned on the outside and no longer pink in the center, stirring occasionally to turn and break up the beef. Pour into a colander and rinse under hot water to remove excess fat; drain well. Return the beef mixture to the saucepan.

Stir in the broth, macaroni, and salt. Increase the heat to high and bring to a boil. Reduce the heat and simmer, covered, for 5 minutes.

Stir in the undrained tomatoes, bell pepper, chili powder, cumin, oregano, and cayenne. Cook, covered, for 10 minutes, or until the macaroni and bell pepper are tender.

To serve, ladle into bowls. Sprinkle with the cilantro and cheese.

WITH CHEESE

PER SERVING			PER SERVING	
Calories 288	Cholesterol 51 mg		Calories 298	Cholesterol 52 mg
Total Fat 5.0 g	Sodium 444 mg		Total Fat 5.0 g	Sodium 511 mg
Saturated 1.5 g	Carbohydrates 32 g		Saturated 1.5 g	Carbohydrates 32 g
Polyunsaturated 0.5 g	Fiber 5 g		Polyunsaturated 0.5 g	Fiber 5 g
Monounsaturated 2.0 g	Sugar 7 g		Monounsaturated 2.0 g	Sugar 7 g
	Protein 28 g			Protein 30 g

meat-and-potatoes meat loaf

SERVES 4; ONE 4$^{1}/_{2}$-INCH SQUARE PER SERVING

That good old standby just got easier—simply combine the ingredients in the baking pan, bake the mixture, and cut it into squares.

1 pound lean ground beef

2 cups refrigerated nonfat hash brown potatoes (about 12 ounces)

2 medium onions, chopped

1 medium green bell pepper, chopped

Whites of 2 large eggs

$^{1}/_{2}$ cup no-salt-added tomato sauce with Italian seasoning

1 teaspoon very low sodium or low-sodium Worcestershire sauce

$^{1}/_{2}$ teaspoon dried oregano, crumbled

$^{1}/_{2}$ teaspoon salt

$^{1}/_{4}$ teaspoon pepper

$^{1}/_{2}$ cup no-salt-added tomato sauce with Italian seasoning

$^{1}/_{4}$ cup no-salt-added ketchup

Preheat the oven to 350°F.

In a 9-inch square baking pan, combine the beef, potatoes, onions, bell pepper, egg whites, $^{1}/_{2}$ cup tomato sauce, Worcestershire sauce, oregano, salt, and pepper. Smooth with the back of a spoon. Pour the remaining $^{1}/_{2}$ cup tomato sauce over the mixture.

Bake for 50 minutes. Spread the ketchup over the meat loaf. Bake for 5 to 10 minutes, or until the meat loaf is no longer pink in the center.

PER SERVING	
Calories 346	Cholesterol 41 mg
Total Fat 10.5 g	Sodium 481 mg
Saturated 4.0 g	Carbohydrates 34 g
Polyunsaturated 0.5 g	Fiber 4 g
Monounsaturated 4.5 g	Sugar 11 g
	Protein 29 g

spicy spaghetti and meatballs

SERVES 4; 1 CUP PASTA PLUS 6 MEATBALLS PER SERVING

Your family will love this lightened version of the Italian classic. If you have extra time, double the meatball mixture and freeze half for future use.

12 ounces dried whole-wheat spaghetti

MEATBALLS

1 pound lean ground beef

2 tablespoons fat-free, low-sodium or low-fat, low-sodium tomato-basil spaghetti sauce

$1/4$ cup grated or finely chopped onion

3 tablespoons plain dry bread crumbs

White of 1 large egg

$1/2$ tablespoon dried basil, crumbled

$1/4$ teaspoon crushed red pepper flakes

$1/4$ teaspoon salt

❖ ❖ ❖ ❖

Vegetable oil spray

1 large green bell pepper, chopped

2 medium garlic cloves, minced

$1^1/2$ cups fat-free, low-sodium or low-fat, low-sodium tomato-basil spaghetti sauce

14.5-ounce can no-salt-added diced tomatoes, undrained

$1/4$ teaspoon crushed red pepper flakes

Italian, or flat-leaf, parsley, snipped (optional)

Prepare the spaghetti using the package directions, omitting the salt and oil. Drain the spaghetti in a colander. Set aside in the colander.

Meanwhile, for the meatballs, in a large bowl, stir together the beef, 2 tablespoons spaghetti sauce, onion, bread crumbs, egg white, basil, $1/4$ teaspoon red pepper flakes, and salt. Shape the mixture into 24 meatballs, each about $1^1/2$ inches in diameter.

PER SERVING	
Calories 586	Cholesterol 41 mg
Total Fat 12.0 g	Sodium 647 mg
Saturated 4.5 g	Carbohydrates 84 g
Polyunsaturated 1.0 g	Fiber 15 g
Monounsaturated 4.5 g	Sugar 14 g
	Protein 40 g

Heat a large nonstick saucepan or Dutch oven over medium heat. Remove from the heat and lightly spray with vegetable oil spray (being careful not to spray near a gas flame). Cook half the meatballs for 8 minutes, turning once. (Meatballs will not be fully cooked in the center.) Transfer the meatballs to a plate. Set aside. Repeat with the remaining meatballs.

Lightly spray the saucepan with vegetable oil spray. Cook the bell pepper and garlic for 3 minutes, stirring occasionally.

Add $1^1/_2$ cups spaghetti sauce, tomatoes, and $^1/_4$ teaspoon red pepper flakes. Bring to a simmer. Reduce the heat and simmer for 8 minutes, or until the bell peppers are tender.

Return the meatballs to the sauce. Simmer for 10 minutes, or until the meatballs are no longer pink in the center.

To serve, reheat the spaghetti if needed by leaving it in the colander and running it under hot water for 20 to 25 seconds. Shake off excess water. Put the spaghetti on plates. Top with the meatballs and sauce. Garnish with the parsley.

roast beef
and red beet salad

SERVES 4; 2 CUPS PER SERVING

Crisp, cold, and colorful—that's how you'll describe this salad. Perfect for dinner at home or a picnic on a warm day, it's almost too easy to be true.

1¼ cups uncooked instant rice or 2 cups chilled cooked rice

Juice of 1 large orange

2 tablespoons plain rice vinegar

2 teaspoons low-salt soy sauce

¼ teaspoon pepper

½ pound lean cooked or deli roast beef, all visible fat discarded

14.5-ounce can no-salt-added sliced beets, chilled

2 large carrots

4 large radishes

¼ cup diced red onion

2 cups chopped escarole or curly endive

Prepare the rice using the package directions, omitting the salt and margarine. Transfer to a large bowl. Cover with plastic wrap while hot; refrigerate until chilled, 2 to 3 hours.

Meanwhile, in a small bowl, stir together the orange juice, vinegar, soy sauce, and pepper.

Cut the beef into matchstick-size strips, drain the beets, grate the carrots (you need about 1 cup carrots, packed), and thinly slice the radishes. Add to the chilled rice. Add the onion and escarole. Toss well.

Pour the orange juice mixture over the rice mixture. Toss well.

PER SERVING	
Calories 272	Cholesterol 48 mg
Total Fat 3.0 g	Sodium 163 mg
Saturated 1.0 g	Carbohydrates 38 g
Polyunsaturated 0 g	Fiber 4 g
Monounsaturated 1.0 g	Sugar 10 g
	Protein 22 g

creamy corn
and ham chowder

SERVES 4; 2 CUPS PER SERVING

Cream-free but oh so creamy, this rich-tasting chowder is full of vegetables and thin strips of ham. Slivered snow peas provide the finishing touch.

   Vegetable oil spray

3 medium carrots, minced

2 small ribs of celery, minced

1 small onion, minced

8 ounces sliced low-fat, lower-sodium ham

2 15.25-ounce cans no-salt-added cream-style corn, undrained

2 cups water

1 tablespoon red wine vinegar

$1/8$ teaspoon pepper, or to taste

12 large snow peas, trimmed and slivered

Heat a medium stockpot over medium-high heat. Remove from the heat and lightly spray with vegetable oil spray (being careful not to spray near a gas flame). Cook the carrots, celery, and onion, covered, for 2 minutes; stir. Cook, covered, for 3 minutes.

Meanwhile, cut the ham into matchstick-size strips. Put $1/4$ cup of the strips in a food processor or blender; set the rest aside.

Add the undrained corn to the processor; process until smooth. Add the corn mixture, water, vinegar, and pepper to the stockpot. Bring to a boil.

Taste a piece of the carrot. If it is tender, stir in the remaining ham. If the carrot is hard, cook for 3 to 4 minutes before stirring in the ham. Cook for 5 minutes.

To serve, ladle soup into bowls. Sprinkle with the snow peas.

PER SERVING	
Calories 257	Cholesterol 24 mg
Total Fat 3.0 g	Sodium 509 mg
Saturated 1.0 g	Carbohydrates 50 g
Polyunsaturated 0.5 g	Fiber 5 g
Monounsaturated 1.5 g	Sugar 14 g
	Protein 15 g

ham and potato
skillet pie

Equally at home on the brunch, lunch, or dinner table, this dish is easy to toss together.

1/3 cup water

1 pound baking potatoes (russet preferred), diced

1 medium onion, chopped

10 ounces frozen cauliflower or broccoli florets, thawed and patted dry

3 ounces lower-sodium, low-fat ham, finely chopped

Egg substitute equivalent to 4 eggs

1/4 teaspoon ground nutmeg

1/4 teaspoon salt

1/4 teaspoon pepper

4 3/4-ounce slices reduced-fat American cheese, torn into small pieces

In a large nonstick skillet, bring the water to a boil over high heat. Add the potatoes and onion. Return to a boil. Reduce the heat and simmer, covered, for 6 minutes, or until the potatoes are tender-crisp.

Stir in the remaining ingredients except the cheese. Reduce the heat to medium-low; cook without stirring for 20 minutes, or until the eggs are almost set.

Meanwhile, preheat the broiler.

Broil 4 to 5 inches from the heat for 2 minutes. Top with the cheese and broil for an additional 1 to 2 minutes, or until the cheese is melted, watching carefully so it doesn't burn.

COOK'S TIP ON DEFROSTING VEGETABLES

Place frozen vegetables in a colander and run them under cold running water for 15 to 20 seconds to defrost quickly. Shake off excess water before using the vegetables.

PER SERVING	
Calories 213	Cholesterol 19 mg
Total Fat 4.0 g	Sodium 786 mg
Saturated 2.5 g	Carbohydrates 31 g
Polyunsaturated 0 g	Fiber 5 g
Monounsaturated 0.5 g	Sugar 10 g
	Protein 20 g

scalloped potatoes
with ham and asparagus

SERVES 4; 1³/₄ CUPS PER SERVING

Scalloped potatoes aren't just a side dish when you add ham and asparagus, then smother the casserole with Swiss cheese.

Vegetable oil spray

1¹/₂ pounds baking potatoes (russets preferred), unpeeled, thinly sliced

8 ounces lower-sodium, low-fat ham, finely chopped

12 ounces asparagus spears, trimmed, cut into 2-inch pieces

1 medium onion, chopped

1 teaspoon dried dillweed, crumbled

6 ounces fat-free evaporated milk

2 tablespoons all-purpose flour

¹/₈ teaspoon salt

2 tablespoons light tub margarine

¹/₄ teaspoon pepper

3 ounces reduced-fat Swiss cheese, torn into small pieces or shredded

Preheat the oven to 350°F. Lightly spray a 9-inch glass baking dish with vegetable oil spray.

Spread one third of the potatoes in the dish. Top with one half each of the ham, asparagus, onion, and dillweed. Repeat the layers, ending with potatoes.

In a small bowl, whisk together the milk, flour, and salt until smooth. Pour over the potatoes. Dot with the margarine. Sprinkle with the pepper. Lightly spray a sheet of aluminum foil with vegetable oil spray. Cover the casserole with the foil with the sprayed side down.

Bake for 40 minutes. Remove the foil. Bake for 25 minutes, or until the potatoes are very tender. Sprinkle the cheese evenly over the casserole. Bake for 5 minutes, or until the cheese is melted. If time allows, remove the casserole from the oven and let stand for 5 to 10 minutes so the flavors can blend and some of the liquid can be absorbed.

PER SERVING	
Calories 334	Cholesterol 39 mg
Total Fat 9.5 g	Sodium 659 mg
Saturated 4.0 g	Carbohydrates 44 g
Polyunsaturated 0.5 g	Fiber 6 g
Monounsaturated 2.5 g	Sugar 11 g
	Protein 24 g

salad of pork, corn, and brussels sprouts with honey-mustard dressing

A honey-mustard mixture cooks into brussels sprouts, adding to the complex flavors of this deliciously sweet and savory entrée salad.

DRESSING

    2 tablespoons honey

    2 tablespoons white wine vinegar

    1 tablespoon Dijon mustard

    ❖ ❖ ❖ ❖

    2 tablespoons water

  20 medium brussels sprouts, trimmed and cut in half lengthwise

    2 cups frozen whole-kernel corn

    1 cup halved grape tomatoes or cherry tomatoes

    ¹/₄ cup minced dried apricots

    ¹/₄ teaspoon salt

  12 ounces cooked lean pork roast, all visible fat discarded, cut into matchstick-size strips

In a large bowl, whisk together the dressing ingredients.

Heat a 12-inch skillet over high heat. Bring the water and 2 tablespoons of the dressing to a boil. Add the brussels sprouts. Cook for 5 minutes, or until the liquid evaporates, stirring occasionally. Reduce the heat to low. Cook, covered, for 5 minutes, or until the sprouts are tender.

Add the sprouts and the remaining ingredients except the pork to the reserved dressing. Toss for 2 to 3 minutes, or until the corn is thawed.

Add the pork; toss.

Cover and refrigerate for 1 to 12 hours before serving.

COOK'S TIP ON MEASURING HONEY

If you lightly spray your measuring spoon or cup with vegetable oil spray before measuring honey, all of it will pour out easily.

PER SERVING	
Calories 352	Cholesterol 66 mg
Total Fat 7.5 g	Sodium 307 mg
Saturated 2.5 g	Carbohydrates 44 g
Polyunsaturated 1.0 g	Fiber 7 g
Monounsaturated 3.0 g	Sugar 19 g
	Protein 32 g

braised pork loin
with apple ratatouille

SERVES 6; 3 OUNCES PORK, $^1/_2$ CUP APPLE RATATOUILLE, AND $^1/_2$ CUP POTATOES
PER SERVING (PLUS ABOUT 8 OUNCES COOKED PORK)

Spicy apple, carrot, and raisin ratatouille is the unusual accompaniment to this pork. You'll have enough roast left over to use in a salad, a casserole, or sandwiches.

> **Vegetable oil spray**
> **2$^1/_2$-pound boneless top loin pork roast, all visible fat discarded**

APPLE RATATOUILLE

> **3 large or 4 medium Granny Smith apples, unpeeled, thinly sliced**
> **1 large carrot, grated**
> **$^1/_3$ cup raisins**
> **2 tablespoons brown sugar**
> **1 tablespoon cider vinegar**
> **$^1/_8$ teaspoon ground nutmeg**
> **$^1/_8$ teaspoon ground cloves**
>
> ❖ ❖ ❖ ❖
>
> **3 large red potatoes (about 1$^1/_2$ pounds), quartered**
> **$^1/_8$ teaspoon salt**

Preheat the oven to 325°F.

Heat a Dutch oven over medium-high heat. Remove from the heat and lightly spray with vegetable oil spray (being careful not to spray near a gas flame). Brown the roast on all sides, about 10 minutes.

Meanwhile, in a medium bowl, stir together the apple ratatouille ingredients. Spoon the mixture beside the roast on two sides. In the same bowl, stir together the potatoes and salt. Put the potatoes around the roast and apples.

Bake, covered, for 1 hour 15 minutes to 1 hour 30 minutes, or until the internal temperature of the roast reaches 170°F, the juices run clear, and the pork is no longer pink in the center.

Transfer the pork and potatoes to a serving platter. Stir the apple mixture to incorporate the cooking juices. Serve with the roast.

PER SERVING	
Calories 361	Cholesterol 62 mg
Total Fat 8.0 g	Sodium 93 mg
Saturated 3.0 g	Carbohydrates 49 g
Polyunsaturated 0.5 g	Fiber 6 g
Monounsaturated 3.5 g	Sugar 27 g
	Protein 28 g

herbed pork tenderloin and root vegetables

SERVES 4; ABOUT 3 OUNCES PORK AND 1¹/₄ CUPS VEGETABLES PER SERVING

Serve this comfort-food roasted dinner with a fresh fruit salad and rye rolls.

Vegetable oil spray

2 medium parsnips, peeled

2 medium carrots, peeled

2 medium turnips or 1 large rutabaga (about 10 ounces), peeled

4 medium beets (about 8 ounces), peeled

1 medium fennel bulb (about 12 ounces) or 3 medium ribs of celery

1 tablespoon olive oil

1 teaspoon garlic powder

¹/₂ teaspoon salt

¹/₂ tablespoon dried thyme, crumbled

1 teaspoon dried rosemary, crushed

1 teaspoon paprika

¹/₂ teaspoon pepper

²/₃ cup fat-free, no-salt-added beef broth

1 pound pork tenderloin, all visible fat discarded

2 tablespoons chopped fennel fronds or fresh thyme (optional)

Preheat the oven to 375°F. Lightly spray a large, shallow roasting pan or heavy rimmed baking sheet with vegetable oil spray.

Cut the parsnips, carrots, turnips, and beets into 1¹/₂-inch pieces. Put in the roasting pan.

Cut off the feathery fronds from the fennel bulb. Set aside 2 tablespoons for garnish, if desired. Trim the bulb; cut lengthwise into ³/₄-inch slices. (If using celery, cut the ribs crosswise into 1¹/₂-inch pieces.) Add to the roasting pan. Drizzle all with the oil.

In a small bowl, stir together the garlic powder, salt, thyme, rosemary, paprika, and pepper. Sprinkle 1 tablespoon over the vegetables, stirring to coat. Set aside the remaining mixture.

PER SERVING	
Calories 307	Cholesterol 63 mg
Total Fat 8.0 g	Sodium 516 mg
Saturated 2.0 g	Carbohydrates 33 g
Polyunsaturated 1.0 g	Fiber 11 g
Monounsaturated 4.0 g	Sugar 12 g
	Protein 28 g

Pour the broth into the pan.

Bake for 30 minutes.

Stir the vegetables and move them to the edges of the pan. Place the pork in the center. Sprinkle with the remaining garlic powder mixture, turning to coat.

Bake for 30 minutes, or until the internal temperature of the pork reaches 160°F and the pork has very little pink in the center.

Transfer the pork to a carving board. Cover lightly with aluminum foil; let stand for 5 minutes. Cut the pork crosswise into thin slices.

To serve, arrange the pork and vegetables on plates. Garnish with the fennel fronds.

thai coconut
and curry soup

Tantalize your taste buds with this soup's many layers of flavor, from soothing lemongrass and rich-tasting light coconut milk to spicy Thai red curry paste and zesty lime.

    2 stalks of lemongrass or 2 teaspoons grated lemon zest

    4 cups fat-free, low-sodium chicken broth

    13.5-ounce can light coconut milk, or 12-ounce can fat-free evaporated milk
        and 1 teaspoon coconut extract

    1 pound pork tenderloin, all visible fat discarded, cut into thin strips

    1 cup shredded carrot

    1 cup canned cut baby corn, packed in water, rinsed and drained

    8-ounce can bamboo shoots, rinsed and drained

    1 tablespoon Thai red curry paste

    2 ounces dried rice noodles or dried angel hair pasta

    6 ounces snow peas, trimmed (about 2 cups)

    ¹/₄ cup loosely packed fresh basil leaves, thick stems discarded, thinly sliced

    1 teaspoon grated lime zest

    2 tablespoons fresh lime juice

Trim and discard about 6 inches from the slender tip end of the lemongrass stalks. Remove the outer layer of leaves from the bottom part of the stalks. Cut the stalks crosswise into ¹/₄-inch slices.

In a large saucepan, bring the lemongrass (if using lemon zest, add later) and chicken broth to a simmer over medium-high heat, stirring occasionally. Reduce the heat and simmer, covered, for 10 to 12 minutes. With a slotted spoon, remove and discard the lemongrass.

Stir in the coconut milk, pork, carrot, corn, bamboo shoots, and red curry paste. Cook, covered, over medium heat for 6 to 7 minutes, or until the pork is no longer pink in the center.

PER SERVING	
Calories 316	Cholesterol 74 mg
Total Fat 9.0 g	Sodium 391 mg
Saturated 4.5 g	Carbohydrates 27 g
Polyunsaturated 0.5 g	Fiber 5 g
Monounsaturated 2.0 g	Sugar 6 g
	Protein 30 g

Increase the heat to medium-high and bring the mixture to a simmer. Stir in the rice noodles. Bring to a boil. Boil, uncovered, for 2 to 3 minutes, or until the noodles are tender, stirring occasionally.

Stir in the snow peas, fresh basil, lime zest, and lime juice. If you are using lemon zest instead of lemongrass, add it here. Reduce the heat to medium. Cook, uncovered, for 1 minute, or until the peas are tender-crisp, stirring occasionally.

korean-style grilled
pork and potato salad

Inspired by bulgogi, a popular Korean barbecued meat, this recipe calls for pork tenderloin soaked in a sesame oil and soy sauce marinade, then grilled to perfection. The list of ingredients is long, but the preparation is simple. You can even prepare the pork and potatoes up to five days in advance, then later whisk together the dressing ingredients and toss in some baby spinach.

1 tablespoon low-salt soy sauce

1 tablespoon toasted sesame oil

2 medium garlic cloves, minced

1/4 teaspoon pepper

1 pound pork tenderloin, all visible fat discarded, cut in half lengthwise

Vegetable oil spray

4 medium red potatoes (about 4 ounces each), unpeeled, cut into 3/4-inch cubes

1 tablespoon sesame seeds

1 teaspoon salt-free all-purpose seasoning blend

2 tablespoons red wine vinegar

1 tablespoon low-salt soy sauce

1 tablespoon Dijon mustard

2 teaspoons olive oil

1 teaspoon toasted sesame oil

1 teaspoon brown sugar

4 to 5 ounces baby spinach leaves (about 4 cups)

In a large airtight plastic bag, combine 1 tablespoon soy sauce, 1 tablespoon sesame oil, garlic, and pepper. Add the pork. Seal the bag and turn to coat the pork. Refrigerate for 15 minutes to 24 hours.

Preheat the grill on medium-high.

Place an 18 × 24-inch sheet of aluminum foil on a flat surface. Lightly spray the foil with vegetable oil spray. Place the potatoes in the middle; sprinkle with

PER SERVING	Cholesterol 75 mg
Calories 290	Sodium 364 mg
Total Fat 9.5 g	Carbohydrates 24 g
Saturated 2.5 g	Fiber 4 g
Polyunsaturated 1.5 g	Sugar 4 g
Monounsaturated 4.5 g	Protein 29 g

the sesame seeds and all-purpose seasoning. Lightly spray the potatoes with vegetable oil spray. Fold the sides of the foil toward the center; fold the top and ends twice to seal.

Put the pork and the potato packets on the grill; cover. Grill the pork for 10 to 12 minutes on each side, or until no longer pink in the center. Transfer the pork to a cutting board; let cool for 5 minutes. Cut into thin slices.

Grill the potatoes for 15 to 20 minutes, or until they are tender. (When checking the potatoes, open the package carefully to avoid steam burns.) Reseal the package and set aside.

Meanwhile, in a large bowl, whisk together the remaining ingredients except the spinach.

To serve, add the spinach, potatoes, and pork to the dressing. Using two large spoons, toss to combine.

grilled pork-and-vegetable pitas

SERVES 4; 2 KEBABS AND 1 PITA BREAD PER SERVING

Served in whole-wheat pitas and topped with Dijon-yogurt sauce, this combination of grilled pork tenderloin and vegetables is simply irresistible!

  3 tablespoons Dijon mustard

  3 tablespoons red wine vinegar

  2 teaspoons olive oil

  2 medium garlic cloves, minced

  1/4 teaspoon pepper

  8 ounces fat-free or low-fat plain yogurt

  1 pound pork tenderloin, all visible fat discarded, cut into 3/4-inch cubes

14 medium button mushrooms, halved

  1 medium red bell pepper, cut into 3/4-inch cubes

  1/2 medium onion, cut into 3/4-inch pieces

  4 6-inch whole-wheat pita breads, halved crosswise

In a small bowl, stir together the mustard, vinegar, oil, garlic, and pepper. Stir 1 tablespoon of this mixture into the container of yogurt. Refrigerate.

Preheat the grill to medium-high heat.

On eight 10-inch metal skewers, alternately thread the pork, mushrooms, bell pepper, and onion.

Grill the kebabs for 2 minutes on each side, or until the pork is browned. Brush the mustard mixture without the yogurt on all sides of the kebabs; grill for 1 to 2 minutes on each side, or until the pork is no longer pink in the center and the vegetables are tender.

To serve, remove the meat and vegetables from a skewer and place in half a pita bread. Top with 2 tablespoons of the refrigerated yogurt sauce. Repeat with the remaining kebabs and yogurt sauce.

PER SERVING	
Calories 402	Cholesterol 76 mg
Total Fat 9.0 g	Sodium 689 mg
Saturated 2.5 g	Carbohydrates 44 g
Polyunsaturated 1.5 g	Fiber 6 g
Monounsaturated 4.0 g	Sugar 8 g
	Protein 36 g

jerked pork with sweet potatoes and pineapple

SERVES 4; 3 OUNCES PORK AND 1 CUP VEGETABLE AND FRUIT MIXTURE PER SERVING

Tender pork slices with roasted sweet potato cubes tossed with clove-flavored pineapple chunks and onion wedges—so Caribbean, so good!

> Vegetable oil spray
>
> 1 pound pork tenderloin, all visible fat discarded
>
> 1/2 tablespoon jerk seasoning
>
> 16-ounce can pineapple chunks packed in their own juice, drained
>
> Whole cloves (about 24)
>
> 1 1/2 pounds sweet potatoes, peeled and cut into 1/2-inch cubes
>
> 1 medium onion, cut into 1/2-inch wedges
>
> 1 tablespoon light tub margarine
>
> 1 teaspoon sugar
>
> 1/2 teaspoon ground cinnamon

Preheat the oven to 425°F.

Lightly spray a nonstick rimmed baking sheet with vegetable oil spray. Put the pork on the baking sheet. Sprinkle the jerk seasoning over the pork.

Pierce each pineapple chunk with a whole clove. Arrange the pineapple, sweet potatoes, and onion around the pork. Lightly spray all with vegetable oil spray.

Bake for 22 to 24 minutes, or until the pork is slightly pink in the center. Transfer the pork to a cutting board. Let stand for 5 minutes before slicing.

Meanwhile, remove and discard the cloves. Gently stir the remaining ingredients into the vegetables and fruit on the baking sheet.

To serve, arrange the pork slices on plates. Spoon the vegetable and fruit mixture onto the plates.

PER SERVING	
Calories 380	Cholesterol 63 mg
Total Fat 5.0 g	Sodium 240 mg
Saturated 1.5 g	Carbohydrates 60 g
Polyunsaturated 0.5 g	Fiber 7 g
Monounsaturated 2.0 g	Sugar 23 g
	Protein 26 g

stuffed pork tenderloin
and pesto couscous

When sliced, this pork tenderloin reveals a secret: a stuffing of vibrant sun-dried tomatoes and carrots. Served on pesto couscous with a pile of roasted mushrooms on the side, this is a one-pot pleasure.

$1/2$ cup dry-packed sun-dried tomatoes, coarsely chopped

$1/2$ cup hot water

1 large carrot, grated

Vegetable oil spray

1 teaspoon olive oil

1 large leek (white and very light green parts only), diced

1 pound pork tenderloin, all visible fat discarded

1 pound small button mushrooms, stems trimmed

2 portobello mushrooms (about 6 ounces), stems discarded, caps thinly sliced

1 medium red bell pepper, diced

1 tablespoon balsamic vinegar

1 cup lightly packed fresh basil, large stems removed

2 tablespoons fat-free or reduced-fat mayonnaise dressing

Juice of 1 medium lemon

$1/4$ teaspoon salt

$1/4$ teaspoon pepper

2 cups hot water

$1^1/2$ cups uncooked couscous

In a large measuring cup, soak the tomatoes in $1/2$ cup hot water for 30 minutes. Drain. Stir the carrot into the tomatoes.

Meanwhile, heat a Dutch oven over medium heat. Remove from the heat and lightly spray with vegetable oil spray (being careful not to spray near a gas flame). Pour in the oil and swirl to coat the bottom. Cook the leeks for 6 to 7 minutes, or until very soft, stirring occasionally. Transfer to a medium bowl.

PER SERVING	
Calories 553	Cholesterol 63 mg
Total Fat 7.0 g	Sodium 283 mg
Saturated 2.0 g	Carbohydrates 82 g
Polyunsaturated 1.5 g	Fiber 7 g
Monounsaturated 2.5 g	Sugar 11 g
	Protein 39 g

Push a boning knife, a thin utility knife, or a long, thin steak knife lengthwise through the center of the tenderloin to make a hole. Force a sharpening steel or the handle of a wooden spoon through the hole to make it larger. Using your fingers, stuff the tenderloin with the tomato mixture, forcing it into the hole. When the mixture reaches the center, begin stuffing from the other end.

Lightly respray the Dutch oven. Cook the meat over medium heat for about 1½ minutes on each side, or until it has just a little color, not a true browning.

Meanwhile, stir the button and portobello mushrooms, bell pepper, and vinegar into the leeks. Pour over the tenderloin. Reduce the heat to medium-low. Cook, covered, for 15 minutes, or until the internal temperature of the pork registers 150° to 155°F on an instant-read meat thermometer. Transfer the meat and vegetables to a serving plate. Cover with aluminum foil.

In a food processor or blender, puree the basil, mayonnaise, lemon juice, salt, and pepper.

In the Dutch oven, stir together the basil mixture, 2 cups hot water, and couscous. Increase the heat to medium. Cook until the mixture begins to simmer. Remove from the heat. Let stand, covered, for 5 minutes. Fluff the couscous with a fork. Spoon onto the serving plate.

COOK'S TIP

If you find it difficult to guide a boning knife all the way through the tenderloin, or if your knife is too short, cut the tenderloin in half to form two equal logs. When cooking, place them touching end to end so the meat cooks like a full-length tenderloin.

horseradish pork
with blue cheese tomatoes

SERVES 4; 3 OUNCES PORK, 1 STUFFED TOMATO, AND $^1/_2$ CUP COUSCOUS PER SERVING

This dish will definitely be a hit with blue-cheese lovers. The tomatoes are stuffed to the brim with it!

1$^1/_2$ tablespoons prepared horseradish

1$^1/_2$ tablespoons Dijon mustard

$^1/_2$ teaspoon pepper

Vegetable oil spray

1 pound pork tenderloin, all visible fat discarded

10-ounce package frozen chopped spinach, thawed, well drained, and squeezed dry

$^1/_4$ cup finely chopped green onions (green and white parts)

2 ounces blue cheese, crumbled

2 teaspoons dried oregano, crumbled

1 medium garlic clove, minced

4 medium tomatoes

1 cup uncooked couscous

$^1/_4$ cup snipped fresh parsley

Preheat the oven to 425°F.

In a medium bowl, stir together the horseradish, mustard, and pepper.

Lightly spray a broiler pan with vegetable oil spray. Put the pork on the broiler pan. Coat the top and sides of the pork with the horseradish mixture.

In the same bowl, stir together the spinach, green onions, blue cheese, oregano, and garlic.

Cut a thin slice from the top of each tomato. Scoop out the pulp, being sure not to pierce the bottom. Spoon the spinach mixture into each tomato. Cover each with aluminum foil to keep the top from drying out. Place the tomatoes on the broiler pan with the pork.

Bake for 25 minutes, or until the pork is just barely pink in the center.

PER SERVING	Cholesterol 74 mg
Calories 445	Sodium 466 mg
Total Fat 9.5 g	Carbohydrates 52 g
Saturated 4.0 g	Fiber 6 g
Polyunsaturated 1.0 g	Sugar 6 g
Monounsaturated 3.0 g	Protein 36 g

Meanwhile, prepare the couscous using the package directions, omitting the salt and oil. Fluff with a fork.

When the pork is done, sprinkle with the parsley. Let stand for 5 minutes. Slice the pork on the diagonal.

To serve, spoon the couscous onto plates. Arrange the pork on the couscous. Serve the tomatoes on the side.

COOK'S TIP ON TOMATOES

You can freeze the pulp you remove from the tomatoes, then use it later in soups or stews.

COOK'S TIP ON PORK TENDERLOIN

When cooking a whole pork tenderloin, tuck the thinner end under to prevent uneven cooking. Remember that if you let pork stand before slicing, it continues to cook after being removed from the oven.

rosemary pork and pears
with dried berries

Here's a different way to include more fruit in your day: baked pear halves filled with deliciously spiced dried fruit. They are a delightful accompaniment for the rosemary pork.

$^1/_3$ cup dried blueberries or cranberries

1 tablespoon light tub margarine

$^1/_2$ teaspoon grated orange zest

$^1/_2$ teaspoon ground cinnamon

Vegetable oil spray

1 pound pork tenderloin, all visible fat discarded

4 medium pears, halved and cored

$^1/_2$ teaspoon dried rosemary, crushed

$^1/_4$ teaspoon salt

$^1/_8$ teaspoon garlic powder

Paprika to taste

$^1/_4$ cup sliced almonds

$^1/_2$ cup uncooked rice

Preheat the oven to 425°F.

In a small bowl, stir together the blueberries, margarine, orange zest, and cinnamon.

Lightly spray a nonstick rimmed baking sheet with vegetable oil spray. Place the pork and pears with the cut side up on the baking sheet. Spoon the berry mixture into the cavity of each pear half. Sprinkle the pork with the rosemary, salt, garlic powder, and paprika.

Bake for 22 minutes, or until the pork is barely pink in the center. Transfer to a cutting board and let stand for about 3 minutes. Thinly slice on the diagonal (about $^1/_8$-inch pieces).

PER SERVING	
Calories 433	Cholesterol 63 mg
Total Fat 9.5 g	Sodium 214 mg
Saturated 1.5 g	Carbohydrates 61 g
Polyunsaturated 1.5 g	Fiber 7 g
Monounsaturated 4.5 g	Sugar 27 g
	Protein 26 g

Meanwhile, heat a small saucepan over medium-high heat. Dry-roast the almonds for 3 to 4 minutes, or until they begin to brown lightly, stirring frequently. Remove the almonds.

In the same saucepan, prepare the rice using the package directions, omitting the salt and margarine. Stir in the almonds.

To serve, spoon the rice onto a serving platter. Top with the pork slices and arrange the pears around the edge.

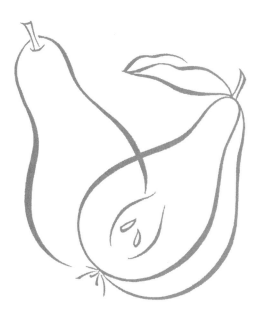

dijon pork with
potatoes and carrots

SERVES 4; 3 OUNCES PORK PLUS 1 1/2 CUPS VEGETABLES PER SERVING

Cleanup is kept to an absolute minimum with the help of a sheet of aluminum foil. Just line a baking sheet with it, combine and roast the ingredients on it, then throw the foil away. There isn't even a mixing bowl to wash.

8 medium red potatoes (about 2 ounces each), cut into 1/2-inch wedges

4 medium carrots, quartered lengthwise, then cut into 2-inch-long pieces

2 small onions, cut into eighths

1 medium green bell pepper, cut into thin strips

1 medium red bell pepper, cut into thin strips

2 medium garlic cloves, minced

1 tablespoon olive oil (extra virgin preferred)

1 pound pork tenderloin, all visible fat discarded

1 1/2 tablespoons Dijon mustard

1/2 teaspoon cracked black pepper

2 teaspoons olive oil (extra virgin preferred)

1/2 teaspoon salt

Preheat the oven to 425°F. Line a baking sheet with aluminum foil.

Put the potatoes, carrots, onions, bell peppers, and garlic on the baking sheet. Toss with 1 tablespoon oil. Arrange in a single layer, leaving enough room in the center for the pork.

Spoon the mustard over the pork; spread evenly over the top and sides. Sprinkle with the pepper. Place the pork on the baking sheet. Tuck the thin end of the pork under for even cooking.

Bake for 10 minutes. Stir the vegetables. Bake for 25 minutes, or until the pork is no longer pink in the center. Turn off the oven. Transfer the pork to a cutting board. Let stand for 3 minutes for easier slicing.

Meanwhile, drizzle the remaining 2 teaspoons oil over the vegetables. Stir gently to coat. Sprinkle with the salt. Stir gently. Leave the vegetables in the oven to keep warm while you slice the pork.

PER SERVING	
Calories 341	Cholesterol 74 mg
Total Fat 10.0 g	Sodium 511 mg
Saturated 2.0 g	Carbohydrates 37 g
Polyunsaturated 1.0 g	Fiber 7 g
Monounsaturated 6.0 g	Sugar 12 g
	Protein 29 g

chipotle pork posole

Mexican in origin, posole (poh-SOH-leh) is a thick, rich-tasting stew made with hominy. The creamy dollop of sour cream, sprinkling of cilantro, and spritz of lime are just the right ingredients to complement the heat of the chipotle peppers.

> Vegetable oil spray
>
> 1 pound pork tenderloin, all visible fat discarded, cut into ¹/₂-inch pieces
>
> 2 medium onions, chopped
>
> 1 medium or large red bell pepper, chopped
>
> 15.5-ounce can yellow hominy, rinsed and drained
>
> 14.5-ounce can no-salt-added stewed tomatoes, undrained
>
> 14.5-ounce can fat-free, low-sodium chicken broth
>
> 2 to 3 canned chipotle peppers packed in adobo sauce, finely chopped and mashed
>
> 1 tablespoon olive oil (extra virgin preferred)
>
> ¹/₈ teaspoon salt
>
> ¹/₄ cup fat-free or light sour cream
>
> ¹/₄ cup snipped fresh cilantro
>
> 1 medium lime, quartered

Heat a Dutch oven over medium-high heat. Remove from the heat and lightly spray with vegetable oil spray (being careful not to spray near a gas flame). Cook the pork for 3 to 4 minutes, or until the outside is no longer pink, stirring almost constantly. Transfer the pork with any accumulated juices to a medium bowl.

Respray the Dutch oven with vegetable cooking spray. Cook the onions and bell pepper for 4 minutes, or until the onions are translucent, stirring occasionally.

Stir in the hominy, undrained tomatoes, broth, chipotle peppers, and reserved pork with any accumulated juices. Increase the heat to high; bring to a boil. Reduce the heat and simmer, covered, for 20 minutes, or until the vegetables are tender.

Remove from the heat. Stir in the oil and salt.

To serve, ladle into bowls. Top each serving with a dollop of sour cream; sprinkle with cilantro. Serve with a lime wedge to squeeze over the stew.

PER SERVING	
Calories 328	Cholesterol 76 mg
Total Fat 7.5 g	Sodium 781 mg
Saturated 2.0 g	Carbohydrates 37 g
Polyunsaturated 0.5 g	Fiber 7 g
Monounsaturated 4.0 g	Sugar 12 g
	Protein 30 g

pork and toasted peanut
fusion wrap

Imagine crisp vegetables topped with crunchy peanuts and stir-fried pork in a fruity spiced sauce, all wrapped in a huge tortilla. Now imagine how wonderful it will taste when you devour it!

^{1}/4 cup seedless raspberry, apricot, or peach all-fruit spread

2 tablespoons sugar

2 tablespoons low-salt soy sauce

1 tablespoon cider vinegar

2 teaspoons grated peeled gingerroot

1 teaspoon cornstarch

^{1}/4 teaspoon crushed red pepper flakes

^{1}/4 cup peanuts (about 1 ounce)

1 pound pork tenderloin, all visible fat discarded, cut into thin strips

4 9^1/2- to 10-inch low-fat flour tortillas

2 cups shredded cabbage or bok choy

8-ounce can sliced water chestnuts, rinsed and drained

In a small bowl, whisk together the fruit spread, sugar, soy sauce, vinegar, gingerroot, cornstarch, and red pepper flakes until the cornstarch is completely dissolved. Set aside.

Heat a 12-inch skillet over medium-high heat. Dry-roast the peanuts for 3 minutes, or until beginning to lightly brown, stirring constantly. Remove the peanuts. Set aside.

In the same skillet, cook the pork over medium-high heat for 3 minutes, or until brown on the outside and pink on the inside, stirring frequently.

Increase the heat to high. Stir in the fruit spread mixture. Bring to a boil; continue boiling for 1 minute, or until the mixture is thickened and reduced slightly and the pork is no longer pink in the center, stirring constantly.

PER SERVING	Cholesterol 74 mg
Calories 434	Sodium 726 mg
Total Fat 9.0 g	Carbohydrates 55 g
Saturated 2.0 g	Fiber 7 g
Polyunsaturated 2.0 g	Sugar 14 g
Monounsaturated 4.0 g	Protein 33 g

Warm the tortillas using the package directions. Place on plates.

To assemble, spoon $^1/_2$ cup cabbage or bok choy down the center of each tortilla. Top with the water chestnuts and peanuts, then with the pork mixture. Fold the sides of the tortillas to the center, overlapping slightly. Secure with wooden toothpicks, if desired. Cut in half diagonally.

TIME-SAVER

You can use bagged angel hair cabbage instead of the shredded cabbage called for in the recipe.

thai pork and noodles

SERVES 4; ABOUT 1¹/4 CUPS PORK MIXTURE AND ³/4 CUP NOODLES PER SERVING

Thai peanut sauce and red curry paste team up in this spicy dish. A sprinkling of chopped peanuts provides crunch and intensifies the flavor of the dish.

  1 pound pork tenderloin, all visible fat discarded, cut into ³/4-inch cubes
  16-ounce package frozen stir-fry vegetables, thawed and drained
  ³/4 cup fat-free, low-sodium chicken broth
  ¹/4 cup Thai peanut sauce
  2 tablespoons low-salt soy sauce
  3 medium garlic cloves, minced
  1 to 2 teaspoons red curry paste or ¹/4 to ¹/2 teaspoon crushed red pepper flakes
  1 tablespoon cornstarch
  ¹/4 cup fat-free, low-sodium chicken broth
  4 ounces rice sticks or long rice vermicelli
  ¹/4 cup snipped fresh cilantro or thinly sliced green onions (green and white parts)
  ¹/4 cup chopped peanuts, dry-roasted

In a slow cooker, stir together the pork, vegetables, ³/4 cup broth, peanut sauce, soy sauce, garlic, and curry paste. Cook, covered, on high for 2 to 2¹/2 hours or on low for 4 hours, or until the pork is no longer pink in the center.

Put the cornstarch in a cup. Add ¹/4 cup broth, stirring to dissolve. Pour into the pork mixture. Cook, covered, on high for 10 minutes, or until the sauce thickens.

Meanwhile, prepare the rice sticks according to the package directions, omitting the salt.

To serve, put the noodles in shallow bowls or plates. Top with the pork mixture. Sprinkle with the cilantro and peanuts.

COOK'S TIP ON RICE STICKS

If rice sticks aren't available, substitute 2 to 3 cups cooked brown rice or angel hair pasta.

PER SERVING	
Calories 411	Cholesterol 74 mg
Total Fat 12.0 g	Sodium 365 mg
Saturated 2.5 g	Carbohydrates 40 g
Polyunsaturated 3.0 g	Fiber 5 g
Monounsaturated 5.5 g	Sugar 5 g
	Protein 34 g

cajun pork chop skillet

SERVES 4; 1 PORK CHOP, $^3/_4$ CUP RICE, AND $^1/_2$ CUP GREEN BEANS PER SERVING

Serve this full-flavored skillet supper with a tossed green salad and crusty whole-grain rolls.

> 1 teaspoon salt-free Cajun or Creole seasoning blend (See Cook's Tip on Cajun or Creole Seasoning Blend, page 7)
>
> $^1/_2$ teaspoon salt
>
> 4 boneless center-cut pork chops, about $^1/_2$ inch thick (about 4 ounces each), all visible fat discarded
>
> Vegetable oil spray
>
> 1 cup uncooked long-grain or jasmine rice
>
> 1 teaspoon salt-free Cajun or Creole seasoning blend
>
> $^1/_4$ teaspoon salt
>
> 14.5-ounce can fat-free, low-sodium chicken broth
>
> 10 ounces frozen cut green beans or mixed vegetables, thawed and drained

Sprinkle 1 teaspoon seasoning blend and $^1/_2$ teaspoon salt over the pork chops.

Heat a large nonstick skillet over medium heat. Remove the skillet from the heat and lightly spray with vegetable oil spray (being careful not to spray near a gas flame). Cook the pork chops for 3 to 4 minutes on each side, or until browned and barely pink in the center. (Do not overcook, or the pork will be tough.) Transfer to a plate. Set aside.

In the skillet, combine the rice, 1 teaspoon seasoning blend, and $^1/_4$ teaspoon salt. Stir in the broth. Bring to a boil. Reduce the heat and simmer, covered, for 15 minutes.

Stir in the green beans. Arrange the pork chops on top. Simmer, covered, for 8 minutes, or until the liquid is absorbed and the pork is no longer pink in the center.

PER SERVING	
Calories 358	Cholesterol 67 mg
Total Fat 7.0 g	Sodium 515 mg
Saturated 2.5 g	Carbohydrates 43 g
Polyunsaturated 0.5 g	Fiber 3 g
Monounsaturated 3.0 g	Sugar 2 g
	Protein 29 g

pork chops and potatoes
in creamy gravy

SERVES 4; 1 PORK CHOP PLUS 1¹/₄ CUPS VEGETABLE MIXTURE PER SERVING

When you want to see contented looks on everyone's face, serve potatoes, carrots, and pimientos smothered in gravy and topped with tender pork chops. With only one pan to clean, you'll be content, too!

4 lean pork chops with bone in (about 5 ounces each), all visible fat discarded
Paprika to taste
Pepper to taste
Vegetable oil spray
2 cups fat-free, low-sodium chicken broth
8 red potatoes (about 2 ounces each), each cut into 8 wedges
2 medium onions, thinly sliced
2 medium carrots, thinly sliced
¹/₄ teaspoon dried tarragon, crumbled
¹/₂ cup fat-free evaporated milk
2 tablespoons all-purpose flour
³/₄ teaspoon salt
4-ounce jar sliced pimientos

Sprinkle one side of the pork chops with paprika and pepper.

Heat a large skillet over high heat. Remove the skillet from the heat and lightly spray with vegetable oil spray (being careful not to spray near a gas flame). Cook the pork chops with the seasoned side down for 1 minute. Remove from the skillet.

In the same skillet, stir together the broth, potatoes, onions, carrots, and tarragon. Bring to a boil. Top with the pork chops with the seasoned side up. Reduce the heat and simmer, covered, for 12 minutes, or until the pork is no longer pink in the center and the potatoes are tender.

Using a large slotted spoon, transfer the vegetables to a serving platter with a rim or to a large shallow bowl. Top with the pork. Cover with aluminum foil to keep warm. Set aside.

PER SERVING	
Calories 302	Cholesterol 47 mg
Total Fat 6.0 g	Sodium 546 mg
Saturated 2.5 g	Carbohydrates 38 g
Polyunsaturated 0.5 g	Fiber 5 g
Monounsaturated 3.0 g	Sugar 13 g
	Protein 27 g

Increase the heat to high. Bring the broth to a boil. Boil for 2 minutes, or until reduced to 1 cup.

Reduce the heat to medium. Whisk in the evaporated milk and flour until well blended. Stir in the salt. (If you use a flat spatula, you can scrape the skillet.) Cook for 2 minutes. Remove from the heat.

Stir in the pimientos. Pour over the vegetables on the serving platter.

pork with bell peppers and orzo

SERVES 4; 1 1/2 TO 1 3/4 CUPS PER SERVING

A simply delicious dessert of assorted tropical fruits is the perfect complement for this pork and mini-pasta dish.

Vegetable oil spray

4 boneless pork loin chops (about 4 ounces each), all visible fat discarded, cut into thin strips

1 large red bell pepper, sliced

1 large bell pepper, any color, sliced

1 large onion, sliced

1/2 tablespoon olive oil

2 cups fat-free, low-sodium chicken broth

1/2 cup dried orzo

1/4 cup chili sauce, or 1/4 cup no-salt-added ketchup and 1/4 teaspoon red hot-pepper sauce

1 tablespoon chopped fresh rosemary

1 teaspoon salt-free garlic-herb seasoning blend

1/4 teaspoon salt

Heat a large, deep nonstick skillet over medium-high heat. Remove from the heat and lightly spray with vegetable oil spray (being careful not to spray near a gas flame). Cook the pork for 3 to 4 minutes, stirring occasionally.

Add the bell peppers, onion, and oil. Reduce the heat to medium. Cook for 2 to 3 minutes, or until the vegetables are tender and the pork is no longer pink in the center, stirring occasionally.

Stir in the remaining ingredients. Increase the heat to medium-high and bring to a simmer. Reduce the heat and simmer, covered, for 15 minutes, or until the pasta is tender, stirring once.

PER SERVING	
Calories 308	Cholesterol 55 mg
Total Fat 8.5 g	Sodium 442 mg
Saturated 2.5 g	Carbohydrates 30 g
Polyunsaturated 1.0 g	Fiber 3 g
Monounsaturated 4.5 g	Sugar 9 g
	Protein 27 g

sweet-and-sour pork with brown rice and bok choy

Mildly tart rice vinegar, pineapple juice, and apricot spread accent brown rice, lean pork, and bok choy in this sweet-and-sour dish. Garnish with carrot curls for extra color and extra nutrition.

> 1 small bunch bok choy (8 to 12 ounces)
>
> Vegetable oil spray
>
> 4 boneless pork loin chops (about 4 ounces each), all visible fat discarded, cut into thin strips
>
> $^1/_2$ medium onion, thinly sliced
>
> 1 cup uncooked instant brown rice
>
> $^3/_4$ cup canned pineapple juice
>
> $^1/_2$ cup fat-free, low-sodium chicken broth
>
> 8-ounce can sliced water chestnuts, rinsed and drained
>
> 2 tablespoons plain rice vinegar, or to taste
>
> $^1/_3$ cup all-fruit apricot spread
>
> $^1/_2$ teaspoon low-salt soy sauce
>
> Carrot curls (optional)

Trim and discard the ends of the bok choy stalks. Slice the stalks crosswise into $^1/_4$-inch pieces. Cut the bok choy leaves into thin strips. Set aside.

Heat a large, deep nonstick skillet over medium-high heat. Remove the skillet from the heat and lightly spray with vegetable oil spray (being careful not to spray near a gas flame). Cook the pork for 3 minutes, stirring occasionally.

Stir in the onion. Cook for 2 to 3 minutes, or until the onion is translucent, stirring occasionally.

Stir in the rice, pineapple juice, broth, water chestnuts, and vinegar. Stir in the bok choy. Bring to a simmer, stirring occasionally. Reduce the heat and simmer, covered, for 10 minutes, or until the rice is tender and the liquid is absorbed.

Stir in the apricot spread. Reduce the heat to low. Cook for 1 to 2 minutes, or until the mixture is warmed through, stirring occasionally. Stir in the soy sauce.

Garnish with carrot curls.

PER SERVING	
Calories 341	Cholesterol 62 mg
Total Fat 7.0 g	Sodium 135 mg
Saturated 2.0 g	Carbohydrates 39 g
Polyunsaturated 1.0 g	Fiber 5 g
Monounsaturated 3.0 g	Sugar 16 g
	Protein 29 g

sausage and barley with pine nuts and golden raisins

Flecks of red and green bell peppers color this unusually flavored dish.

1 1/4 cups water

3/4 cup uncooked quick-cooking pearl barley

1/2 cup pine nuts

6 ounces reduced-fat bulk breakfast sausage

1 medium onion, chopped

1 medium green bell pepper, chopped

1 medium red bell pepper, chopped

1/3 to 1/2 cup golden raisins

1/2 teaspoon ground cumin

1/2 teaspoon salt

1/4 teaspoon cayenne

In a small saucepan, bring the water to a boil over high heat. Stir in the barley and return to a boil. Reduce the heat and simmer, covered, for 10 minutes. Remove from the heat. Let stand for 5 minutes to absorb the liquid.

Meanwhile, heat a 12-inch nonstick skillet over medium-high heat. Dry-roast the pine nuts for 2 minutes, or until lightly golden, stirring frequently. Remove the pine nuts.

In the same skillet, cook the sausage for 3 minutes, breaking up large pieces and stirring frequently.

Add the onion and bell peppers. Cook for 6 minutes, or until the onion is translucent and beginning to lightly brown, stirring frequently. Pour into a colander and rinse under hot water to remove excess fat. Drain well.

Stir in the remaining ingredients, including the barley and pine nuts. Remove from the heat. Let stand, covered, for 5 minutes to absorb flavors.

PER SERVING	
Calories 338	Cholesterol 21 mg
Total Fat 8.5 g	Sodium 547 mg
Saturated 1.5 g	Carbohydrates 53 g
Polyunsaturated 3.5 g	Fiber 9 g
Monounsaturated 3.0 g	Sugar 17 g
	Protein 15 g

sausage and potato frittata

SERVES 4; 1 WEDGE PER SERVING

Using a small amount of highly seasoned reduced-fat sausage provides hefty flavor without a hefty saturated fat and calorie count.

Vegetable oil spray

8 ounces reduced-fat bulk breakfast sausage

1/3 cup water

1 pound baking potatoes (russet preferred), unpeeled, thinly sliced

2 medium onions, chopped

1 medium carrot, chopped

1 medium zucchini, sliced

1/2 teaspoon dried oregano, crumbled

1/4 teaspoon crushed red pepper flakes

Egg substitute equivalent to 4 eggs

1/2 cup shredded reduced-fat sharp Cheddar cheese

Heat a 12-inch skillet over medium-high heat. Remove from the heat and lightly spray with vegetable oil spray (being careful not to spray near a gas flame). Cook the sausage for 2 minutes, or until browned on the outside and no longer pink in the center, stirring occasionally to turn and break up the sausage. Pour into a colander to drain; discard any grease. Rinse the sausage under hot water to remove excess fat; drain well. Set on paper towels. Wipe the skillet with a paper towel.

In the same skillet, bring the water to a boil. Stir in the potatoes, onions, carrot, zucchini, oregano, and red pepper flakes. Reduce the heat and simmer, covered, for 6 minutes, or until the potatoes are tender-crisp.

Stir in the sausage. Pour the egg substitute over all. Reduce the heat to medium-low. Cook, covered, for 12 minutes, or until the egg mixture is almost set. Remove from the heat.

Sprinkle with the cheese. Let stand, covered, for 2 minutes, or until the cheese is melted. Cut into 4 wedges.

PER SERVING	
Calories 257	Cholesterol 36 mg
Total Fat 3.5 g	Sodium 554 mg
Saturated 2.0 g	Carbohydrates 32 g
Polyunsaturated 0 g	Fiber 5 g
Monounsaturated 0.5 g	Sugar 10 g
	Protein 24 g

mushroom-stuffed
veal marsala

Lightly cooked romaine and radicchio accompany wafer-thin slices of veal scaloppini stuffed with mushrooms and couscous in this thoroughly modern version of a classic dish.

Vegetable oil spray

2 teaspoons olive oil

1 large shallot, minced

8 large button mushrooms, minced

1 cup fat-free, low-sodium chicken broth

³/₄ cup uncooked couscous

¹/₄ teaspoon salt

¹/₈ teaspoon pepper

4 slices veal scaloppini (about 4 ounces each), all visible fat discarded

¹/₄ cup marsala, or 2 tablespoons balsamic vinegar plus 2 tablespoons water

1 medium head romaine, cut crosswise into 1-inch-wide strips (about 6 cups)

1 small head radicchio, cut crosswise into ¹/₄-inch strips (about 2 cups)

Heat a 12-inch skillet or Dutch oven over medium heat. Remove from the heat and lightly spray with vegetable oil spray (being careful not to spray near a gas flame). Add the oil and swirl to coat the bottom. Cook the shallot and mushrooms for 5 minutes, or until the mushrooms are very soft, stirring occasionally.

Stir in the broth, couscous, salt, and pepper. Bring to a boil. Remove from the heat. Let stand, covered, for 7 to 8 minutes, or until the couscous is tender and all or nearly all the liquid is absorbed.

Meanwhile, pound the veal until it is very thin (about ¹/₈ inch thick). Spread one fourth of the mushroom mixture on a piece of veal. Roll up jelly-roll style and secure with a wooden toothpick. Repeat with the remaining veal and stuffing.

Heat the skillet over medium heat. Remove from the heat and lightly spray with vegetable oil spray (being careful not to spray near a gas flame). Brown the

PER SERVING	Cholesterol 94 mg
Calories 360	Sodium 276 mg
Total Fat 6.5 g	Carbohydrates 39 g
Saturated 1.5 g	Fiber 3 g
Polyunsaturated 1.0 g	Sugar 5 g
Monounsaturated 3.0 g	Protein 32 g

veal on all sides, turning carefully to keep as much filling in place as possible. (Tongs work well for this. A little filling will come out.)

Remove from the heat. Pour in the marsala, turning each veal log to coat. Reduce the heat to medium-low. Cook, covered, for 8 minutes, or until the veal is no longer pink in the center and most of the liquid is evaporated. Transfer the veal to plates. Remove the toothpicks.

In the same skillet, cook the romaine and radicchio for 2 to 5 minutes, or until thoroughly wilted, stirring constantly. (Tongs work well for this.) Spoon the mixture beside each veal log.

curried lamb and
couscous skillet

SERVES 4; ABOUT 1^1/$_2$ CUPS PER SERVING

Whole-wheat couscous, which has three times the fiber of regular couscous, soaks up the exotic, spicy flavor of Madras curry powder in this quick-cooking supper.

^{3}/$_4$ cup fat-free or low-fat plain yogurt

2 teaspoons Madras curry powder, or 2 teaspoons regular curry powder plus ^{1}/$_8$ teaspoon cayenne

1-pound boneless leg of lamb, all visible fat discarded, cut into ^{3}/$_4$-inch cubes
Vegetable oil spray

16-ounce package frozen bell pepper and onion strips, thawed and drained

14.5-ounce can fat-free, low-sodium chicken broth

1 cup uncooked whole-wheat couscous

1 teaspoon Madras curry powder, or 1 teaspoon regular curry powder plus ^{1}/$_8$ teaspoon cayenne

^{1}/$_2$ teaspoon salt

3 tablespoons snipped fresh cilantro or thinly sliced green onions (green and white parts)

^{1}/$_2$ cup mango chutney

^{1}/$_4$ cup sliced almonds, dry-roasted (optional)

Place a strainer over a small bowl; put a paper towel or coffee filter in the strainer. Spoon the yogurt into the lined strainer. Let stand at room temperature for 10 to 20 minutes to drain.

Meanwhile, put 2 teaspoons curry powder in a medium bowl. Add the lamb, stirring to coat. Set aside for about 5 minutes.

Heat a large, deep skillet over medium-high heat. Remove from the heat and lightly spray with vegetable oil spray (being careful not to spray near a gas flame). Cook the lamb for 3 minutes, or until browned but still pink in the center, stirring constantly. Transfer to a bowl. Set aside.

WITH ALMONDS

PER SERVING		PER SERVING	
Calories 509	Cholesterol 66 mg	Calories 543	Cholesterol 66 mg
Total Fat 7.0 g	Sodium 417 mg	Total Fat 10.0 g	Sodium 417 mg
Saturated 2.0 g	Carbohydrates 78 g	Saturated 2.5 g	Carbohydrates 79 g
Polyunsaturated 1.0 g	Fiber 9 g	Polyunsaturated 1.5 g	Fiber 10 g
Monounsaturated 2.5 g	Sugar 26 g	Monounsaturated 4.5 g	Sugar 27 g
	Protein 33 g		Protein 34 g

Add the bell pepper and onion strips to the skillet; cook for 1 minute, stirring constantly.

Stir in the broth; bring to a boil over medium-high heat. Cook for 1 minute, or until the peppers are tender.

Stir in the couscous, 1 teaspoon curry powder, salt, and the reserved lamb. Remove from the heat and let stand, covered, for 5 minutes, or until the liquid is absorbed.

To serve, transfer to plates. Top with the drained yogurt. Sprinkle with the cilantro. Serve with the chutney and almonds.

vegetarian

Wild Mushroom and Onion Pizza

❖

Naples-Style Pizza

❖

Angel Hair Pasta with Swiss
Chard and Gorgonzola

❖

Garden-Fresh Vegetable Linguini

❖

Ratatouille Pasta

❖

Macaroni Primavera
with Ricotta Cheese

❖

Penne with Vegetables
and Sun-Dried Tomatoes

❖

Tricolored Vegetable and Bean
Lasagna

❖

Vegetable Lasagna

❖

Vegetable Stroganoff

❖

Milanese Tortellini en Brodo

❖

Asparagus, Tomato,
and Bow-Tie Pasta Salad

❖

Butternut Squash Risotto
with Pistachios

❖

Creamy Long-Grain
and Wild Rice Supper

❖

Black Bean and Zucchini Cobbler

❖

Black Bean Tortilla Casserole

❖

Roasted Vegetable
and Black Bean Salad
with Cilantro Dressing

❖

Vegetable Chili Hot Pot

❖

Bean and Cheese Enchiladas

❖

White Bean and Rotini Salad
with Blue Cheese

❖

Eggplant and Tomato Stew

❖

Red Beans and Rice Gumbo-Style

❖

Cassoulet with Zesty
Tomato Sauce

❖

Overstuffed Pitas

❖

Italian Vegetable Soup

❖

Tagine of Red Lentils,
Brown Rice, and Tomatoes

❖

Lentils Bourguignon

❖

Fennel Braised with Red Lentils

❖

Potato-Crusted
Vegetable Quiche

❖

(continued on following page)

Broccoli-and-Cheese Bread
Pudding

❖

Spinach and Feta Pie

❖

Frittata Primavera

❖

Cheddar Frittata with Black
Beans and Cilantro

❖

Walnut-Crusted Goat Cheese
and Fruit Salad

❖

Grilled Vegetable Sandwiches
with Goat Cheese

❖

Broiled Mozzarella Veggie
Sandwiches

❖

Mega Veggie Wraps

❖

Mushroom and Barley Chowder

❖

Italian Barley and Artichoke
Salad with Olives

❖

Vegetable and Barley Stew

❖

Home-Style Broccoli and Potato
Soup

❖

Curried Vegetable Chowder

❖

Summery Fruit Salad
with Quinoa

❖

Quinoa and Toasted Peanut Salad

❖

Asian Noodle Soup with
Mini Portobellos

❖

Stir-Fried Tofu with Bok Choy
and Soba Noodles

❖

Lettuce Cups with Soft Tofu
and Vegetables

❖

Couscous with Vegetables
and Ricotta Cheese

❖

Golden Vegetable Ragout with
Currant-Studded Couscous

❖

Couscous and Vegetable Salad
with Feta

❖

Carrot and Pear Soup with
Basil Chiffonade

❖

Slow-Cooker Edamame Stew

❖

Bulgur and Vegetable Skillet
with Fresh Herbs

❖

Vegetarian Chili

❖

Mushroom Marinara Polenta

❖

Meatless Lasagna

wild mushroom
and onion pizza

Sun-dried tomato wraps provide a crispy, crackerlike crust for this sauceless pizza.

> 4 9- to 10-inch sun-dried tomato wraps
>
> Vegetable oil spray
>
> 2 teaspoons olive oil
>
> 3 small onions, thinly sliced, separated into rings
>
> 8 ounces shiitake, oyster, or cremini (brown) mushrooms, sliced
>
> $1/4$ cup chopped mixed fresh herbs, such as parsley, basil, thyme, and chives
>
> $1/4$ cup thinly sliced oil-packed sun-dried tomatoes, well drained and patted dry
>
> $1/4$ teaspoon salt
>
> $1^1/2$ cups shredded part-skim mozzarella cheese

Preheat the oven to 450°F.

Lightly spray both sides of the wraps with vegetable oil spray. Arrange them on a large baking sheet. Bake for 4 minutes; turn over. Bake for 3 to 4 minutes, or until crisp. If the wraps puff up during baking, use a potholder or oven mitt to gently press down and flatten them.

Meanwhile, heat a large nonstick skillet over medium-high heat. Pour in the oil and swirl to coat the bottom. Cook the onions, covered, for 2 minutes, or until wilted. Cook, uncovered, for 3 to 5 minutes, or until soft and golden brown, stirring occasionally.

Stir in the mushrooms. Cook for 3 to 5 minutes, or until softened, stirring frequently. Remove from the heat. Stir in the herbs, tomatoes, and salt.

Spoon the mixture over the wraps. Sprinkle with the cheese.

Bake for 4 to 5 minutes, or until the cheese melts. Cut into slices.

PER SERVING	
Calories 312	Cholesterol 25 mg
Total Fat 11.5 g	Sodium 508 mg
Saturated 5.0 g	Carbohydrates 37 g
Polyunsaturated 0.5 g	Fiber 4 g
Monounsaturated 4.0 g	Sugar 8 g
	Protein 16 g

naples-style pizza

Serve this tasty pizza with a tossed green or Caesar salad.

    12-inch thin prepared pizza crust (10 ounces)

    1/3 cup pizza sauce

    1 tablespoon chopped fresh basil or 1 teaspoon dried, crumbled

    1/2 teaspoon dried oregano, crumbled

    2 thin slices red onion, separated into rings

    1 medium green or yellow bell pepper, thinly sliced into rings

    4 Italian plum tomatoes, seeded and thinly sliced into rings

    10-ounce package frozen chopped spinach, thawed and squeezed dry

    1 cup shredded part-skim mozzarella cheese

Preheat the oven to 450°F or lightly oil the grill rack and preheat the grill on medium-low.

Put the pizza crust on a large cookie sheet or baking sheet. Spread the sauce over the crust. Top with the remaining ingredients in the order listed.

Bake for 10 to 12 minutes, or until the crust is golden brown and the cheese is melted. If grilling, place the prepared pizza on the grill rack. Grill, covered, for 5 to 6 minutes, or until the cheese is melted and the pizza is hot.

COOK'S TIP ON SEEDING TOMATOES

To quickly seed tomatoes, cut them in half crosswise and use your finger to scoop out the seeds.

PER SERVING	Cholesterol 16 mg
Calories 309	Sodium 677 mg
Total Fat 8.5 g	Carbohydrates 41 g
Saturated 4.0 g	Fiber 5 g
Polyunsaturated 0.5 g	Sugar 6 g
Monounsaturated 1.5 g	Protein 18 g

angel hair pasta with swiss chard and gorgonzola

If you have been attracted to the jewel-tone colors of the different Swiss chard varieties and wondered how to use the vegetable, this great recipe is your answer.

> 2 quarts water
>
> 12 cups Swiss chard leaves, cut into 1-inch strips (about 1 1/2 pounds or 3 bunches), or 12 cups fresh baby spinach
>
> 6 ounces dried angel hair pasta
>
> 2 teaspoons salt-free all-purpose seasoning blend
>
> 4 ounces fat-free or low-fat ricotta cheese
>
> 2 ounces Gorgonzola cheese, crumbled
>
> 1/2 cup walnut halves
>
> 2 tablespoons imitation bacon bits
>
> 1/2 teaspoon pepper
>
> 1/4 teaspoon salt
>
> 1/4 cup fat-free milk or fat-free half-and-half (optional)

In a large pot, bring the water to a boil over high heat. Stir in the Swiss chard and pasta. Cook over medium-high heat for 3 to 4 minutes, or until tender, stirring occasionally. If using spinach, add it during the last 2 minutes of the pasta cooking time. Pour the mixture into a colander, reserving 1/4 cup cooking liquid if desired instead of milk or half-and-half; drain well.

Meanwhile, in a large bowl, stir together all the remaining ingredients except the reserved cooking liquid or milk.

Add the pasta mixture, stirring until the cheese is melted and the ingredients are evenly distributed. If the mixture seems too dry, gradually stir in the cooking liquid or milk until the desired moistness.

PER SERVING	Cholesterol 15 mg
Calories 342	Sodium 666 mg
Total Fat 13.5 g	Carbohydrates 40 g
Saturated 4.0 g	Fiber 4 g
Polyunsaturated 6.5 g	Sugar 4 g
Monounsaturated 1.5 g	Protein 17 g

WITH MILK

PER SERVING	Cholesterol 15 mg
Calories 347	Sodium 674 mg
Total Fat 13.5 g	Carbohydrates 41 g
Saturated 4.0 g	Fiber 4 g
Polyunsaturated 6.5 g	Sugar 5 g
Monounsaturated 1.5 g	Protein 18 g

garden-fresh
vegetable linguini

Feta cheese and a splash of fresh lemon juice transform pasta and vegetables into a stellar dish.

8 cups water

6 ounces dried linguini, broken into thirds

4 ounces sugar snap peas, trimmed

4 ounces asparagus spears, trimmed, broken into 2-inch pieces

6 ounces grape tomatoes or cherry tomatoes, halved

1/3 cup snipped fresh parsley

1/4 cup finely chopped green onions (green and white parts)

1/2 teaspoon salt

6 ounces nonfat or low-fat feta cheese, drained and crumbled

1 tablespoon fresh lemon juice

1/4 to 1/2 teaspoon pepper, or to taste

In a large saucepan, bring the water to a boil over high heat. Add the pasta, stir, and return to a boil. Boil for 6 minutes.

Stir in the peas and asparagus. Cook for 3 minutes, or until the peas are tender-crisp.

Meanwhile, in a large bowl, stir together the tomatoes, parsley, green onions, and salt.

Drain the pasta mixture in a colander, shaking off excess water. Gently stir into the tomato mixture.

Gently stir the feta, lemon juice, and pepper into the mixture.

PER SERVING	
Calories 241	Cholesterol 0 mg
Total Fat 1.0 g	Sodium 635 mg
Saturated 0 g	Carbohydrates 41 g
Polyunsaturated 0.5 g	Fiber 3 g
Monounsaturated 0 g	Sugar 7 g
	Protein 16 g

ratatouille pasta

SERVES 4; ABOUT 1¹/₄ CUPS PASTA PLUS 1 CUP SAUCE PER SERVING

Basically Italian, this dish gets a spicy kick from salsa. The sauce also may be spooned over toasted French bread, bruschetta style. Try small pieces for an appetizer or large pieces for open-face sandwiches.

10 ounces dried whole-wheat spaghetti
1 tablespoon salt-free all-purpose seasoning blend
1 tablespoon olive oil
1 medium onion, chopped
1 medium eggplant, peeled and diced into ¹/₂-inch pieces (about 3 cups)
4 medium garlic cloves, minced
14.5-ounce can no-salt-added stewed tomatoes, undrained
¹/₂ cup salsa (medium hot preferred)
¹/₂ cup water or low-sodium vegetable broth
2 tablespoons capers, rinsed and drained
¹/₄ cup thinly sliced or chopped fresh basil, heavy stems removed

In a stockpot, prepare the pasta using the package directions, omitting the salt and oil and adding the seasoning blend. Drain in a colander. Set aside.

Pour the oil into the pot and swirl to coat the bottom. Reduce the heat to medium. Cook the onion for 3 minutes, stirring occasionally.

Add the eggplant and garlic. Cook for 5 minutes, stirring occasionally.

Stir in the undrained tomatoes, salsa, water, and capers. Reduce the heat and simmer, covered, for 25 minutes, or until the vegetables are tender.

To serve, run the pasta, still in the colander, under hot water for 20 to 25 seconds to reheat. Drain well, shaking off excess water. Transfer the pasta to plates. Spoon the sauce over the pasta. Sprinkle with the basil.

COOK'S TIP ON CAPERS

Capers are packed in brine. To remove excess salt and the briny flavor, rinse them in a strainer.

PER SERVING	
Calories 366	Cholesterol 0 mg
Total Fat 4.5 g	Sodium 310 mg
Saturated 0.5 g	Carbohydrates 73 g
Polyunsaturated 1.0 g	Fiber 15 g
Monounsaturated 2.5 g	Sugar 16 g
	Protein 13 g

macaroni primavera
with ricotta cheese

The question is whether to cook the vegetables for the sauce in this dish. The answer is that it doesn't matter—the sauce is excellent whether the vegetables are cooked or raw.

1 tablespoon olive oil

1 cup coarsely chopped button mushrooms

2 medium garlic cloves, minced

1 1/2 cups low-sodium vegetable broth

1/2 to 1 tablespoon balsamic vinegar, or to taste

14.5-ounce can quartered artichoke hearts, rinsed and drained

1 cup coarsely chopped tomatoes

1 medium zucchini, shredded

1 medium yellow squash, shredded

1 cup chopped cauliflower

1/4 teaspoon pepper

4 ounces dried whole-wheat elbow macaroni

4 ounces nonfat or low-fat ricotta cheese

2 ounces shredded or grated Parmesan cheese

1/4 cup loosely packed fresh basil, tough stems removed, leaves thinly sliced

1/4 cup loosely packed fresh oregano, coarsely chopped

For the cooked version, heat a large, deep nonstick skillet over medium-high heat. Add the oil and swirl to coat the bottom. Cook the mushrooms and garlic for 3 to 4 minutes, or until the mushrooms are tender.

Pour in the broth and vinegar. Stir in the artichokes, tomatoes, zucchini, yellow squash, cauliflower, and pepper. Bring to a simmer.

Stir in the pasta. Reduce the heat and simmer, covered, for 10 minutes, or until the pasta is tender. Reduce the heat to low and cook, uncovered, for 1 to 2 minutes to cool the mixture slightly, stirring constantly.

WITH COOKED VEGETABLES

PER SERVING	
Calories 285	Cholesterol 13 mg
Total Fat 8.0 g	Sodium 493 mg
Saturated 3.0 g	Carbohydrates 38 g
Polyunsaturated 0.5 g	Fiber 6 g
Monounsaturated 4.0 g	Sugar 8 g
	Protein 18 g

WITH RAW VEGETABLES

PER SERVING	
Calories 278	Cholesterol 13 mg
Total Fat 8.0 g	Sodium 475 mg
Saturated 3.0 g	Carbohydrates 37 g
Polyunsaturated 0.5 g	Fiber 6 g
Monounsaturated 4.0 g	Sugar 8 g
	Protein 18 g

Stir in the ricotta cheese, Parmesan, basil, and oregano. Cook for 1 to 2 minutes, or until the cheeses are melted, stirring occasionally.

macaroni with balsamic-flavored vegetables and ricotta cheese

For the raw-vegetable version, omit the broth. In a large bowl, stir together all the ingredients except the macaroni. Cover and refrigerate.

Cook the macaroni using the package directions, omitting the salt and oil. Drain well. Add to the vegetable mixture, stirring until the cheeses are melted.

penne with vegetables and sun-dried tomatoes

SERVES 4; 2 CUPS PER SERVING

This easy dish is as colorful as it is flavorful.

  4 cups water
16 ounces dried whole-wheat penne pasta
  2 14.5-ounce cans low-sodium vegetable broth
  $^1/_4$ teaspoon crushed red pepper flakes
12 medium asparagus spears, trimmed and cut into 1-inch pieces
  8 ounces broccoli rabe, cut into 1-inch pieces, or 12 additional medium asparagus spears, trimmed and cut into 1-inch pieces
  2 tablespoons dry-packed sun-dried tomato bits
  1 tablespoon olive oil (extra virgin preferred)
  $^1/_4$ teaspoon salt
  $^1/_4$ cup water (optional)
  1$^1/_4$ cups shredded part-skim mozzarella or Gouda cheese (smoked preferred)
     Black pepper (optional)

In a large, deep skillet, bring the water to a boil over high heat. Stir in the pasta. Reduce the heat and simmer for 5 minutes. Pour the pasta into a colander and drain well.

Put the broth and red pepper flakes in the skillet. Bring to a boil over high heat. Return the pasta to the skillet. Reduce the heat and simmer for 3 minutes.

Stir in the asparagus, broccoli rabe, sun-dried tomatoes, oil, and salt. Simmer for 5 minutes, or until the pasta and vegetables are tender and most of the sauce is absorbed. Add $^1/_4$ cup water if the broth is absorbed before the pasta is tender.

To serve, put the pasta mixture on plates. Sprinkle with the cheese and pepper.

COOK'S TIP ON BROCCOLI RABE

This somewhat bitter and pungent relative of cabbage and turnips is also known as *broccoli raab, broccoli rape, rapini,* and even *gai lon* and *Chinese flowering cabbage.* Slice the stalks crosswise, leaving the tiny broccoli-like florets and the dark green leaves intact.

PER SERVING	
Calories 559	Cholesterol 20 mg
Total Fat 10.5 g	Sodium 371 mg
Saturated 4.5 g	Carbohydrates 93 g
Polyunsaturated 1.0 g	Fiber 11 g
Monounsaturated 4.5 g	Sugar 7 g
	Protein 30 g

tricolored vegetable and bean lasagna

SERVES 8; SCANT 2 CUPS PER SERVING

The colors of the Italian flag—red, white, and green—are represented in this untraditional lasagna. Much of its rich creaminess comes from the beans. This casserole reheats beautifully and tastes even better the second day.

Vegetable oil spray

2 cups fat-free half-and-half

1 cup reduced-fat Alfredo sauce

9 oven-ready dried lasagna noodles

2 10-ounce packages frozen chopped spinach, thawed and squeezed dry

1 cup shredded nonfat or part-skim mozzarella cheese

3 cups frozen cauliflower florets, thawed (about 15 ounces)

15-ounce can low-sodium Great Northern beans, rinsed and drained

15-ounce container fat-free or light ricotta cheese

1 tablespoon salt-free Italian seasoning

7- to 8-ounce jar roasted red bell peppers, rinsed, drained, and sliced

Preheat the oven to 375°F. Lightly spray a 13 × 9 × 2-inch baking pan with vegetable oil spray.

In a small bowl, stir together the half-and-half and Alfredo sauce.

To assemble, spread about half the sauce in the pan. Make a layer of noodles by placing 2 noodles lengthwise side by side, then placing the third noodle crosswise at the other end of the pan. Spread the spinach evenly over the noodles, cover with 1 cup sauce, and sprinkle with 1/4 cup mozzarella. Cover with another layer of 3 noodles. Arrange the cauliflower and beans over the noodles. Spoon the ricotta cheese evenly on top, and sprinkle with the Italian seasoning and another 1/4 cup mozzarella. Cover with the remaining noodles and the remaining sauce. Arrange the roasted bell peppers over the surface. Sprinkle with the remaining 1/2 cup mozzarella. Cover the pan tightly with aluminum foil.

Bake for 45 minutes, or until the noodles are tender and the lasagna is warmed through.

PER SERVING	
Calories 318	Cholesterol 22 mg
Total Fat 5.0 g	Sodium 778 mg
Saturated 3.0 g	Carbohydrates 43 g
Polyunsaturated 0.5 g	Fiber 6 g
Monounsaturated 0 g	Sugar 10 g
	Protein 26 g

vegetable lasagna

SERVES 6; 3 × 4¹/₂-INCH PIECE PER SERVING

Fresh basil complements artichoke hearts and roasted red bell peppers in this satisfying dish.

Vegetable oil spray (olive oil spray preferred)

26-ounce jar fat-free, low-sodium spaghetti sauce, such as tomato-basil

14-ounce can artichoke hearts, drained and coarsely chopped

7- to 8-ounce jar roasted red bell peppers, rinsed, drained, and coarsely chopped

15-ounce container fat-free or low-fat ricotta cheese

2 tablespoons chopped fresh basil or 2 teaspoons dried, crumbled

¹/₄ teaspoon crushed red pepper flakes (optional)

4 oven-ready dried lasagna noodles

1 cup shredded part-skim mozzarella cheese

¹/₄ cup chopped or very thinly sliced fresh basil or snipped fresh Italian, or flat-leaf, parsley (optional)

Preheat the oven to 400°F. Lightly spray a 9-inch square baking pan with vegetable oil spray.

In a large bowl, stir together the spaghetti sauce, artichoke hearts, and roasted bell peppers.

In a medium bowl, stir together the ricotta cheese, 2 tablespoons basil, and red pepper flakes.

To assemble, spread a scant cup of the spaghetti sauce mixture in the pan. Make a layer of 2 noodles over the sauce. Spread half the ricotta mixture over the noodles. Top with 1 cup sauce mixture and half the mozzarella. Repeat the layers with the remaining 2 noodles, remaining ricotta mixture, sauce mixture, and mozzarella.

Lightly spray a sheet of aluminum foil with vegetable oil spray. Cover the pan with the foil, sprayed side down, to prevent the cheese from sticking.

Bake for 25 minutes. Remove the foil. Bake for 20 to 25 minutes, or until hot and bubbly. Let stand for 5 minutes before serving. Garnish with ¹/₄ cup basil.

PER SERVING	
Calories 213	Cholesterol 17 mg
Total Fat 3.0 g	Sodium 633 mg
Saturated 2.0 g	Carbohydrates 26 g
Polyunsaturated 0 g	Fiber 2 g
Monounsaturated 1.0 g	Sugar 10 g
	Protein 18 g

vegetable stroganoff

SERVES 4; ABOUT 1 CUP SAUCE AND 1¹/4 CUPS NOODLES PER SERVING

Cremini mushrooms, sometimes labeled as "baby portobellos" or "baby bellas," give this stroganoff a meaty texture and pleasantly earthy flavor.

8 ounces dried no-yolk egg noodles

1 tablespoon light stick margarine

12 ounces asparagus spears, trimmed and cut into 1-inch pieces

8 ounces cremini (brown) mushrooms, sliced

¹/2 cup finely chopped onion or shallots

10.75-ounce can reduced-fat, reduced-sodium condensed cream of mushroom soup

¹/2 cup fat-free milk

2 tablespoons dry sherry or water

1 teaspoon dried thyme, crumbled

¹/2 teaspoon salt

¹/4 teaspoon pepper

Pepper to taste (optional)

Prepare the noodles using the package directions, omitting the salt and oil. Drain in a colander. Set aside.

Meanwhile, in a large, deep skillet, melt the margarine over medium heat. Stir in the asparagus, mushrooms, and onion. Cook for 6 minutes, or until the vegetables are tender, stirring occasionally.

Stir in the soup, milk, sherry, thyme, salt, and ¹/4 teaspoon pepper. Reducing the heat if needed, simmer for 5 minutes, stirring occasionally.

Transfer the noodles to plates. Top with the mushroom mixture. Serve with the additional pepper.

PER SERVING	
Calories 328	Cholesterol 7 mg
Total Fat 3.5 g	Sodium 652 mg
Saturated 1.0 g	Carbohydrates 58 g
Polyunsaturated 0.5 g	Fiber 5 g
Monounsaturated 0.5 g	Sugar 9 g
	Protein 12 g

milanese tortellini
en brodo

"En brodo" is just a more exotic way to say "in broth." Serve this meatless Italian stew with crusty whole-grain rolls and a Caesar salad.

2 teaspoons olive oil

2 medium garlic cloves, minced

2 14.5-ounce cans low-sodium vegetable broth

9-ounce package refrigerated mushroom and cheese tortellini

14.5-ounce can no-salt-added diced tomatoes, undrained

1 teaspoon dried basil, crumbled

¹/₄ teaspoon crushed red pepper flakes or red hot-pepper sauce

3 cups packed torn escarole or kale

¹/₄ cup shredded or grated Parmesan or asiago cheese

Heat a large saucepan over medium heat. Pour in the olive oil and swirl to coat the bottom. Cook the garlic for 1 minute, stirring occasionally.

Stir in the broth. Bring to a boil.

Stir in the tortellini. Reduce the heat and simmer for 6 minutes.

Stir in the undrained tomatoes, basil, and red pepper flakes. Return to a simmer and cook for 3 minutes, or until the tortellini is tender.

Stir in the escarole. Simmer for 1 minute, or until the escarole is wilted.

To serve, ladle into soup bowls. Sprinkle with the cheese.

COOK'S TIP ON ESCAROLE

Escarole, part of the endive family, is slightly bitter. Its sturdy texture holds up well in soups and stews. Discard any tough outer leaves.

PER SERVING	
Calories 270	Cholesterol 27 mg
Total Fat 8.0 g	Sodium 468 mg
Saturated 4.0 g	Carbohydrates 37 g
Polyunsaturated 0.5 g	Fiber 5 g
Monounsaturated 2.0 g	Sugar 4 g
	Protein 13 g

asparagus, tomato, and bow-tie pasta salad

Hot weather and cool salads go hand in hand. This brilliantly colored and deeply flavored version is perfect for patio entertaining.

    10 cups water
     8 ounces dried bow-tie pasta
     6 ounces asparagus spears, trimmed, cut into 2-inch pieces
     4 ounces grape tomatoes, halved, or cherry tomatoes, quartered
    24 pitted black olives
     2 tablespoons balsamic vinegar (white balsamic preferred)
     1 tablespoon olive oil (extra virgin preferred)
     2 teaspoons Dijon mustard
     1 medium garlic clove, minced
     1 teaspoon dried tarragon, crumbled
    ¹/4 teaspoon salt
    ¹/4 teaspoon pepper
     4 ounces feta cheese, rinsed and crumbled

In a stockpot or large saucepan, bring the water to a boil over high heat. Add the pasta and boil for 8 minutes. Stir in the asparagus; cook for 2 minutes, or until the asparagus is just tender-crisp. Drain the mixture in a colander. Run cold water over the mixture to stop the cooking process and to cool it quickly. Drain well.

In a large bowl, combine the remaining ingredients except the feta cheese. Add the pasta and asparagus. Toss gently to coat. Add the feta cheese. Toss gently.

COOK'S TIP

You can cook the pasta and the asparagus up to 24 hours in advance. For peak flavor, however, don't assemble the salad until serving time. White balsamic vinegar provides a lighter taste and allows the true colors of the vegetables and pasta to shine through. Dark balsamic vinegar is equally flavorful, but it gives a slightly darker color to the pasta.

PER SERVING	
Calories 365	Cholesterol 25 mg
Total Fat 12.5 g	Sodium 698 mg
Saturated 5.0 g	Carbohydrates 50 g
Polyunsaturated 1.0 g	Fiber 3 g
Monounsaturated 5.5 g	Sugar 7 g
	Protein 13 g

butternut squash risotto
with pistachios

SERVES 4; ABOUT 1½ CUPS PER SERVING

Pistachios are an unexpected garnish that adds texture to the dish.

1 tablespoon olive oil

12 to 14 ounces butternut squash, peeled, cut into ½-inch cubes (see tip, opposite)

⅓ cup chopped shallots

3 medium garlic cloves, minced

3 cups low-sodium vegetable broth or fat-free, low-sodium chicken broth

1 cup uncooked arborio rice

½ cup dry white wine (regular or nonalcoholic), low-sodium vegetable broth, or fat-free, low-sodium chicken broth

½ cup low-sodium vegetable broth or fat-free, low-sodium chicken broth (optional)

½ cup grated Parmesan cheese (Parmigiano-Reggiano preferred)

½ cup unsalted dry-roasted shelled pistachios

Heat a large, deep skillet over medium heat. Pour the oil into the skillet and swirl to coat the bottom. Cook the squash, shallots, and garlic for 5 minutes, stirring occasionally.

Meanwhile, in a 4-cup glass measuring cup or microwave-safe bowl, microwave 3 cups broth at high power for 4 to 5 minutes, or until simmering. Or heat the broth in a medium saucepan over medium heat for 3 to 4 minutes.

Add the rice to the skillet. Cook for 1 minute, stirring constantly.

Pour in the wine. Cook for 2 minutes, or until the wine is absorbed, stirring constantly.

Stir in 1 cup of the simmering broth. Simmer until most of the liquid is absorbed, stirring occasionally. Repeat twice, using 2 more cups broth. Keep the rice mixture at a gentle simmer, stirring occasionally. Cook until the squash and rice are tender and the texture is creamy, about 25 minutes total, adding the remaining ½ cup broth if needed.

Remove from the heat. Stir in the cheese and pistachios.

WITH OPTIONAL BROTH

PER SERVING		PER SERVING	
Calories 485	Cholesterol 8 mg	Calories 487	Cholesterol 8 mg
Total Fat 14.0 g	Sodium 232 mg	Total Fat 14.0 g	Sodium 238 mg
Saturated 3.5 g	Carbohydrates 71 g	Saturated 3.5 g	Carbohydrates 71 g
Polyunsaturated 2.5 g	Fiber 8 g	Polyunsaturated 2.5 g	Fiber 8 g
Monounsaturated 7.0 g	Sugar 6 g	Monounsaturated 7.0 g	Sugar 6 g
	Protein 15 g		Protein 15 g

creamy long-grain and wild rice supper

SERVES 4; ABOUT 1¹/₂ CUPS PER SERVING

As easy to prepare as it is unusual, this dish gets its special flavor from dried cranberries. Serve it with a crisp green salad with a noncreamy dressing, followed by low-fat fruit-studded bran muffins for dessert.

2¹/₃ cups water

6-ounce package long-grain and wild rice mix

12 to 14 ounces butternut squash, cut into ¹/₂-inch cubes

2 cups frozen cut green beans

¹/₂ cup dried cranberries or dried cherries

3 ounces fat-free or light cream cheese, cut into ¹/₂-inch cubes

¹/₃ cup coarsely chopped pecans, dry-roasted

In a large saucepan, stir together the water, rice, and contents of the seasoning packet. Bring to a boil over high heat.

Stir in the squash, green beans, and cranberries. Return to a boil. Reduce the heat and simmer, covered, for 25 minutes, or until the liquid is absorbed and the vegetables and rice are tender.

Add the cream cheese, stirring until melted.

To serve, transfer the mixture to bowls. Sprinkle with the pecans.

COOK'S TIP ON BUTTERNUT SQUASH

Use a vegetable peeler to peel the hard outer skin from butternut squash. Use a large chef's knife to cut the squash crosswise into ¹/₂-inch slices. Discard the seeds and cut the slices into ¹/₂-inch cubes.

PER SERVING	
Calories 363	Cholesterol 4 mg
Total Fat 8.0 g	Sodium 701 mg
Saturated 1.0 g	Carbohydrates 67 g
Polyunsaturated 2.5 g	Fiber 10 g
Monounsaturated 4.0 g	Sugar 16 g
	Protein 10 g

black bean and
zucchini cobbler

A layered zucchini crust is the eye-catching top of this sensational Southwestern casserole.

Vegetable oil spray

6-inch corn tortilla

15-ounce can no-salt-added black beans, rinsed if desired and drained

2 medium ears of corn, kernels cut off, or 1^1/$_2$ cups frozen whole-kernel corn

2 small tomatoes, minced

1 medium red bell pepper, minced

3 medium green onions (green and white parts), diced

1 to 2 tablespoons diced canned jalapeño pepper, undrained

1 teaspoon ground cumin

1 teaspoon paprika

^{1}/$_4$ teaspoon salt

2 medium zucchini, thinly sliced on the diagonal (about ^{1}/$_8$ inch thick)

1 tablespoon fresh lime juice

8 ounces fat-free or low-fat plain yogurt

Preheat the oven to 350°F.

Lightly spray a 2-quart casserole dish with vegetable oil spray. Put the tortilla in the dish.

In a medium bowl, stir together the beans, corn kernels, tomatoes, bell pepper, green onions, jalapeño, cumin, paprika, and salt. Spread the mixture over the tortilla; gently press down. (This helps the tortilla absorb some of the liquid.)

Arrange the zucchini so the pieces slightly overlap to form attractive layered rows over the bean mixture. Sprinkle with the lime juice. Spoon the yogurt over the zucchini. Using the back of a spoon, carefully spread it evenly over the top.

Bake in the center of the oven for 35 minutes. Turn on the broiler. Leaving the rack in the center, broil for 3 to 4 minutes, or until the yogurt is browned.

PER SERVING	
Calories 207	Cholesterol 1 mg
Total Fat 1.5 g	Sodium 265 mg
Saturated 0 g	Carbohydrates 39 g
Polyunsaturated 0.5 g	Fiber 8 g
Monounsaturated 0.5 g	Sugar 15 g
	Protein 13 g

black bean tortilla
casserole

SERVES 4; 4 1/2-INCH SQUARE PER SERVING

If you're a some-like-it-hot kind of person, try the spiciest variety of salsa or picante sauce for this satisfying dish, use more crushed red pepper flakes, or sprinkle with canned jalapeño slices.

1 cup frozen chopped bell pepper, thawed and drained

1 cup frozen chopped onion, thawed and drained

15- to 16-ounce can no-salt-added black beans, rinsed if desired and drained

14.5-ounce can no-salt-added diced tomatoes, undrained

1/2 cup salsa or picante sauce

Vegetable oil spray

8 6-inch corn tortillas

1 cup shredded light Mexican cheese blend or Monterey Jack cheese

Heaping 1/8 teaspoon crushed red pepper flakes

1/4 cup snipped fresh cilantro

Preheat the oven to 400°F.

In a large bowl, stir together the bell pepper, onion, beans, undrained tomatoes, and salsa.

Lightly spray a 9-inch square baking pan with vegetable oil spray. Spoon 1 cup bell pepper mixture into the pan. Arrange 4 tortillas in the pan, overlapping as necessary. Spoon half the remaining sauce over the tortillas. Top with 1/2 cup cheese. Repeat.

Lightly spray a sheet of aluminum foil with vegetable oil spray. Cover the pan with the foil, sprayed side down, to prevent the cheese from sticking.

Bake for 30 minutes. Remove the foil. Bake for 5 minutes, or until hot and bubbly. Let stand for 5 minutes. Sprinkle with red pepper flakes and cilantro. Cut into 4 squares.

PER SERVING	
Calories 272	Cholesterol 10 mg
Total Fat 5.5 g	Sodium 431 mg
Saturated 3.0 g	Carbohydrates 40 g
Polyunsaturated 1.5 g	Fiber 8 g
Monounsaturated 1.0 g	Sugar 10 g
	Protein 17 g

roasted vegetable and black bean salad with cilantro dressing

SERVES 4; 1¹/₄ CUPS PER SERVING

Cleanup is a breeze when even the salad dressing is mixed in the cooking pan. Serve the salad warm, or let it marinate in the refrigerator and serve it chilled.

4 portobello mushrooms (about 12 ounces), stems discarded, caps cut into
¹/₂-inch slices

1 large red bell pepper, thinly sliced

1 large onion, thinly sliced

2 large ears of corn or 2 cups frozen or no-salt-added canned whole-kernel corn, thawed if frozen or drained if canned

2 teaspoons salt-free all-purpose seasoning blend

Olive oil spray

15-ounce can no-salt-added black beans, rinsed if desired and drained

¹/₃ cup red wine vinegar

2 tablespoons olive oil

2 tablespoons snipped fresh cilantro

2 medium garlic cloves, minced

1 teaspoon brown sugar

¹/₂ teaspoon salt

Preheat the oven to 400°F.

Put the mushrooms, bell pepper, and onion in a 13 × 9 × 2-inch baking pan.

Cut the kernels off the corn cob if using fresh. Add the corn to the pan. Sprinkle with the seasoning blend. Lightly spray the tops of the vegetables with olive oil spray. Stir well.

Roast for 15 to 20 minutes, or until tender, stirring once. Let the mixture cool on a cooling rack for 5 minutes.

Stir in the remaining ingredients.

PER SERVING	Cholesterol 0 mg
Calories 264	Sodium 310 mg
Total Fat 8.0 g	Carbohydrates 42 g
Saturated 1.0 g	Fiber 9 g
Polyunsaturated 1.0 g	Sugar 14 g
Monounsaturated 5.0 g	Protein 10 g

vegetable chili hot pot

Dappled with pinto beans and simmered with intense spices, this exuberant combination of vegetables is truly a palate-pleaser.

2 teaspoons olive oil

1 small onion, diced

1 medium fresh jalapeño pepper, seeded and ribs discarded, minced

2 medium garlic cloves, minced

2 tablespoons chili powder, or to taste

1 teaspoon ground cumin

1 teaspoon dried oregano, crumbled

$^1/_4$ teaspoon ground nutmeg

$^1/_4$ teaspoon cayenne (optional)

8 ounces napa cabbage (about $^1/_2$ small head), thinly sliced

3 large tomatoes, coarsely diced

2 large zucchini, grated (about 2 cups)

2 portobello mushrooms, gills and stems discarded, caps coarsely diced

2 medium ears of corn, kernels cut off, or $1^1/_2$ cups frozen whole-kernel corn

3 small red potatoes (10 to 12 ounces), diced

15-ounce can no-salt-added pinto beans, rinsed if desired and drained

2 cups hot water

Juice from 1 medium orange

1 tablespoon balsamic vinegar

$^1/_2$ teaspoon salt

Heat a stockpot or Dutch oven over medium heat. Pour in the oil and swirl to coat the bottom. Cook the onion for 6 to 7 minutes, or until it begins to brown, stirring occasionally.

Stir in the jalapeño and garlic. Cook for 1 minute, stirring constantly. Add the chili powder, cumin, oregano, nutmeg, and cayenne. Cook for 1 minute, stirring constantly.

Stir in the remaining ingredients. Cook, covered, for 10 minutes. Stir well. Cook, covered, for 10 minutes. Uncover and cook for 15 minutes, or until the potatoes are tender, stirring occasionally.

PER SERVING	
Calories 317	Cholesterol 0 mg
Total Fat 4.5 g	Sodium 369 mg
Saturated 0.5 g	Carbohydrates 62 g
Polyunsaturated 1.0 g	Fiber 14 g
Monounsaturated 2.0 g	Sugar 21 g
	Protein 15 g

bean and cheese
enchiladas

Serve these scrumptious enchiladas with slices of ripe papaya sprinkled with fresh lime juice.

Vegetable oil spray

14.5-ounce can no-salt-added diced tomatoes, undrained

15-ounce can no-salt-added pinto beans, rinsed if desired and drained

$1/4$ cup plus 2 tablespoons shredded Mexican cheese blend or reduced-fat Monterey Jack cheese

$1/4$ cup snipped fresh cilantro

8 6-inch corn tortillas

10-ounce can enchilada sauce

$1/2$ cup shredded Mexican cheese blend or reduced-fat Monterey Jack cheese

$1/4$ cup snipped fresh cilantro

Preheat the oven to 375°F. Lightly spray a $13 \times 9 \times 2$-inch glass baking dish with vegetable oil spray.

Drain the tomatoes, reserving the liquid in a medium bowl.

In another medium bowl, stir together the drained tomatoes, beans, $1/4$ cup plus 2 tablespoons cheese, and $1/4$ cup cilantro. Spoon $1/3$ cup bean mixture down the center of each tortilla. Roll up jelly-roll style and place with the seam side down in the baking dish.

Add the enchilada sauce to the reserved tomato liquid. Spoon over the tortillas.

Bake, covered, for 15 minutes. Sprinkle with the remaining $1/2$ cup cheese. Bake, uncovered, for 10 minutes, or until the cheese is melted.

To serve, sprinkle with the remaining $1/4$ cup cilantro.

PER SERVING	
Calories 300	Cholesterol 26 mg
Total Fat 9.0 g	Sodium 434 mg
Saturated 4.5 g	Carbohydrates 41 g
Polyunsaturated 1.0 g	Fiber 8 g
Monounsaturated 2.5 g	Sugar 7 g
	Protein 15 g

white bean and rotini
salad with blue cheese

Blue cheese provides a refreshing change from the traditional in this colorful pasta salad.

> 3/4 cup dried rotini
>
> 16-ounce can no-salt-added navy beans
>
> 2 tablespoons fresh lemon juice
>
> 2 tablespoons olive oil (extra virgin preferred)
>
> 1/2 medium garlic clove, minced
>
> 3/4 teaspoon salt
>
> 1/4 teaspoon pepper
>
> 1 medium zucchini, cut into matchstick-size strips
>
> 1 medium red bell pepper, cut into matchstick-size strips
>
> 1 tablespoon chopped fresh basil or 1 teaspoon dried, crumbled
>
> 2 ounces blue or feta cheese, crumbled

Prepare the pasta using the package directions, omitting the salt and oil.

Meanwhile, drain the beans in a colander. When the pasta is cooked, add it to the colander. Run cold water over the mixture until the pasta is cool. Drain well. Shake off any excess liquid.

In a large bowl, stir together the lemon juice, olive oil, garlic, salt, and pepper. Add the zucchini, bell peppers, and basil. Toss to coat. Add the beans and pasta. Toss to coat.

To serve, spoon the salad onto plates. Sprinkle with the cheese.

PER SERVING	
Calories 329	Cholesterol 11 mg
Total Fat 11.5 g	Sodium 642 mg
Saturated 3.5 g	Carbohydrates 43 g
Polyunsaturated 1.0 g	Fiber 6 g
Monounsaturated 6.0 g	Sugar 7 g
	Protein 14 g

eggplant and tomato stew

SERVES 4; 1³/4 CUPS PER SERVING

This hearty, full-flavored stew gets its great flavor from a perfect mix of vegetables and spices.

Vegetable oil spray

1 medium onion, chopped

1 medium red, yellow, or green bell pepper, cut into 1-inch pieces

14.5-ounce can no-salt-added diced tomatoes with green peppers and onions, undrained

8 ounces eggplant, peeled and diced (about 1 small)

8 ounces whole button mushrooms, quartered

1/2 cup red wine (regular or nonalcoholic) or water

1¹/2 tablespoons sugar

1 teaspoon ground cinnamon

1/2 teaspoon ground cumin

1/4 teaspoon ground allspice

1/4 teaspoon cayenne (optional)

15-ounce can no-salt-added dark kidney beans, rinsed and drained

4 ounces dried rotini

1 tablespoon olive oil (extra virgin preferred)

1/2 teaspoon salt

Heat a Dutch oven over medium-high heat. Remove from the heat and lightly spray with vegetable oil spray (being careful not to spray near a gas flame). Cook the onion and bell pepper for 3 to 4 minutes, or until translucent, stirring occasionally.

Stir in the undrained tomatoes, eggplant, mushrooms, wine, sugar, cinnamon, cumin, allspice, and cayenne. Increase the heat to high. Bring to a boil. Reduce the heat and simmer, covered, for 30 minutes, or until the eggplant is very tender.

Stir in the beans and rotini. Simmer for 10 minutes, or until tender. Remove from the heat.

Stir in the oil and salt.

PER SERVING	
Calories 339	Cholesterol 0 mg
Total Fat 4.5 g	Sodium 346 mg
Saturated 0.5 g	Carbohydrates 60 g
Polyunsaturated 0.5 g	Fiber 10 g
Monounsaturated 2.5 g	Sugar 16 g
	Protein 14 g

red beans and rice
gumbo-style

Adding okra to red beans and rice gives new flavor to an old favorite. Instant brown rice, a boon for the rush-hour cook, provides whole-grain goodness and a nutty flavor.

1 teaspoon olive oil

1 large onion, chopped

1 medium green bell pepper, chopped

2 medium ribs of celery, chopped

3 cups frozen cut okra

14.5-ounce can no-salt-added diced tomatoes, undrained (optional)

15-ounce can no-salt-added red beans, such as kidney beans, rinsed and drained

1¹/₂ cups low-sodium vegetable broth

1 cup uncooked instant brown rice

¹/₂ tablespoon salt-free garlic-herb seasoning blend

³/₄ teaspoon ground cumin

³/₄ teaspoon dried thyme, crumbled

³/₄ to 1 teaspoon chili powder

¹/₂ teaspoon liquid smoke (optional)

¹/₄ teaspoon salt

¹/₂ tablespoon red hot-pepper sauce (optional)

Heat a large nonstick saucepan over medium-high heat. Pour the oil into the saucepan and swirl to coat the bottom. Cook the onion, bell pepper, and celery for 3 to 5 minutes, or until tender, stirring occasionally.

Stir in the remaining ingredients except the hot-pepper sauce. Bring to a simmer, stirring occasionally. Reduce the heat and simmer, covered, for 10 to 15 minutes, or until the rice is tender and almost all the liquid is absorbed.

Stir in the hot-pepper sauce.

PER SERVING	Cholesterol 0 mg
Calories 252	Sodium 201 mg
Total Fat 2.5 g	Carbohydrates 49 g
Saturated 0 g	Fiber 9 g
Polyunsaturated 0.5 g	Sugar 8 g
Monounsaturated 1.0 g	Protein 12 g

WITH TOMATOES

PER SERVING	Cholesterol 0 mg
Calories 273	Sodium 254 mg
Total Fat 2.5 g	Carbohydrates 53 g
Saturated 0 g	Fiber 11 g
Polyunsaturated 0.5 g	Sugar 11 g
Monounsaturated 1.0 g	Protein 13 g

cassoulet with zesty
tomato sauce

SERVES 6; 1¹/₂ CUPS PER SERVING

This cassoulet bakes slowly, in the traditional manner, but does away with the time-consuming step of soaking the dried beans.

7 cups low-sodium vegetable broth

2 cups dried mixed beans, such as navy beans, pinto beans, kidney beans, and lentils

1 large rutabaga, peeled and diced (about 12 ounces)

8 ounces button mushrooms, sliced

2 medium turnips, peeled and diced (about 1 pound)

1 large onion, diced

¹/₂ cup dry red wine (regular or nonalcoholic) or low-sodium vegetable broth

6-ounce can no-salt-added tomato paste

2 medium garlic cloves, minced

1 teaspoon dried basil, crumbled

1 teaspoon dried rosemary, crushed

¹/₂ to 1 teaspoon crushed red pepper flakes

¹/₂ teaspoon salt

¹/₄ teaspoon pepper

Preheat the oven to 350°F.

In a Dutch oven, combine all the ingredients. Bring to a boil over high heat, stirring occasionally.

Bake, covered, for 1¹/₂ to 2 hours, or until the beans and vegetables are tender. (No stirring should be necessary unless the mixture needs more liquid during baking. If so, stir in ¹/₂ cup water at a time, as needed.)

COOK'S TIP

Look in the dried bean section of the supermarket for packaged mixed dried beans.

PER SERVING	Cholesterol 0 mg
Calories 357	Sodium 338 mg
Total Fat 1.5 g	Carbohydrates 65 g
Saturated 0 g	Fiber 23 g
Polyunsaturated 0.5 g	Sugar 15 g
Monounsaturated 0 g	Protein 23 g

overstuffed pitas

These bountiful Greek-salad sandwiches come in handy on steamy summer days. Don't underestimate the power of that little squirt of lemon—it provides a refreshing punch.

$1/2$ cup fat-free or low-fat plain yogurt

2 tablespoons fat-free or reduced-fat mayonnaise dressing

1 medium garlic clove, minced

$1/2$ teaspoon dried oregano, crumbled

$1/4$ teaspoon salt

$1/4$ teaspoon ground cumin, or to taste

3 cups chopped romaine

15-ounce can no-salt-added chick-peas, rinsed if desired and drained

$1/2$ medium cucumber, peeled and diced

4 thin slices of red onion

4 ounces grape tomatoes, halved, or cherry tomatoes, quartered

3 ounces feta cheese with sun-dried tomatoes and basil, crumbled

4 6-inch whole-wheat or white pita breads, cut in half to make pockets

2 medium lemons, quartered

In a large bowl, whisk together the yogurt, mayonnaise, garlic, oregano, salt, and ground cumin.

Add the romaine, chick-peas, cucumber, and onion. Toss gently to coat.

Add the tomatoes and feta. Toss gently.

Microwave the pita halves on a microwave-safe plate or paper towels on 100 percent power (high) for 10 to 15 seconds, or until warm.

To serve, fill the pita pockets with the romaine mixture. Serve with the lemon wedges.

PER SERVING	
Calories 473	Cholesterol 16 mg
Total Fat 9.5 g	Sodium 741 mg
Saturated 3.5 g	Carbohydrates 75 g
Polyunsaturated 2.0 g	Fiber 16 g
Monounsaturated 2.0 g	Sugar 13 g
	Protein 24 g

italian vegetable soup

When you need to combat cold weather, try this veggie-packed stewlike soup.

Vegetable oil spray

2 medium onions, chopped

1 large green bell pepper, chopped

1 medium rib of celery, thinly sliced

4 cups water

15.5-ounce can no-salt-added dark kidney beans or navy beans,
rinsed if desired and drained (optional)

14.5-ounce can no-salt-added stewed tomatoes, undrained

8 ounces button mushrooms, sliced

1¹/₂ tablespoons dried basil, crumbled

4 ounces dried vermicelli or other very thin pasta, broken into thirds

2 ounces fresh spinach leaves

1 tablespoon sugar

1 tablespoon balsamic vinegar

¹/₂ teaspoon salt

2 teaspoons olive oil (extra virgin preferred)

1 cup shredded part-skim mozzarella cheese

Heat a Dutch oven over medium-high heat. Remove from the heat and lightly spray with vegetable oil spray (being careful not to spray near a gas flame). Cook the onions, pepper, and celery for 8 minutes, or until the onions begin to lightly brown, stirring occasionally.

Stir in the water, beans, undrained tomatoes, mushrooms, and basil. Increase the heat to high. Bring to a boil. Stir in the vermicelli. Return to a boil. Reduce the heat and simmer, covered, for 15 minutes.

Stir in the spinach, sugar, vinegar, and salt. Cook for 1 minute, or until the spinach is tender. Stir in the oil. Ladle the soup into bowls and sprinkle with the cheese.

WITH BEANS

PER SERVING		PER SERVING	
Calories 305	Cholesterol 16 mg	Calories 398	Cholesterol 16 mg
Total Fat 7.5 g	Sodium 499 mg	Total Fat 7.5 g	Sodium 503 mg
Saturated 3.5 g	Carbohydrates 47 g	Saturated 3.5 g	Carbohydrates 65 g
Polyunsaturated 0.5 g	Fiber 6 g	Polyunsaturated 0.5 g	Fiber 10 g
Monounsaturated 3.0 g	Sugar 18 g	Monounsaturated 3.0 g	Sugar 20 g
	Protein 15 g		Protein 22 g

tagine of red lentils, brown rice, and tomatoes

Borrowing its blend of spices and its name from Morocco, this tagine (stew) is cooked to thick, savory excellence.

1 teaspoon ground cumin

1/2 teaspoon ground cinnamon

1/4 teaspoon pepper

4 cups hot water

1 cup uncooked brown rice

1 cup split red lentils, sorted for stones and shriveled lentils and rinsed

2 tablespoons fresh lemon juice

1/4 teaspoon salt

3 medium carrots, minced

1 1/2 cups cherry tomatoes, halved

1 small onion, diced

1/4 cup snipped fresh parsley

4 slices nonfat or part-skim mozzarella cheese (2/3 to 3/4 ounce each)

Preheat the oven to 350°F.

Heat a Dutch oven over high heat. Add the cumin, cinnamon, and pepper; cook for 1 minute, stirring constantly. Stir in the water, rice, lentils, lemon juice, and salt. Bring to a boil.

Stir in the carrots, tomatoes, and onion.

Bake, covered, for about 45 minutes, or until the rice is tender and the lentils are soft but not mushy.

Stir in the parsley. Top with the cheese.

Bake, covered, for 5 minutes.

COOK'S TIP ON RED LENTILS

Red lentils, which cook in less time than green lentils, actually are orange-red and have a distinctive peppery flavor.

PER SERVING	
Calories 424	Cholesterol 4 mg
Total Fat 2.5 g	Sodium 432 mg
Saturated 0.5 g	Carbohydrates 78 g
Polyunsaturated 1.0 g	Fiber 20 g
Monounsaturated 0.5 g	Sugar 11 g
	Protein 25 g

lentils bourguignon

Where's the beef? Not in this hearty bourguignon. As the lentils and barley cook, they absorb a homemade sauce flavored with a generous red wine reduction.

 2 cups robust red wine (burgundy preferred)
 2 medium onions, chopped
 5 medium garlic cloves, thinly sliced
 3 tablespoons no-salt-added tomato paste
 6 ounces button mushrooms, thickly sliced
 3 medium carrots, thickly sliced
 2 medium ribs of celery, thickly sliced
 6 cups water, or 3 cups water plus 3 cups fat-free, low-sodium chicken broth
 3 medium tomatoes, coarsely chopped
 1¹/₂ cups dried lentils, sorted for stones and shriveled lentils and rinsed
 1 cup uncooked pearl barley
 2 tablespoons chopped fresh sage
 2 tablespoons red wine vinegar
 2 sprigs of fresh thyme
 ¹/₄ teaspoon pepper
 ¹/₂ teaspoon salt

In a stockpot, cook the wine, onions, and garlic over high heat for 12 to 15 minutes, or until the liquid part is reduced to about ¹/₂ cup.

Add the tomato paste, stirring until dissolved. Stir in the mushrooms, carrots, and celery. Reduce the heat to medium. Cook, covered, for 5 minutes.

Stir in the remaining ingredients except the salt. Bring to a boil. Reduce the heat and simmer, covered, for 30 minutes. Uncover and simmer for 15 minutes, or until all excess liquid evaporates (no liquid should be pooled, but the bottom of the pot should be wet) and the lentils are tender. Stir in the salt.

PER SERVING	
Calories 435	Cholesterol 0 mg
Total Fat 1.5 g	Sodium 298 mg
Saturated 0.5 g	Carbohydrates 84 g
Polyunsaturated 0.5 g	Fiber 24 g
Monounsaturated 0 g	Sugar 13 g
	Protein 23 g

fennel braised
with red lentils

This dish is packed with incredible flavors that will wake up your taste buds. Serve it with a tossed green salad and crusty sourdough bread.

1 large or 2 small fennel bulbs (about 1 pound, including stalks)

1 tablespoon olive oil

1 large sweet onion (Vidalia or Walla Walla preferred), cut through the core into thin wedges

3 medium garlic cloves, minced

2 3/4 cups low-sodium vegetable broth

1 cup dried red lentils, sorted for stones and shriveled lentils and rinsed

1/3 cup crumbled Gorgonzola or blue cheese

Pepper to taste

Cut off and chop about 2 tablespoons of feathery fronds from the fennel bulb for garnish. Set aside. Trim the fennel bulb and cut crosswise into thin slices.

Heat a large, deep skillet over medium-high heat. Pour the oil into the skillet and swirl to coat the bottom. Cook the fennel bulb and onion for 3 minutes, or until the onion is translucent, stirring once.

Stir in the garlic. Cook for 1 minute.

Stir in the broth; bring to a simmer.

Stir in the lentils. Reduce the heat and simmer, uncovered, for about 17 minutes, or until the lentils and vegetables are tender, stirring occasionally.

To serve, ladle the mixture into bowls. Sprinkle with the cheese and fennel fronds. Serve with the pepper.

COOK'S TIP ON FENNEL

To trim fennel bulbs, remove the fronds, then cut off the stalks as well as the tough base at the bottom of the bulb. The fronds can be used for garnish, as in this dish, and the stalks are a distinctive addition to broths.

PER SERVING	
Calories 284	Cholesterol 8 mg
Total Fat 6.5 g	Sodium 237 mg
Saturated 2.5 g	Carbohydrates 43 g
Polyunsaturated 0.5 g	Fiber 12 g
Monounsaturated 2.5 g	Sugar 5 g
	Protein 17 g

potato-crusted vegetable quiche

Remake an old brunch favorite by switching to a crust of paper-thin cheese-covered potato slices. If you have any leftover veggies in the refrigerator, feel free to add them to the filling.

Vegetable oil spray

2 large baking potatoes (russet preferred), peeled and sliced very thin ($^1/_{10}$ of an inch or thinner)

3 ounces reduced-fat, reduced-sodium Swiss cheese (about 2 4 × 6-inch slices)

2 medium red bell peppers, diced

1 large green bell pepper, diced

2 large carrots, grated

$^1/_4$ cup finely chopped onion

1 small fresh jalapeño pepper, seeds and ribs discarded, minced

Egg substitute equivalent to 6 eggs

$^1/_2$ cup fat-free milk

$^1/_4$ teaspoon salt

Preheat the oven to 375°F. Lightly spray a 10-inch deep-dish pie pan with vegetable oil spray.

Starting by placing one slice of potato in the center, make circles of overlapping potatoes around it until the bottom of the pan is covered by a single layer of potatoes (little or none of the bottom should show).

Finish the crust by arranging a row of potato slices around the side of the pan. To keep these slices from slipping, rest their bottom edges on the flat potatoes. Place a second circle of potato slices around the side of the pan, and then make another layer on the bottom of the pan. Lightly spray the bottom and side with vegetable oil spray. Gently press a sheet of aluminum foil over the potatoes to hold them in place.

Bake for 20 minutes. Remove from the oven and discard the foil.

PER SERVING	
Calories 238	Cholesterol 16 mg
Total Fat 5.0 g	Sodium 395 mg
Saturated 3.0 g	Carbohydrates 30 g
Polyunsaturated 0 g	Fiber 5 g
Monounsaturated 0 g	Sugar 10 g
	Protein 19 g

Tearing the cheese as you go, sprinkle the pieces on the crust, covering as much of the bottom as possible.

Bake, uncovered, for 10 minutes.

Meanwhile, in a medium bowl, stir together the remaining ingredients.

Remove the pan from the oven. Pour in the vegetable-egg mixture. Reduce the temperature to 325°F.

Bake, uncovered, for 30 to 35 minutes, or until the top springs back when pressed lightly in the center.

Let cool for 5 to 10 minutes before serving. Run a knife around the side of the pan before cutting the quiche into wedges.

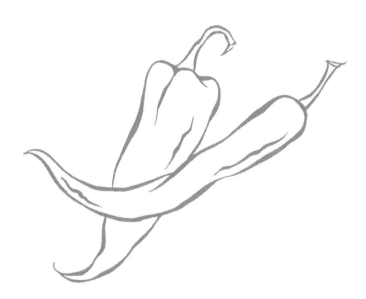

broccoli-and-cheese
bread pudding

One of the best things about this strata-type casserole is its versatility. You can prepare it early in the day and pop it into the oven at dinnertime, or prepare it in the evening, then bake it for brunch.

  Vegetable oil spray
  4 cups cubed (¾-inch pieces) whole-grain bread (about 5 slices)
  8 ounces frozen broccoli florets (about 2 cups), thawed and drained
  1 cup shredded reduced-fat Cheddar cheese
  12-ounce can fat-free evaporated milk
  Whites of 5 large eggs
  1 teaspoon herbes de Provence or fines herbes, or ½ teaspoon dried basil
  and ½ teaspoon dried thyme, crumbled
  ¼ teaspoon salt
  ⅛ teaspoon pepper

Lightly spray an 8- or 9-inch square glass baking dish with vegetable oil spray. Put the bread cubes in the dish.

Cut the broccoli into bite-size pieces. Place the broccoli and cheese on the bread cubes.

In a medium bowl, whisk together the remaining ingredients. Pour over the bread mixture. Using a large spatula, press down so the milk mixture moistens the other ingredients. Let stand at room temperature for 30 minutes, or cover and refrigerate for up to 8 hours before baking.

Preheat the oven to 350°F.

Bake for 40 to 45 minutes, or until the center is set (custard doesn't jiggle when gently shaken). Let stand for 5 minutes before cutting into squares.

PER SERVING	
Calories 266	Cholesterol 18 mg
Total Fat 6.5 g	Sodium 660 mg
Saturated 4.0 g	Carbohydrates 28 g
Polyunsaturated 0.5 g	Fiber 4 g
Monounsaturated 1.5 g	Sugar 13 g
	Protein 24 g

spinach and feta pie

This skillet pie is packed with rice, spinach, feta cheese, and herbs. A fresh lemon spritz gives it extra punch.

1$^1/_4$ cups water

2 medium onions, chopped

$^1/_2$ cup uncooked white rice

10 ounces frozen chopped spinach, thawed and squeezed dry

Egg substitute equivalent to 4 eggs

$^1/_4$ cup fat-free milk

2 ounces feta cheese with sun-dried tomatoes and basil

1 teaspoon dried oregano, crumbled

$^1/_2$ teaspoon salt

2 ounces feta cheese with sun-dried tomatoes and basil

2 medium lemons, quartered

In a medium broilerproof skillet, bring the water to a boil over high heat. Stir in the onions and rice. Return to a boil. Reduce the heat and simmer, covered, for 15 minutes.

Stir in the spinach, egg substitute, milk, 2 ounces feta, oregano, and salt. Reduce the heat to medium-low. Cook, covered, for 20 minutes, or until the eggs are almost set. Sprinkle the remaining 2 ounces feta over the pie.

Meanwhile, preheat the broiler.

Broil for 2 minutes, or until the cheese begins to melt slightly. Remove from the oven and let stand for 5 minutes to allow the flavors to blend and for easier cutting. (The egg mixture will continue to cook while the pie broils and stands.) Cut into 4 wedges. Serve with lemon to squeeze on top.

PER SERVING	
Calories 249	Cholesterol 21 mg
Total Fat 6.5 g	Sodium 705 mg
Saturated 4.0 g	Carbohydrates 31 g
Polyunsaturated 0 g	Fiber 4 g
Monounsaturated 0 g	Sugar 7 g
	Protein 16 g

frittata primavera

The word *frittata* is Italian. After one taste, you'll think that translates as "an easy omelet filled with good stuff."

Vegetable oil spray

6 large button mushrooms, sliced

2 large carrots, grated

1 medium shallot, minced

10 ounces frozen chopped spinach, thawed and squeezed dry

4 1/2 ounces refrigerated angel hair pasta, cut into 3- to 4-inch pieces

Egg substitute equivalent to 6 eggs

1/2 cup fat-free milk

1/8 teaspoon salt

1/8 teaspoon pepper

Whites of 2 large eggs, room temperature

2 tablespoons shredded or grated Parmesan cheese

Heat a 10-inch nonstick skillet over medium heat. Remove from the heat and lightly spray with vegetable oil spray (being careful not to spray near a gas flame). Cook the mushrooms, carrots, and shallot for 5 to 6 minutes, or until the mushrooms are thoroughly softened, stirring occasionally.

Meanwhile, in a medium bowl, combine the spinach, pasta, egg substitute, milk, salt, and pepper, stirring with a fork to break up the spinach and combine well.

In a small bowl, with an electric mixer at high speed, beat the egg whites until stiff peaks form.

Slowly add the hot mushroom mixture to the spinach mixture, stirring constantly. Fold in the egg whites.

Lightly spray the skillet with vegetable oil spray. Pour the mixture into the skillet. Cook over medium heat for 4 minutes. Reduce the heat to medium-low. Cook, without stirring, for 15 minutes. Sprinkle with the Parmesan.

PER SERVING	
Calories 205	Cholesterol 2 mg
Total Fat 2.0 g	Sodium 475 mg
Saturated 0.5 g	Carbohydrates 28 g
Polyunsaturated 0.5 g	Fiber 5 g
Monounsaturated 0.5 g	Sugar 6 g
	Protein 20 g

Meanwhile, preheat the broiler. If your skillet handle is not broilerproof, wrap it in aluminum foil. Broil the frittata about 6 inches from the heat for 3 minutes, or until golden brown.

To serve, cut into 4 wedges.

COOK'S TIP ON FROZEN SPINACH

One way to remove the excess water from thawed spinach is to use a ricer. Put a large handful of spinach in the ricer; holding the ricer over the sink, squeeze the handles and extract as much liquid as possible through the holes. Turn the ricer upside down to get rid of any water that pooled on top. Remove the drained spinach and repeat with the remaining spinach. Another way is to put the spinach in a colander, press the spinach with a spoon to drain all the liquid you can, then squeeze the spinach with your hands to get rid of the remaining liquid. After either method, use two forks to fluff the spinach.

COOK'S TIP ON BEATING EGG WHITES

Even a single drop of egg yolk prevents egg whites from forming peaks when beaten, so separate eggs very carefully.

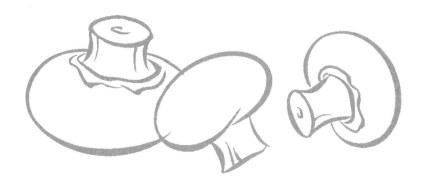

cheddar frittata with black beans and cilantro

SERVES 4; 1 FRITTATA WEDGE AND SCANT $^1/_2$ CUP BLACK BEANS PER SERVING

Frittatas make great last-minute meals. This one offers a combination of black beans, cilantro, and fresh lime as an accompaniment.

> **Egg substitute equivalent to 4 eggs**
> $^1/_2$ **cup shredded reduced-fat sharp Cheddar cheese**
> **4.5-ounce can chopped green chile peppers, undrained**
> **2 small tomatoes, seeded and diced**
> $^1/_2$ **cup finely chopped green onions (green and white parts)**
> **2.25-ounce can sliced ripe olives, drained**
> $^1/_2$ **teaspoon ground cumin**
> $^1/_4$ **to** $^1/_8$ **teaspoon cayenne**
> **Vegetable oil spray**
> $^1/_2$ **cup shredded reduced-fat sharp Cheddar cheese**
> **15-ounce can no-salt-added black beans, rinsed if desired and drained**
> **2 tablespoons snipped fresh cilantro**
> **2 medium limes, quartered**

In a large bowl, gently stir together the egg substitute, $^1/_2$ cup cheese, undrained green chiles, tomatoes, green onions, olives, cumin, and cayenne.

Heat a 12-inch skillet over medium-high heat. Remove from the heat and lightly spray with vegetable oil spray (being careful not to spray near a gas flame). Pour the mixture into the skillet and spread evenly. Immediately reduce the heat to medium-low. Cook, covered, for 14 minutes, or until the mixture begins to puff. The center will be moist.

Meanwhile, preheat the broiler.

Sprinkle the remaining $^1/_2$ cup cheese over the frittata.

Broil for 2 minutes, or until the cheese is melted. (This allows the frittata to continue to cook without drying out.)

To serve, cut the frittata into 4 wedges. Place the wedges on plates. Spoon a scant $^1/_2$ cup black beans beside each wedge. Sprinkle the cilantro over the beans. Squeeze the lime over the beans.

PER SERVING	
Calories 245	Cholesterol 15 mg
Total Fat 7.0 g	Sodium 569 mg
Saturated 4.0 g	Carbohydrates 24 g
Polyunsaturated 0 g	Fiber 7 g
Monounsaturated 2.5 g	Sugar 7 g
	Protein 20 g

walnut-crusted goat cheese and fruit salad

SERVES 4; 2 SLICES GOAT CHEESE, $1/2$ ENGLISH MUFFIN, AND ABOUT 2 CUPS SALAD PER SERVING

Tangy goat cheese contrasts nicely with the sweetness of the mixed berries in this colorful salad.

- 4 ounces soft goat cheese
- $1/4$ cup finely chopped walnuts
- 2 whole-wheat English muffins, split
- Vegetable oil spray
- $1/4$ teaspoon ground cinnamon
- 6 cups torn mixed salad greens or mesclun
- 1 cup sliced strawberries
- 1 cup blueberries
- $1/3$ cup fat-free or light honey Dijon or raspberry vinaigrette salad dressing
- 2 tablespoons thinly sliced or chopped fresh mint (optional)

Preheat the broiler.

Cut the goat cheese crosswise into 8 slices. Place on a baking sheet. Spoon the walnuts onto the cheese; using your fingers, lightly press the walnuts into the cheese. Place the muffin halves with cut sides up on the baking sheet. Lightly spray the cheese and muffin halves with vegetable oil spray. Using a fine strainer, sprinkle the cinnamon evenly over the cheese and muffin halves.

Broil 6 to 7 inches from the heat for 2 minutes, or until the walnuts and muffins are lightly toasted. (Watch carefully to avoid burning the walnuts.)

In a large bowl, toss the salad greens, strawberries, blueberries, and dressing.

To serve, arrange the salad on plates. Place 2 slices of goat cheese on each salad. Cut the muffin halves into quarters and arrange around the edges of the salads. Sprinkle the salads with mint.

PER SERVING	
Calories 269	Cholesterol 13 mg
Total Fat 12.0 g	Sodium 558 mg
Saturated 5.0 g	Carbohydrates 32 g
Polyunsaturated 4.0 g	Fiber 7 g
Monounsaturated 2.5 g	Sugar 11 g
	Protein 11 g

grilled vegetable sandwiches with goat cheese

SERVES 4; 1 SANDWICH PER SERVING

Grilled vegetables and goat cheese are a dynamic duo in this hefty sandwich.

> Vegetable oil spray or olive oil spray
> 4 large portobello mushrooms, trimmed
> 4 small (4-inch) or 2 large Japanese eggplants (about 12 ounces)
> 2 large red or yellow bell peppers
> 1/3 cup fat-free or light Italian salad dressing
> 8 slices Italian or sourdough bread, 1/2 inch thick
> 3 ounces crumbled soft goat cheese
> 1 cup packed arugula or mixed salad greens

Spray the grill rack with vegetable oil spray. Preheat the grill on medium-high.

If desired, using a tablespoon, scrape out and discard the gills on the undersides of the mushroom caps. If the eggplants are long, cut crosswise in half. Trim the ends and cut the eggplants lengthwise into 1/4- to 1/3-inch slices. Cut the bell peppers lengthwise in half; discard the stems and seeds. Lightly brush the dressing over both sides of the vegetables and bread.

Grill the vegetables, covered, for 5 minutes. Turn the vegetables over.

Arrange the bread around the edges. Grill, covered, for 2 minutes. Turn the bread over. Grill, covered, for 2 to 3 minutes, or until the vegetables are tender and the bread is golden brown.

To assemble the sandwiches, place vegetables, goat cheese, and arugula on 4 slices of bread. Top with the remaining bread.

COOK'S TIP ON EGGPLANT

Japanese eggplants are thinner than regular eggplants and often are a very light purple. If they are not available, substitute four 1/2-inch-thick center-cut slices of a large eggplant.

PER SERVING	
Calories 226	Cholesterol 10 mg
Total Fat 6.5 g	Sodium 559 mg
Saturated 3.5 g	Carbohydrates 34 g
Polyunsaturated 1.0 g	Fiber 5 g
Monounsaturated 1.5 g	Sugar 8 g
	Protein 10 g

broiled mozzarella veggie sandwiches

Toss vegetables with aromatic fresh basil and salty kalamata olives before mounding them on sourdough bread and smothering them with mozzarella. The result is a zesty open-face sandwich that abounds with color and flavor.

Vegetable oil spray

1 medium red or yellow bell pepper, thinly sliced

1 medium zucchini, sliced

4 ounces button mushrooms, sliced

1 small onion, thinly sliced

10 kalamata olives, coarsely chopped

2 tablespoons chopped fresh basil, heavy stems removed, or 2 teaspoons dried, crumbled

4 slices sourdough bread

1 tablespoon plus 1 teaspoon Dijon mustard

1 medium tomato, cut into 8 thin slices

1 cup shredded nonfat or part-skim mozzarella cheese

Preheat the broiler.

Heat a 12-inch nonstick skillet over medium-high heat. Remove from the heat and lightly spray with vegetable oil spray (being careful not to spray near a gas flame). Cook the bell pepper, zucchini, mushrooms, and onion for 8 minutes, or until the onion is translucent, stirring occasionally. Remove from the heat. Stir in the olives and basil.

Meanwhile, lightly spray one side of each bread slice with vegetable oil spray. Place with the sprayed side up on a baking sheet.

Broil for 1 minute, or until golden brown. Remove from the broiler, leaving the broiler on.

To assemble, spread the mustard on the bread. Top with the tomato and cooked vegetables. Sprinkle with the mozzarella.

Broil for 1 minute, or until the cheese is melted.

PER SERVING	
Calories 194	Cholesterol 5 mg
Total Fat 3.5 g	Sodium 792 mg
Saturated 0.5 g	Carbohydrates 26 g
Polyunsaturated 0.5 g	Fiber 4 g
Monounsaturated 2.5 g	Sugar 5 g
	Protein 14 g

mega veggie wraps

Make this easy sandwich even easier by using your favorite already-cleaned-and-cut veggies from the salad bar.

> Vegetable oil spray
> 8 cups cut mixed vegetables (about 2 pounds, depending on vegetables used)
> 1/2 cup fat-free or light honey Dijon dressing
> 1/3 cup chopped fresh basil, heavy stems removed, chives, or mixed fresh herbs
> 4 9-inch sun-dried tomato wraps or whole-wheat tortillas
> 1 1/2 cups shredded nonfat or part-skim mozzarella or nonfat smoked Cheddar cheese

Heat a large, deep skillet over medium-high heat. Remove from the heat and lightly spray with vegetable oil spray (being careful not to spray near a gas flame). Add the vegetables. Lightly spray the vegetables with vegetable oil spray. Cook, covered, for 3 minutes, or until they begin to soften. Cook, uncovered, for 3 to 5 minutes, or until tender-crisp, stirring constantly.

Remove from the heat. Stir in the dressing and basil.

Warm the wraps using the package directions.

To assemble, spoon one fourth of the vegetable mixture vertically down the center of each wrap; don't spread all the way to the top and bottom. Sprinkle the cheese over the vegetables. Fold the top and bottom of each wrap toward the filling. Fold the sides toward the center.

PER SERVING	
Calories 317	Cholesterol 8 mg
Total Fat 2.0 g	Sodium 800 mg
Saturated 0 g	Carbohydrates 56 g
Polyunsaturated 0.5 g	Fiber 7 g
Monounsaturated 0 g	Sugar 22 g
	Protein 20 g

mushroom and barley
chowder

SERVES 4; 1 1/2 CUPS PER SERVING

Dried porcini and fresh exotic mushrooms combine to give this hearty soup a distinctive flavor. Use kitchen shears to cut the dried mushrooms easily.

    1 teaspoon acceptable vegetable oil

1/2 cup chopped onion

    4-ounce package sliced exotic mushrooms, such as shiitake, oyster, or cremini (brown)

    2 medium garlic cloves, minced

    2 14.5-ounce cans low-sodium vegetable broth or fat-free, low-sodium chicken broth

    2 tablespoons finely snipped dried porcini mushrooms

    2 medium carrots, thinly sliced

2/3 cup uncooked quick-cooking barley

    1 teaspoon dried thyme, crumbled

3/4 teaspoon salt

1/4 teaspoon pepper

1 3/4 cups fat-free milk

    2 tablespoons all-purpose flour

1/2 cup shredded fat-free or reduced-fat Cheddar cheese (about 2 ounces)

Heat a large nonstick saucepan over medium heat. Pour the oil into the saucepan and swirl to coat the bottom. Cook the onion for 3 to 4 minutes, or until translucent, stirring occasionally.

Stir in the sliced mushrooms and garlic. Cook for 3 minutes.

Stir in the broth and dried mushrooms. Bring to a boil.

Stir in the carrots, barley, thyme, salt, and pepper. Return to a boil. Reduce the heat and simmer for 10 minutes, or until the barley and vegetables are tender, stirring occasionally.

In a small bowl, whisk together the milk and flour. Stir into the barley mixture. Simmer for 3 minutes, or until thickened, stirring occasionally.

To serve, ladle the soup into bowls. Sprinkle with the cheese.

PER SERVING	
Calories 257	Cholesterol 5 mg
Total Fat 2.0 g	Sodium 697 mg
Saturated 0.5 g	Carbohydrates 44 g
Polyunsaturated 0.5 g	Fiber 8 g
Monounsaturated 1.0 g	Sugar 10 g
	Protein 16 g

italian barley and artichoke salad with olives

SERVES 4; 1¹/₂ CUPS PER SERVING

Move over, pasta. Barley takes the spotlight in this pasta-style salad of tomatoes, bell peppers, artichoke hearts, olives, and mozzarella.

2 cups water

1 cup uncooked quick-cooking barley

14-ounce can quartered artichoke hearts (chilled preferred)

12 pitted kalamata olives

1 medium yellow bell pepper

¹/₂ cup grape tomatoes or cherry tomatoes (about 4 ounces)

4 ounces nonfat or part-skim mozzarella cheese

1 tablespoon dried basil, crumbled

1¹/₂ to 2 tablespoons cider vinegar

2 tablespoons olive oil (extra virgin preferred)

1 medium garlic clove, minced

¹/₈ teaspoon salt

In a medium saucepan, bring the water to a boil over high heat. Stir in the barley. Reduce the heat and simmer, covered, for 10 minutes, or until the barley is just tender but firm.

Transfer the barley to a colander. Run under cold water to cool completely. Drain well. Place in a medium bowl.

Meanwhile, rinse, drain, and coarsely chop the artichokes and olives; chop the bell pepper; quarter the tomatoes; and cut the cheese into ¹/₄-inch cubes. Add to the barley. Add the remaining ingredients and toss to blend.

COOK'S TIP

You can make this salad up to 24 hours in advance, in which case we suggest using the full 2 tablespoons of cider vinegar. The slightly smaller amount is better if you plan to eat the salad right after preparing it.

PER SERVING	
Calories 354	Cholesterol 5 mg
Total Fat 10.5 g	Sodium 760 mg
Saturated 1.5 g	Carbohydrates 51 g
Polyunsaturated 1.5 g	Fiber 11 g
Monounsaturated 7.5 g	Sugar 4 g
	Protein 16 g

vegetable and barley
stew

The slow-cooker technique of this recipe coaxes out the full flavors of the vegetables, infusing the broth and the barley with them. Suit your whims and inspirations from the produce section of your grocery store or local farmer's market by incorporating different vegetables, such as parsnips, beets, or summer squash.

6 cups low-sodium vegetable broth

15-ounce can no-salt-added kidney beans, rinsed if desired and drained

14.5-ounce can no-salt-added diced tomatoes

2 cups fresh corn kernels, frozen whole-kernel corn, or canned no salt-added whole-kernel corn, rinsed if desired and drained

1 cup frozen pearl onions, thawed

2 medium ribs of celery, sliced

1/2 cup uncooked pearl barley

1 teaspoon salt-free all-purpose seasoning blend

1 teaspoon dried oregano, crumbled

1/2 teaspoon dried basil, crumbled

1/4 teaspoon pepper

Put all ingredients in a slow cooker, stirring to combine. Cook, covered, on high heat for 4 to 5 hours or on low heat for 8 to 10 hours, or until the barley and vegetables are tender.

PER SERVING	
Calories 219	Cholesterol 0 mg
Total Fat 1.0 g	Sodium 101 mg
Saturated 0 g	Carbohydrates 45 g
Polyunsaturated 0.5 g	Fiber 8 g
Monounsaturated 0 g	Sugar 8 g
	Protein 11 g

home-style broccoli
and potato soup

If you like baked potatoes with all the fixings, you will love this soup.

   Vegetable oil spray

   4 ounces button mushrooms, sliced

   ¹/₂ cup chopped green onions (green and white parts)

   1 pound baking potatoes (russet preferred), diced

   ¹/₂ cup water

   2¹/₄ cups fat-free milk

   1¹/₂ cups frozen broccoli florets, thawed

   ¹/₂ cup frozen whole-kernel corn, thawed

   ¹/₄ teaspoon dried thyme, crumbled

   ¹/₄ teaspoon cayenne

   ³/₄ cup nonfat or light sour cream

   1 medium green onion, chopped (green and white parts)

   ³/₄ teaspoon salt

   ¹/₈ teaspoon pepper

   ¹/₂ cup shredded reduced-fat sharp Cheddar cheese

Heat a Dutch oven over medium-high heat. Remove from the heat and lightly spray with vegetable oil spray (being careful not to spray near a gas flame). Cook the mushrooms and ¹/₂ cup green onions for 2 minutes, stirring occasionally.

   Stir in the potatoes and water. Increase the heat to high. Bring to a boil.

   Reduce the heat and simmer, covered, for 7 minutes, or until the potatoes are tender-crisp.

   Stir in the milk, broccoli, corn, thyme, and cayenne. Increase the heat to high and bring just to a boil. Reduce the heat and simmer, covered, for 5 minutes, or until the potatoes are tender.

   Remove from the heat. Stir in the remaining ingredients except the cheese.

   To serve, ladle the soup into soup bowls. Sprinkle with the cheese.

PER SERVING	
Calories 264	Cholesterol 18 mg
Total Fat 3.0 g	Sodium 655 mg
Saturated 2.0 g	Carbohydrates 45 g
Polyunsaturated 0 g	Fiber 6 g
Monounsaturated 0.5 g	Sugar 14 g
	Protein 18 g

curried vegetable chowder

Bright orange carrots simmer with red bell pepper bits before green peas, fresh cilantro, and green onions join them in creamy coconut milk colored with curry powder.

1/2 cup water

10 ounces baking potatoes (russet preferred), peeled and cut into 1/2-inch cubes

2 medium carrots, thinly sliced

1 medium red bell pepper, chopped

1/4 teaspoon cayenne

13.5-ounce can light coconut milk

1 cup fat-free half-and-half

1 cup frozen green peas

1 teaspoon curry powder

1 teaspoon salt

1/2 teaspoon ground cumin

1/2 cup snipped fresh cilantro

1/2 cup chopped green onions (green and white parts)

In a large saucepan, bring the water to a boil over high heat. Stir in the potatoes, carrots, bell pepper, and cayenne. Bring to a boil. Reduce the heat and simmer, covered, for 8 minutes, or until the potatoes are tender.

Increase the heat to medium. Stir in the coconut milk, half-and-half, peas, curry powder, salt, and cumin. Cook for 5 minutes, or until heated through. Stir in the cilantro and green onions.

PER SERVING	
Calories 350	Cholesterol 1 mg
Total Fat 12.0 g	Sodium 227 mg
Saturated 1.5 g	Carbohydrates 53 g
Polyunsaturated 8.0 g	Fiber 7 g
Monounsaturated 2.0 g	Sugar 23 g
	Protein 10 g

summery fruit salad with quinoa

Combine a tasty blend of summer fruit with quinoa, a balsamic-lemon dressing, and lots of crunch from walnuts, jícama, and celery for an unusual entrée. Allow plenty of time to chill the ingredients for optimum taste.

1 cup uncooked quinoa, thoroughly rinsed and drained

1/2 medium to large cantaloupe

1 small jícama (8 to 9 ounces)

1 1/2 cups seedless grapes

2 large ribs of celery

8 ounces nonfat lemon yogurt

2 tablespoons fat-free or reduced-fat mayonnaise dressing

1 tablespoon balsamic vinegar

1/4 teaspoon salt

1/2 cup plus 2 tablespoons coarsely chopped walnuts, dry-roasted

3 tablespoons thinly sliced or chopped fresh mint plus 5 sprigs for garnish

1 lime, cut into 5 wedges

Cook the quinoa according to the package directions, omitting the salt and oil. Transfer the quinoa to a large bowl, preferably chilled. Once the quinoa is cooled to room temperature, cover the bowl with plastic wrap; refrigerate until completely chilled.

Meanwhile, dice the cantaloupe, peel and dice the jícama, halve the grapes, and slice the celery on the diagonal. Refrigerate in separate containers until thoroughly chilled.

At serving time, in a small bowl, whisk together the yogurt, mayonnaise, vinegar, and salt. Stir the mixture into the quinoa.

Drain the cantaloupe if needed. Stir the cantaloupe, jícama, grapes, walnuts, and 3 tablespoons mint into the quinoa.

PER SERVING	
Calories 350	Cholesterol 1 mg
Total Fat 12.0 g	Sodium 227 mg
Saturated 1.5 g	Carbohydrates 53 g
Polyunsaturated 8.0 g	Fiber 7 g
Monounsaturated 2.0 g	Sugar 23 g
	Protein 10 g

To serve, place two 1-cup scoops of the salad on each plate. Garnish each serving with a sprig of mint and a lime wedge to squeeze over the salad.

COOK'S TIP

Rinsing quinoa is needed to get rid of the bitter-tasting coating. If you have a large metal bowl, put it in the refrigerator or freezer to chill while you prepare the quinoa.

quinoa and toasted
peanut salad

SERVES 4; 1 1/2 CUPS PER SERVING

Quinoa (KEEN-wah) contains more protein than any other grain. It makes a great base for this salad, tossed with toasted peanuts, crunchy vegetables, dried fruits, and a sweet soy dressing.

2/3 cup unsalted peanuts (about 3 ounces)

1 cup water

1/2 cup uncooked quinoa, thoroughly rinsed and drained

1 medium red bell pepper, chopped

2 cups broccoli florets, broken into small pieces (about 1/2 large bunch)

8-ounce can sliced water chestnuts, rinsed and drained

1/2 cup chopped dried mixed fruits

3 tablespoons low-salt soy sauce

2 tablespoons sugar

2 tablespoons cider vinegar

1 teaspoon grated orange zest

1/2 teaspoon ground cumin

Heat a small saucepan over medium-high heat. Dry-roast the peanuts for 4 minutes, or until beginning to turn golden brown, stirring frequently. Transfer to a medium bowl.

In the same saucepan, bring the water to a boil over high heat. Stir the quinoa into the boiling water. Return to a boil. Reduce the heat and simmer, covered, for 15 minutes, or until the liquid is absorbed. Cool quickly by spreading the quinoa in a thin layer on a sheet of aluminum foil; let stand for 5 minutes.

Add all the ingredients to the peanuts; stir.

PER SERVING	Cholesterol 0 mg
Calories 335	Sodium 318 mg
Total Fat 14.0 g	Carbohydrates 47 g
Saturated 2.0 g	Fiber 8 g
Polyunsaturated 4.5 g	Sugar 10 g
Monounsaturated 6.5 g	Protein 11 g

asian noodle soup
with mini portobellos

SERVES 4; 2 CUPS PER SERVING

While shopping at your local farmer's market or gourmet grocery store, look for interesting exotic mushrooms (fresh and dried) for this substantial soup.

2 teaspoons acceptable vegetable oil

2 medium shallots, chopped

8 ounces mini portobello mushrooms or exotic mushrooms, such as morel, shiitake, chanterelle, enoki, or wood ear, sliced

6 cups low-sodium vegetable broth

12 to 14 ounces silken or soft tofu, drained if necessary, cut into $1/2$-inch cubes

8 dried shiitake, morel, or porcini mushrooms, stems discarded, caps quartered

1 tablespoon low-salt soy sauce

1 teaspoon toasted sesame oil

$1/4$ teaspoon ground ginger

2 ounces dried somen noodles or angel hair pasta

8 ounces sugar snap peas

4 medium green onions (green and white parts), thinly sliced

Heat a large saucepan over medium heat. Pour the oil into the saucepan and swirl to coat the bottom. Cook the shallots for 1 to 2 minutes, or until tender-crisp, stirring occasionally.

Stir in the fresh mushrooms. Increase the heat to medium-high and cook for 4 to 5 minutes, or until tender, stirring occasionally.

Stir in the broth, tofu, dried mushrooms, soy sauce, sesame oil, and ground ginger. Bring to a simmer, stirring occasionally. Reduce the heat and simmer, covered, for 15 minutes, or until the dried mushrooms are tender.

Increase the heat to medium-high. Stir in the somen noodles. Cook, uncovered, for 3 to 4 minutes, or until the noodles are tender, stirring occasionally.

Stir in the peas and green onions. Cook for 1 to 2 minutes, or until the peas are tender-crisp.

PER SERVING	
Calories 230	Cholesterol 0 mg
Total Fat 6.5 g	Sodium 439 mg
Saturated 0.5 g	Carbohydrates 32 g
Polyunsaturated 3.0 g	Fiber 5 g
Monounsaturated 2.5 g	Sugar 5 g
	Protein 13 g

stir-fried tofu
with bok choy
and soba noodles

SERVES 4; 1 1/2 CUPS PER SERVING

Tender-crisp, nutrient-rich bok choy is stir-fried with silky tofu, then combined with a spicy sesame-ginger sauce and soba noodles.

       8 stalks bok choy

       1 teaspoon acceptable vegetable oil

       2 teaspoons minced peeled gingerroot

       1 large yellow bell pepper, thinly sliced

   1/2 medium onion, thinly sliced

       12 to 14 ounces low-fat extra-firm tofu, drained if needed, cut into 1/2-inch cubes

       2 cups low-sodium vegetable broth

       2 tablespoons low-salt soy sauce

       2 teaspoons toasted sesame oil

   1/2 to 1 teaspoon crushed red pepper flakes

       4 ounces dried soba noodles or whole-wheat angel hair pasta

       4 green onions (green and white parts), thinly sliced

Trim the ends off the bok choy; cut the stalks and leaves crosswise into 1/2-inch slices, keeping the stalks and leaves separate.

Heat a large, deep nonstick skillet or nonstick wok over medium-high heat. Pour the vegetable oil into the skillet and swirl to coat the bottom. Cook the gingerroot for 10 to 15 seconds, stirring constantly. Watch the ginger carefully so it doesn't burn.

Stir in the bell pepper and onion. Cook for 2 to 3 minutes, or until the vegetables are tender-crisp, stirring constantly.

Stir in the bok choy stalks (not the leaves yet) and tofu. Cook for 2 to 3 minutes, or until the bok choy is tender-crisp and the tofu is warmed through, stirring constantly yet gently to keep from breaking up the tofu.

PER SERVING	
	Cholesterol 0 mg
Calories 202	Sodium 368 mg
Total Fat 4.5 g	Carbohydrates 30 g
Saturated 0.5 g	Fiber 3 g
Polyunsaturated 2.0 g	Sugar 5 g
Monounsaturated 2.0 g	Protein 13 g

Stir in the vegetable broth, soy sauce, sesame oil, and red pepper flakes. Bring to a boil, stirring occasionally.

Stir in the soba noodles. Reduce the heat and simmer for 3 to 4 minutes, or until the noodles are tender and the mixture is warmed through, stirring occasionally.

Stir in the bok choy leaves and green onions. Cook for 1 to 2 minutes, or until they are wilted, stirring occasionally.

lettuce cups with soft tofu and vegetables

SERVES 4; 1¹/4 CUPS FILLING AND 4 LETTUCE LEAVES PER SERVING

A few quick pulses of a food processor and you'll have dinner all wrapped up! No knives and forks are needed for eating this fun food.

15-ounce can no-salt-added chick-peas, rinsed if desired and drained

2 medium carrots, cut into 1- or 2-inch pieces

8 medium radishes, stems and roots trimmed

¹/2 cup frozen green peas, thawed

¹/2 cup sliced green onions (green and white parts)

2 tablespoons reduced-fat peanut butter

3 tablespoons red wine vinegar

2 tablespoons low-salt soy sauce

1 teaspoon toasted sesame oil

12 ounces soft tofu, drained if necessary, cut into ¹/2-inch cubes

2 heads of iceberg lettuce

In a food processor, use the pulse button and coarsely chop the chick-peas. Transfer to a large bowl. Chopping each separately, repeat with the carrots, radishes, and peas. Add each to the chick-peas. Stir in the green onions.

Put the peanut butter, vinegar, soy sauce, and sesame oil in the food processor. Process for 15 to 20 seconds, or until blended. Stir into the chick-pea mixture.

Gently stir in the tofu cubes. Cover and refrigerate for at least 15 minutes before serving. (The refrigerated mixture will keep in an airtight container for up to 4 days.)

Cut each head of lettuce in half vertically through the core. Carefully peel off 4 outside layers from each half.

To serve, place 4 lettuce cups on each plate. Spoon a scant ¹/3 cup of the vegetable mixture into each one. Let each person roll up the wraps before eating them.

PER SERVING	
Calories 348	Cholesterol 0 mg
Total Fat 9.5 g	Sodium 299 mg
Saturated 1.0 g	Carbohydrates 48 g
Polyunsaturated 4.0 g	Fiber 13 g
Monounsaturated 4.0 g	Sugar 12 g
	Protein 19 g

couscous with vegetables
and ricotta cheese

Showcase some of the most popular vegetables—carrots, corn, and broccoli—in this quick meal. Delicate couscous gets a bright orange color from turmeric and is a great complement—both in color and in taste—to the vegetables. The goat cheese, which melts beautifully when stirred in, blends all the ingredients.

1 1/2 cups low-sodium vegetable broth

1 cup baby carrots

2 cups frozen whole-kernel corn

2 cups fresh or frozen broccoli florets

2 teaspoons salt-free all-purpose seasoning blend

1/4 teaspoon salt

1/4 teaspoon turmeric (optional)

3/4 cup uncooked couscous

4 ounces fat-free or low-fat ricotta cheese

2 ounces shredded or grated Parmesan cheese

In a large saucepan, bring the broth and carrots to a simmer over medium-high heat. Reduce the heat and continue simmering, covered, for 5 minutes, or until the carrots are tender-crisp.

Stir in the corn, broccoli, seasoning blend, salt, and turmeric. Return to a simmer, stirring occasionally. Reduce the heat and continue simmering, covered, for 5 minutes, or until the broccoli is tender-crisp.

Stir in the couscous. Remove from the heat and let stand, covered, for 5 minutes, or until all the liquid is absorbed and the couscous is tender.

Add the cheeses. Stir until melted and thoroughly combined.

COOK'S TIP

This dish is best when eaten soon after it is prepared.

PER SERVING	
Calories 340	Cholesterol 14 mg
Total Fat 6.0 g	Sodium 509 mg
Saturated 3.0 g	Carbohydrates 55 g
Polyunsaturated 1.0 g	Fiber 5 g
Monounsaturated 1.5 g	Sugar 7 g
	Protein 19 g

golden vegetable ragout
with currant-studded
couscous

SERVES 4; ABOUT 1¹/₄ CUPS VEGETABLE MIXTURE
AND ³/₄ CUP COUSCOUS PER SERVING

Ready in a jiffy, this vegetable dish gets its gorgeous color and exotic flavor from the seasonings.

1¹/₂ tablespoons olive oil

¹/₂ cup sliced shallots or red onions

8 ounces baby pattypan squash (1-inch), halved if larger than 1 inch in diameter, or 1¹/₂ cups sliced crookneck or zucchini squash

2 cups halved baby carrots

2 small heads Belgian endive, quartered, or 1¹/₂ cups packed torn escarole

2 medium garlic cloves, minced

1 cup low-sodium vegetable broth or fat-free, low-sodium chicken broth

1 teaspoon ground coriander

1 teaspoon ground cumin

¹/₂ teaspoon saffron threads or turmeric

¹/₂ teaspoon salt

¹/₄ teaspoon ground cinnamon

1¹/₂ cups low-sodium vegetable broth or fat-free, low-sodium chicken broth

¹/₃ cup currants or raisins

1 cup uncooked whole-wheat couscous

Heat a large, deep skillet or saucepan over medium heat. Pour the oil into the skillet and swirl to coat the bottom. Cook the shallots for 3 minutes, stirring occasionally.

Stir in the squash, carrots, endive, and garlic. Cook for 1 minute.

Stir in 1 cup broth, coriander, cumin, saffron, salt, and cinnamon. Bring to a simmer. Reduce the heat and simmer, covered, for 6 to 8 minutes, or until the vegetables are tender-crisp.

PER SERVING	
Calories 402	Cholesterol 0 mg
Total Fat 7.5 g	Sodium 407 mg
Saturated 1.0 g	Carbohydrates 77 g
Polyunsaturated 1.5 g	Fiber 19 g
Monounsaturated 4.0 g	Sugar 14 g
	Protein 15 g

Meanwhile, in a microwave-safe bowl, stir together 1¹/₂ cups broth and the currants. Microwave on 100 percent power (high) for 3 minutes, or until simmering. If you prefer, heat the mixture in a medium saucepan over medium-high heat for 3 minutes, or until simmering.

Stir in the couscous; let stand, covered, for 5 minutes, or until the liquid is absorbed. Fluff with a fork.

To serve, ladle the vegetable mixture into bowls. Top each serving with a scoop of couscous.

couscous and vegetable
salad with feta

Thanks to the convenience of precut fresh mixed vegetables sold in packages or at the supermarket's salad bar, this tasty salad takes only minutes to prepare. You can even make it up to 24 hours before serving.

    1 tablespoon olive oil (basil flavored or extra virgin preferred)
    4 cups assorted cut vegetables (12 to 14 ounces)
    14.5-ounce can low-sodium vegetable broth or fat-free, low-sodium chicken broth
    1 cup uncooked whole-wheat couscous
    8 large red-leaf lettuce or romaine leaves
    3/4 cup crumbled feta or soft goat cheese (about 3 ounces)
    1/3 cup light Italian or Caesar salad dressing
    1/2 cup thinly sliced fresh basil leaves (about half a 3/4-ounce package)
    1/8 teaspoon pepper, or to taste

Heat a large saucepan over medium-high heat. Pour the oil into the saucepan and swirl to coat the bottom. Cook the vegetables for 4 minutes, stirring frequently.

Stir in the broth. Bring to a boil. Reduce the heat and simmer for 2 to 3 minutes, or until the vegetables are tender-crisp.

Stir in the couscous. Remove from the heat. Let stand, covered, for 5 minutes, or until the liquid is absorbed. Stir and let stand, uncovered, until room temperature, or cover and refrigerate until cold.

To serve, arrange the lettuce leaves on plates. Stir the cheese, dressing, and basil into the couscous mixture. Spoon onto the lettuce. Sprinkle with pepper.

COOK'S TIP

A mix of broccoli florets, carrot strips, sliced mushrooms, sliced red or green onions, diced assorted bell peppers, and chopped zucchini is a good choice for this salad.

PER SERVING	
Calories 365	Cholesterol 25 mg
Total Fat 11.0 g	Sodium 700 mg
Saturated 5.0 g	Carbohydrates 56 g
Polyunsaturated 1.0 g	Fiber 10 g
Monounsaturated 4.0 g	Sugar 6 g
	Protein 15 g

carrot and pear soup
with basil chiffonade

SERVES 4; 2 CUPS PER SERVING

The brilliant color combination of jade-green soybeans and deep orange carrots and orange juice set against a backdrop of snow-white rice noodles is enticing.

2 teaspoons olive oil

4 medium shallots, chopped

2 teaspoons minced peeled gingerroot

2 large carrots, cut crosswise into 1/4-inch slices

1 large pear, peeled and cut into 1/2-inch cubes

6 cups low-sodium vegetable broth

2 cups frozen shelled soybeans (edamame)

1/2 cup fresh orange juice

1/4 teaspoon pepper

2 ounces dried rice noodles or angel hair pasta

1/4 cup loosely packed fresh basil, thinly sliced, or 1/2 teaspoon dried, crumbled

1/4 teaspoon salt

Heat a large saucepan over medium heat. Pour the oil into the saucepan and swirl to coat the bottom. Cook the shallots and ginger for 1 to 2 minutes, or until the shallots are tender-crisp, stirring occasionally.

Stir in the carrots and pear. Cook for 2 to 3 minutes, or until the carrots are tender-crisp, stirring occasionally.

Stir in the broth, soybeans, orange juice, and pepper. Increase the heat to medium-high and bring to a simmer, stirring occasionally. Reduce the heat and simmer, covered, for 10 minutes.

Stir in the rice noodles, basil, and salt. Simmer, uncovered, for 5 minutes, or until the noodles and soybeans are tender.

COOK'S TIP ON CHIFFONADE

A chiffonade is very thin strips of fresh herbs or leafy vegetables, such as the basil in this recipe or lettuce. Stack several pieces, then tightly roll them into a cylinder. Slice crosswise into very thin strips for an attractive presentation.

PER SERVING	
Calories 288	Cholesterol 0 mg
Total Fat 7.5 g	Sodium 242 mg
Saturated 1.5 g	Carbohydrates 40 g
Polyunsaturated 3.0 g	Fiber 8 g
Monounsaturated 2.5 g	Sugar 13 g
	Protein 15 g

slow-cooker edamame stew

A bowlful of this chunky vegetable stew really satisfies on a cold winter day.

1 pound butternut squash

4 medium red potatoes (about 1 pound)

2 cups frozen shelled edamame (soybeans), thawed

2 cups low-sodium vegetable broth

14.5-ounce can no-salt-added stewed tomatoes, undrained

1 cup carrot juice

4 medium garlic cloves, minced

2 teaspoons salt-free lemon-dill seasoning

$^1/_2$ teaspoon salt

$^1/_4$ teaspoon pepper

Using a vegetable peeler, peel the squash. With a sturdy knife, carefully cut the squash in half lengthwise (the squash will be very hard and may be slippery). Remove the seeds. Cut the squash into $^3/_4$-inch cubes; put in a slow cooker.

Cut the unpeeled potatoes into $^3/_4$-inch cubes; stir into the slow cooker with the remaining ingredients.

Cook on high for 4 to 5 hours or on low for 8 to 10 hours, or until the vegetables and edamame are tender.

COOK'S TIP ON EDAMAME

Edamame is the Japanese name for fresh green soybeans. The edible beans grow in almost-inedible pods. (Eating the pods wouldn't harm you, but they are fibrous and not very appealing.) Look in the produce area and with the frozen foods for these delicately sweet beans.

PER SERVING	
Calories 307	Cholesterol 0 mg
Total Fat 5.0 g	Sodium 387 mg
Saturated 1.0 g	Carbohydrates 54 g
Polyunsaturated 2.5 g	Fiber 13 g
Monounsaturated 1.0 g	Sugar 15 g
	Protein 17 g

bulgur and vegetable
skillet with fresh herbs

Brightly colored with carrots, edamame, and fresh herbs, this nutritious dish proves that bulgur enhances dishes other than tabbouleh.

- 1 tablespoon olive oil
- 1 small onion, chopped
- 2 medium garlic cloves, minced
- 3/4 cup uncooked bulgur
- 1/2 cup uncooked long-grain white rice
- 2 medium carrots, sliced
- 1 cup frozen shelled soybeans (edamame) or baby lima beans
- 2 1/2 cups low-sodium vegetable broth
- 1/2 teaspoon salt
- 1/4 cup chopped mixed fresh herbs, such as thyme, basil, chives, and parsley
- 1/4 cup slivered almonds, dry-roasted
  Pepper to taste

Heat a medium saucepan over medium heat. Pour the oil into the saucepan and swirl to coat the bottom. Cook the onion and garlic for 4 minutes, stirring occasionally.

Stir in the bulgur and rice. Cook for 1 minute.

Stir in the carrots and soybeans. Cook for 1 minute.

Stir in the broth and salt. Increase the heat to high and bring to a simmer. Reduce the heat and simmer, covered, for 15 minutes, or until the liquid is absorbed and the vegetables are tender.

Stir in the herbs and almonds. Sprinkle with pepper to taste.

PER SERVING	
Calories 347	Cholesterol 0 mg
Total Fat 10.0 g	Sodium 345 mg
Saturated 1.5 g	Carbohydrates 52 g
Polyunsaturated 2.5 g	Fiber 10 g
Monounsaturated 5.5 g	Sugar 5 g
	Protein 14 g

vegetarian chili

For a refreshing change from the old standby, try this chili with the aroma and taste of Middle Eastern fare.

Vegetable oil spray

2 medium onions, chopped

15.5-ounce can no-salt-added dark kidney beans, rinsed if desired and drained

14.5-ounce can no-salt-added diced stewed tomatoes, undrained

1 1/2 cups water

4.5-ounce can chopped green chiles, rinsed and drained

2 tablespoons chili powder

2 teaspoons ground cumin

1 teaspoon ground cinnamon

12-ounce package frozen ground meatless crumbles

1 tablespoon sugar

1/3 cup snipped fresh parsley

1 tablespoon olive oil (extra virgin preferred)

1 teaspoon ground cumin

1/4 teaspoon salt

Heat a Dutch oven over medium-high heat. Remove from the heat and lightly spray with vegetable oil spray (being careful not to spray near a gas flame). Cook the onions for 3 to 4 minutes, or until translucent, stirring occasionally.

Stir in the beans, undrained tomatoes, water, green chiles, chili powder, 2 teaspoons cumin, and cinnamon. Increase the heat to high. Bring to a boil. Reduce the heat and simmer, covered, for 15 minutes, or until heated through.

Stir in the meatless crumbles and sugar. Cook for 1 minute. Remove from the heat.

Stir in the remaining ingredients. Cover and let stand for 5 to 10 minutes to absorb flavors.

COOK'S TIP ON CANNED GREEN CHILES
Rinsing these mild peppers reduces their sodium content.

PER SERVING	
Calories 324	Cholesterol 0 mg
Total Fat 4.5 g	Sodium 646 mg
Saturated 0.5 g	Carbohydrates 47 g
Polyunsaturated 0.5 g	Fiber 15 g
Monounsaturated 2.5 g	Sugar 15 g
	Protein 27 g

mushroom marinara polenta

Balsamic vinegar gives this quick-cooking, meatless polenta dish a seductively tangy taste.

16-ounce tube fat-free basil and garlic, mushroom, or sun-dried tomato polenta

4 teaspoons olive oil, divided use

1/3 cup chopped shallots or onion

8 ounces cremini (brown) or button mushrooms, stems discarded, caps sliced

3 medium garlic cloves, minced

2 cups fat-free, low-sodium spaghetti sauce, such as tomato-basil

1 1/2 tablespoons balsamic vinegar

1 cup shredded or grated nonfat or part-skim mozzarella cheese

1/4 cup chopped fresh basil or Italian, or flat-leaf, parsley

Preheat the oven to 200°F.

Cut the polenta crosswise into 12 slices.

Heat a large skillet over medium heat. Pour in 1 teaspoon oil and swirl to coat the bottom. Add half the polenta. Cook for 3 minutes on each side, or until golden brown. Transfer to an ovenproof plate; keep the polenta warm in the oven. Repeat with 1 teaspoon oil and remaining polenta.

Pour the remaining 2 teaspoons oil into the skillet. Cook the shallots for 2 minutes, stirring occasionally. Stir in the mushrooms and garlic; cook for 3 minutes. Stir in the spaghetti sauce and vinegar; bring to a simmer. Lowering the heat as necessary, simmer for 10 minutes, stirring frequently.

To serve, spoon the sauce over the polenta. Sprinkle with the cheese and basil.

PER SERVING	
Calories 241	Cholesterol 5 mg
Total Fat 4.5 g	Sodium 625 mg
Saturated 0.5 g	Carbohydrates 34 g
Polyunsaturated 0.5 g	Fiber 3 g
Monounsaturated 3.5 g	Sugar 11 g
	Protein 15 g

meatless lasagna

Soy burger provides a meaty-tasting vegetarian alternative to the usual ground beef or sausage lasagna.

Vegetable oil spray (olive oil spray preferred)

6 Italian plum tomatoes, coarsely chopped

$1/2$ small onion, cut into chunks

3 medium garlic cloves, coarsely chopped

$1/2$ tablespoon dried oregano

1 teaspoon dried basil

$1/4$ teaspoon pepper, or to taste

$1/4$ teaspoon salt

4 ounces soy burger

6 large button mushrooms, chopped

1 cup fat-free or low-fat cottage cheese, undrained

$1/4$ cup snipped fresh parsley

6 oven-ready lasagna noodles

4 slices nonfat or part-skim mozzarella cheese ($2/3$ to $3/4$ ounce each)

Preheat the oven to 350°F. Lightly spray an 8-inch square glass baking dish with vegetable oil spray.

In a food processor or blender, process the tomatoes, onion, garlic, oregano, basil, pepper, and salt until smooth except for the tomato seeds. (You should have about 2 cups. If you do not, add enough water to make up the difference. If you have more, discard the extra or save it for another use.) Pour 1 cup into a small bowl.

Crumble the soy burger into the bowl; stir.

In another small bowl, thoroughly combine the mushrooms, cottage cheese, and parsley.

Pour $1/2$ cup of the sauce without the soy burger into the baking dish. Spread to cover the bottom. Place 2 noodles over the sauce (they won't quite cover it).

PER SERVING	Cholesterol 6 mg
Calories 242	Sodium 693 mg
Total Fat 1.0 g	Carbohydrates 37 g
Saturated 0 g	Fiber 5 g
Polyunsaturated 0.5 g	Sugar 6 g
Monounsaturated 0 g	Protein 22 g

Spoon the sauce and soy-burger mixture over the noodles, spreading evenly. Cover with 2 noodles. Top with the mushroom mixture. Center the remaining 2 noodles on top. Spread the remaining sauce over the noodles, being sure to cover the entire surface with at least a little sauce. Top with the mozzarella.

Lightly spray a large piece of aluminum foil with vegetable oil spray. Tightly cover the baking dish, pulling the foil taut so it doesn't touch the cheese. (Spraying the foil helps keep the cheese undisturbed if the foil happens to touch.)

Bake for 45 minutes without removing the foil. Take the dish from the oven and carefully remove the foil, lifting it on the side away from you so you don't get a steam burn. Don't let the foil touch the cheese.

Bake, uncovered, for about 15 minutes, or until the top is bubbly and beginning to brown. Let stand for 10 to 15 minutes so the noodles absorb most of the liquid. Cut into 4 squares.

COOK'S TIP ON PUREEING VEGETABLES

Cutting up the vegetables before pureeing them, especially if you use a blender, increases the efficiency of the process.

appendix a
EATING FOR A HEALTHY HEART

Smart eating and physical activity are two of the most important steps you can take toward good health. They are also two of the simplest things you can do, "do" being the operative word. It's up to you to get moving and choose to eat healthfully.

Eating trends change faster than hemlines. Nutrition is one of the fastest-growing fields of research. As scientific discovery evolves, along the way experts often disagree. Even long-held dietary beliefs can—and usually do—change. Many unanswered questions remain and countless variables have yet to be identified by scientists, so dietary advice is sure to continue to change as more is learned. It's no wonder that you may be ready to throw up your hands and give up trying to understand or keep up with it all!

Eating right really isn't all that complicated, though. Forget about "all or nothing" and "good or bad" approaches. There are no foods so bad that they can't be part of a healthful diet for most of us. Eating smart doesn't mean you have to deprive yourself of the foods you love. Likewise, there are no magically good foods. Too much of even a good thing isn't good for you.

You don't have to be a scientist to eat well, either. You can learn how to make heart-healthy food choices. The medical experts at the American Heart Association are here to help. They share their best current recommendations, which are based on what the soundest science indicates and what is known today. You'll find everything outlined simply for you on the following pages.

What does it take to eat smart? Every day you're confronted with so many foods to choose from and an overwhelming amount of conflicting dietary advice. The American Heart Association's medical and nutritional experts realize that life is complicated enough without having to make hard decisions about what to eat! They've created a simple eating plan, based on the best available science, that can help most Americans over the age of two enjoy good health and reduce the risk for cardiovascular disease (commonly known as *heart disease*) and other chronic health problems.

The keys to the American Heart Association lifelong eating plan are balance and moderation. You can and should love what you eat. Extremes aren't good for you and certainly aren't much fun. Apply the guidelines to your overall eating pattern over several days and don't fret over every morsel or every meal that passes your lips. If you occasionally have a breakfast high in saturated fat, balance it with a low-fat dinner. Remember, there are no forbidden foods. Everything in moderation can be part of a healthful, balanced diet. If you crave a high-fat treat, just eat reasonable amounts and balance the rest of your diet with plenty of the good stuff.

Deep down, you have a pretty good idea about which foods are the "good stuff." You know you can't eat burgers and fries for every meal, any more than you can be healthy on just lettuce and grapefruit. Still, some advice is sure to be welcome in figuring out exactly how to achieve a healthful balance. The following are the American Heart Association's Dietary Guidelines in a nutshell. These guidelines are designed for most Americans over the age of two. (Growing children, teenagers, pregnant women, the elderly, and people with medical problems such as diabetes and heart disease have special needs and should talk to their healthcare provider or a registered dietitian for additional guidance.)

1. **Enjoy a wide variety of foods.**

   - Six or more daily servings of grain and whole-grain products, legumes, and starchy vegetables

   - Five or more daily servings of colorful fruits and vegetables

   - Three or more daily servings of fat-free or low-fat milk products for most adults (two or more for children; four or more for teenagers, pregnant or breastfeeding mothers, and older adults)

   - Two daily servings of lean meat, poultry, seafood, or vegetarian protein sources, including at least two servings of fish per week

2. Choose a diet moderate in fat (30 percent of total calories) and low in most saturated and hydrogenated fats (10 percent of total calories). Include a balance of healthful monounsaturated and polyunsaturated fats, such as in nut and seed oils, for the remaining fat in your diet. Keep your daily cholesterol intake to under 300 milligrams.

3. If you drink alcohol, do so in moderation—no more than one drink per day if you're a woman and no more than two if you're a man.

4. Be physically active to keep fit.

5. Use salt in moderation, keeping your daily intake under 2,400 milligrams. That's about a level teaspoonful.

6. Choose a diet in which 55 to 60 percent of calories come from carbohydrates, emphasizing the complex carbohydrates found in fruits, vegetables, legumes, and whole grains. These foods should supply 25 to 30 grams of fiber daily. Limit high-calorie foods high in simple sugars and low in nutrients, such as sodas and candy.

Enough rules and numbers. What does all this mean, and why is it so important? Let's dig into the meat of these recommendations.

the healthy heart food pyramid

An easy way to put all the dietary guidelines into action is to use the Healthy Heart Food Pyramid. It's a dandy, at-a-glance tool to help visualize the variety and quantity of foods you need to eat each day.

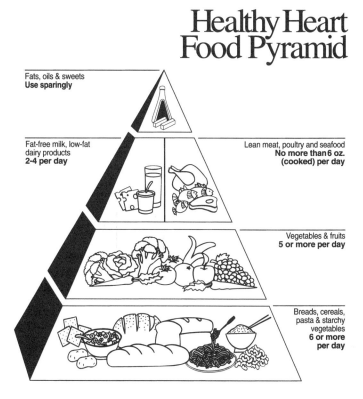

Healthy Heart Food Pyramid

Fats, oils & sweets
Use sparingly

Fat-free milk, low-fat dairy products
2-4 per day

Lean meat, poultry and seafood
**No more than 6 oz.
(cooked) per day**

Vegetables & fruits
5 or more per day

Breads, cereals, pasta & starchy vegetables
**6 or more
per day**

The first step is a foundation of breads, cereals, pasta, and starchy vegetables. These foods—most people call them *starches*—satisfy hunger and are good substitutes for other foods that are high in calories and saturated fats. Starchy vegetables and legumes, such as potatoes, black beans, pinto beans, lima beans, lentils, corn, green peas, and sweet potatoes, are part of this group.

When choosing breads, cereals, and grain products, opt for whole grains and whole-grain products whenever possible instead of refined products, such as in white flours and rices. Like legumes, whole grains give us lots of vitamins and minerals as well as soluble fiber, which helps lower low-density lipoprotein (LDL), or "bad," cholesterol. (See page 294 for more information on fiber.) They taste good, too, with earthy, nutty flavors and chewy textures. Most grain products are also enriched with folic acid, a B vitamin that may reduce the risk of heart disease and stroke.

Plenty of exciting choices are available among grains, breads, and cereals. Try brown and wild rices, barley, wheat berries, whole-wheat couscous, bulgur (cracked) wheat, rye, buckwheat, kamut, millet, polenta, and quinoa. Oats are a terrific whole-grain food. Look for whole-grain breads (whole-wheat flour or another whole grain is listed as the first ingredient on the label), including pitas, flour and corn tortillas, English muffins, matzos, rolls, and bagels. When making muffins, quick breads, pancakes, cookies, and cakes, you can substitute whole-wheat pastry flour (available at most health food stores) for all or part of the all-purpose flour for added nutrition.

---

one serving size =

1 slice of bread

$1/2$ of a 2-ounce bagel

$1/2$ cup oatmeal, wheat cereal, or polenta

1 cup flaked cereal

$1/2$ cup cooked rice, pasta, or grain

$1/2$ cup cooked legumes or starchy vegetables,
    such as pinto beans or sweet potatoes

The second step is fruits and vegetables. The more the merrier, say our experts at the American Heart Association. Those people who eat the most fruits and vegetables may have lower risk for heart disease, stroke, and high blood pressure as well as certain cancers. Produce is generally low in calories and fat but loaded with vitamins, minerals, fiber, and a host of micronutrients.

Micronutrients? That's a catchall term scientists use for the hundreds of phytochemicals, plant sterols, antioxidants such as beta-carotene, and other good things found in the most colorful fruits and vegetables. The various micronutrients in produce—many of which haven't been identified—appear to work together to give us those health benefits. Eating real food is the best way to reap the rewards. Popping supplement pills doesn't do the same thing—and, in fact, some supplements may be harmful.

Eat the widest possible variety of deeply colored fruits and vegetables. Choices include orange carrots, pumpkins, mangoes, apricots, and cantaloupe. Green choices include leafy greens, broccoli, peppers, cabbage, green beans, snow peas, and sugar snap peas. For reds, purples, and blues, eat blueberries, strawberries, cranberries, tomatoes, plums, apples, and grapes.

On the third step up the pyramid are fat-free and low-fat milk products. Fat-free milk is the best source for calcium your body can use. In fact, it's pretty tough to get enough calcium without it. Most Americans are sorely deficient in calcium. That concerns medical experts because calcium isn't essential just for strong bones and teeth in growing children. Grown-ups—both men and women—may have the most to gain from dairy products.

In addition to its virtues as a calcium source, milk also is an excellent supplier of protein, vitamins, and other minerals.

Be sure to choose fat-free or low-fat milk products. Whole milk is high in saturated fats, cholesterol, and calories. That's why the best choices, after the toddler years, are milk products with 0 to 1 percent fat. All fat-free and low-fat dairy products aren't the same good choices, however. Look out for unwanted extra calories and sweeteners in some yogurts and in frozen dairy desserts.

Even if you have trouble digesting milk, you can usually enjoy cultured milk products, such as yogurts and cheeses, and milk in small amounts. If you don't like the taste of milk, there are plenty of creative ways to sneak dairy products into cooked dishes. Cook your oatmeal in milk, for instance, or add milk powder to your flour when baking or to any dish, such as yogurt smoothies and pureed cream soups, when you want to boost its calcium content.

Near the top of the pyramid are lean meats, poultry, and seafood. These protein-rich foods are some of the best sources for essential B vitamins and minerals, such as zinc and iron. B vitamins may play a significant role in lowering the risk for heart disease.

Our experts at the American Heart Association urge you to eat protein in moderation. Too many people favor mammoth plate-size portions of meat, forgetting that a sensible serving is the size of a deck of cards. Protein is important, but too much is not a good idea. Most Americans eat considerably more than the recommended 10 to 15 percent of daily calories in protein, and they are getting too much saturated fat and cholesterol in the fatty cuts and processed forms of meat chosen. To reduce excess saturated fats, select lean cuts of beef, pork, lamb, and game meats, trim all visible fat, and remove the skin from poultry.

Seafood generally has less saturated fat than meat and poultry and offers a bonus. You've probably been hearing a lot about omega-3 fatty acids. These fatty acids are a type of polyunsaturated fat that appears to promote heart health by inhibiting blood clotting, reducing triglyceride levels, and lowering the risk for heart attacks and strokes. Omega-3 fatty acids are high in fish such as salmon, albacore tuna, mackerel, lake trout, herring, and sardines. The smart advice is to enjoy at least two servings of fish, especially fatty fish, each week.

A healthful way to avoid saturated fats is to take advantage of economical vegetarian protein sources such as dried beans, lentils, and soybeans. Animal proteins are considered high-quality "complete proteins" because they supply all the essential amino acids your body needs to make protein. Plant sources of protein, however, can be combined to provide the complete set of amino acids. They can also be bolstered with small amounts of animal proteins, such as milk or cheese. The classic pairings of beans and grains found in many cuisines are good examples of using vegetable products to make complete proteins without any saturated fat. For most people, it's not necessary to pair complementary proteins in the same meal. Any time in the course of the day will do it.

one serving size =

3 ounces cooked (4 ounces raw) lean meat, poultry, or seafood

$1/4$ cup canned tuna, sardines, or salmon (packed in water)

$1/2$ cup cooked beans or lentils

2 tablespoons peanut butter

1 egg

3 ounces soy products, such as tofu and soy burger

At the tip of the pyramid are foods highest in calories—sweets and fats. These foods are often low in nutrients, so try to avoid eating too much of them. To keep your balance on the steep tip of the pyramid, take a look at what makes the most healthful choices.

Sweets. Sweets aren't inherently bad, nor do they cause heart disease or diabetes. They can, however, be empty calories, consisting of lots of added sugar and, often, fat, without supplying much in the way of nutrition. Even decadent sweets can be part of a healthful diet. All together now: "In moderation!" They're best reserved for special treats eaten in small amounts.

Sugars are carbohydrates, our body's main source of energy. All carbs are not the same, however.

Simple carbohydrates are found in table sugars, corn syrup, honey, fruit syrups, and other processed sugars. Eating too much of them may be associated with higher triglyceride and lower high-density lipoprotein (HDL) cholesterol (the "good cholesterol") levels, which may increase the risk for heart disease. Unfortunately, that has led many people to shun carbohydrates altogether. In fact, carbs should supply 55 to 60 percent of your calories.

Complex carbohydrates are found naturally in vegetables, fruits, and whole grains. They're usually low in calories, saturated fats, and cholesterol, yet rich in vitamins and minerals—and make the more nutritious choices for energy foods. Complex carbs are also the main source for dietary fiber, which includes both insoluble and soluble fiber. Insoluble fiber, such as bran, commonly called *roughage,* is known for its contribution to intestinal health. The biggest benefits, however, come from the soluble fibers in these foods. Those soluble fibers appear to help lower LDL-cholesterol levels. Because high-fiber foods can be very filling, people who eat the most dietary fiber may tend to overeat less. It's no surprise our American Heart Association experts recommend consuming 25 to 30 grams of dietary fiber each day.

Fats. The types of fat you eat are as important to your health as the amount, so be especially careful to choose well. *Fat* has become a bad word to many, but fats are not all the same, nor are they all bad. On the contrary, they're crucial for good nutrition.

Plenty of people have come to fear fats and think that healthful eating means a low-fat diet. Not so. The experts at the American Heart Association recommend a diet *moderate* in fats, with fats supplying no more than 30 percent of calories. (That's 65 grams of total fat for those eating 2,000 calories a day, 80 grams for 2,500-calorie diets.) Very low fat diets may not provide important nutrients. Such diets can be risky for some people in the short term, raising triglycerides and lowering HDL cholesterol.

Many people also think that because fats are the most calorie-dense food, supplying 9 calories per gram, eating fat makes them fat. Wrong again. Too many calories, no matter what their source, lead to weight gain. Low-fat foods can be just as high in calories as fatty foods (sometimes higher) because of added sweeteners.

Here's a look at the different types of fat and the ones that the most healthful choices.

types of dietary fat

All fats in foods are made up of fatty acids, which can be saturated, monounsaturated, or polyunsaturated. We use the shortened term *fat* for *fatty acids* in this book.

Saturated and hydrogenated trans fats are the greatest concern to medical experts at the American Heart Association. That's because, when eaten in high amounts, these fats can raise LDL (bad) cholesterol and total cholesterol. High amounts of trans fats may also lower HDL (good) cholesterol, and that may lead to heart disease and strokes. The Association's experts recommend that these fats make up less than one third of the total fats you eat, or less than 10 percent of your daily calories. (That's no more than 20 grams of saturated fats if you eat 2,000 calories a day, and 25 grams if you eat 2,500 calories.) The lower the intake of trans fat, the better, however. When choosing hydrogenated margarines, look for the softest ones. Check the label to be sure that liquid vegetable oil is the first ingredient listed and that the margarine contains no more than 2 grams of saturated fat per tablespoon.

Saturated fats are found in meat fat, poultry fat and skin, whole-milk products and butter, coconut, cocoa butter, and tropical vegetable oils, such as palm kernel, palm, and coconut oils. Most saturated fats are solid at room temperature.

Trans fats are found in varying amounts in vegetable oils that have been hydrogenated (packed with hydrogen to make them more saturated) to make them solid for use in shortening and margarine. You'll also find trans fats in products made with hydrogenated and partially hydrogenated oils, such as cookies, crackers, doughnuts, and commercially fried foods.

Unsaturated fats—polyunsaturated and monounsaturated—are fats the American Heart Association experts recommend eating as substitutes for saturated and trans fats. They suggest aiming for 5 to 8 teaspoons of these a day.

Polyunsaturated fats are found mainly in corn, soybean, canola, and safflower oils, in cold-water fish oils, and in sunflower, sesame, and flax seeds and oils. Polyunsaturated oils are liquid at all temperatures. When used in place of saturated fats, polyunsaturated fats can lower blood cholesterol levels. Some omega-3s, a type of polyunsaturated fat found mostly in fish, may help reduce the risk of heart disease and stroke by decreasing blood clotting and lowering triglyceride levels.

Monounsaturated fats are found primarily in olives, peanuts, almonds, walnuts, and avocados and their oils. These oils are liquid at room temperature but solidify when refrigerated. When used in place of saturated fats, monounsaturated fats appear to reduce levels of bad cholesterol while raising the good cholesterol, thereby helping lower the risk of heart disease.

---

1 teaspoon vegetable oil (4.6 grams total fat) =

1 teaspoon regular margarine

2 teaspoons diet margarine

1 tablespoon salad dressing

2 teaspoons regular mayonnaise or
  peanut butter

1 tablespoon seeds

1/6 medium avocado

10 small or 5 large olives

---

cholesterol basics

Blood cholesterol and dietary cholesterol are not the same. Your liver produces almost all the cholesterol your body needs. The measurement of your blood cholesterol is expressed as total cholesterol, low-density lipoprotein (LDL), and high-density lipoprotein (HDL).

LDL cholesterol transports cholesterol through the bloodstream. It's known as the "bad" cholesterol because it can build up and form waxy plaque deposits and plug up your arteries. This buildup increases your risk for heart disease and stroke.

HDL cholesterol, or "good" cholesterol, removes excess cholesterol from the blood and takes it back to the liver for disposal. High HDL cholesterol levels provide protection from heart disease.

Dietary cholesterol refers to the cholesterol in the foods you eat. It is found only in animal foods, such as organ meats, animal fats, egg yolks, and shellfish. Although dietary cholesterol can raise your blood cholesterol level, there is more to the story. The most significant influence on your blood cholesterol is the amount of saturated and trans fats you eat. Foods high in cholesterol are often, but not always, also high in saturated fats. Coconut oil, which is the most saturated fat you can buy, is plant-based and thus has no cholesterol. Watching your saturated fat and trans fat intake is paramount.

Eggs, an economical source of high-quality protein, B vitamins, iron, and other minerals, are the main source of dietary cholesterol for some people. Eggs can fit into a heart-healthy diet that's otherwise low in cholesterol. Keep in mind, however, that one egg yolk has about 213 milligrams (egg whites have no cholesterol). Dietary cholesterol can increase LDL cholesterol in some people, although not as much as saturated fats do. Because cholesterol absorption varies widely among individuals, and most foods high in saturated fats are also high in cholesterol anyway, the American Heart Association recommends eating no more than 300 milligrams of cholesterol per day. Your doctor may recommend less if you have certain heart problems.

steps beyond the pyramid

calorie balance

The Healthy Heart Food Pyramid offers good advice about healthful foods to eat, but only you can take the last steps. It's up to you to balance how much food you eat with the calories your body needs. It's different for each person. The number of calories you burn depends on your metabolism, weight, gender, amount of lean muscle mass, amount of food eaten, age, even the temperature of your environment. Most of all, it depends on how active you are. Of course, if you are pregnant or nursing or have a medical condition, those factors need to be given special consideration.

Your goal is to eat about the same number of calories as your body burns as fuel. Any excess calories you eat will be stored as fat, and few of us want that! When looking at the calorie counts in foods, pay close attention to portion sizes. Notice, for example, that one bread serving is half of a two-ounce bagel. How many of us wolf down an entire bagel *four times* that size and think we've eaten just one serving? Jumbo servings mean a jumbo you!

If your weight is creeping up, you're probably not getting enough exercise and are probably eating more than you need. We recommend maintaining a moderate level of physical activity, with 30 to 60 minutes of brisk walking or other type of activity most days of the week. (See Appendix D: Risk Factors for Heart Disease for information on managing your weight and healthful weight-loss programs.)

Here's a guide to calculate your daily calorie needs. Don't worry if you go over or under it a bit each day; you're looking for a balance over several days. The final determinant of your success will be your own body and the number on your bathroom scale!

ACTIVITY LEVEL	CALORIES REQUIRED PER POUND OF BODY WEIGHT	
	Men	Women
Sedentary	16	14
Light	18	16
Moderate	21	18
Active	26	22

* Sedentary: occupations that involve sitting most of the day
* Light: activities that involve standing most of the day
* Moderate: includes walking, gardening, and housework
* Active: includes dancing, skating, and manual labor

alcohol

We recommend that if you drink alcohol, do so in moderation. This means no more than two drinks per day for men and one drink per day for women. (A drink is 12 ounces of beer, 4 ounces of wine, 1.5 ounces of 80-proof spirits, or 1 ounce of 100-proof spirits.)

Compared to nondrinkers, those who consume small to moderate amounts of any alcoholic drink have, on average, lower death rates and a 30 to 50 percent reduced risk of heart disease. Alcohol increases the protective HDL cholesterol, but so can exercise. Alcohol may reduce blood clotting, but so can the aspirin your doctor may prescribe for you. If you don't drink, we do not advise you to start. Talk with your doctor about whether drinking is right for you.

Alcohol can be addictive. Heavy drinking and alcohol abuse shorten life and increase your risk for high blood pressure, congestive heart failure, and stroke, as well as contribute to a host of other health and social problems. Alcoholic drinks can also be a source of excess calories. If you have a medical condition worsened by alcohol, are pregnant, have a personal or family history of alcoholism, or are taking any medication that could react adversely with alcohol, you're urged not to drink.

salt

Salt is one factor in the complex interplay that maintains your body's delicate balance of fluids and other electrolytes. Your body needs some salt, but exactly how much isn't known. No daily requirement has been established, and salt needs appear to be highly variable.

What is known is that eating large amounts of salt can increase the risk of high blood pressure and heart disease in some people. Blood pressure response to salt is very unpredictable among individuals. Those who appear to be most sensitive to salt eat diets low in potassium, magnesium, and calcium and have high blood pressure or an increased risk for high blood pressure. People with a family history of high blood pressure, middle-aged men, black women, and the elderly are at especially high risk.

Most scientists agree that Americans probably eat much more salt than is needed, most of it in processed foods. To help prevent and manage blood pressure and heart problems, we recommend that you eat no more than 2,400 milligrams of salt each day. That's about 1 teaspoon of table salt. Limiting salt intake to that amount can lower blood pressure in overweight or hypertensive people, can help older people on medication better control their blood pressure, and can lower the risk of developing high blood pressure in salt-sensitive people.

You now know how important it is to eat a well-balanced diet, watch for saturated fats, and be physically active. You also understand the whys and hows of eating for a healthy heart. Armed with solid information and a commitment to be in control of your own well-being, you are ready to move on to the really fun part: planning and preparing a lifetime of delicious one-dish meals.

For the latest information on heart health,
visit the American Heart Association
website at www.americanheart.org
or phone 1-800-AHA-USA1
(1-800-242-8721)

appendix b
MEAL PLANNING

The joy of one-dish cooking is that it's easy to do well—even if you can't cook, hate to cook, or just don't feel like cooking. Once you've assembled the ingredients, dinner is virtually done.

For many people, the hardest part about getting a good homecooked dinner on the table each night is the planning and organizing. Thinking ahead is key. Face it: If you wait until dinnertime to consider what to make for dinner, you've jinxed even your best intentions. At the end of the day, blood sugars are low, everyone's cranky and tired, and you're ready for some downtime. If you have nothing up your sleeve (or in the pantry, refrigerator, or freezer) for dinner, the lure of junk food may simply be too great.

Instead, if you have a plan, everything can effortlessly fall into place. These one-dish meals provide complete healthful menus built into the recipes. Once you decide on a recipe, the meal planning is done for you. Each dish already contains at least one serving of a fruit or vegetable, plus carbohydrate and protein. That's why we also call this method all-in-one cooking. Even on the most hectic evenings, you'll know you can get a well-rounded meal on the table without much effort. For even more nutrients, serve the one-dish meal with a fruit or vegetable, a dairy product, or a starch, such as a whole-grain roll, tortilla, or muffin.

great go-withs
for one-dish meals

Getting better health from the foods you eat means maximizing nutrients in every bite. With literally hundreds of good things in different foods, eating the largest variety seems wise, doesn't it? It certainly makes for meals that are never monotonous!

When rounding out the one-dish meals in this book, choose foods that add assorted colors, textures, temperatures, and tastes. If you, like most other Americans, have a hard time fitting in enough fruits and vegetables, add them first. Just remember to factor in the calories, saturated fat, cholesterol, or sodium from the added foods. Here are some ideas to get you started:

- **Edible garnishes made from colorful, juicy fruits and vegetables. Some possibilities are wedges or slices of melon, papaya, mango, kiwifruit, pineapple, oranges, peaches, or apples, or even a handful of berries. Or try bell peppers, chiles, zucchini, broccoli or cauliflower florets, snow peas, miniature corn, baby carrots, or cherry tomatoes.**

- Crunchy vegetable or fruit salsas.

- Dark leafy green salads with low-fat dressing.

- Sliced juicy tomatoes sprinkled with fresh herbs, black pepper, and balsamic vinegar.

- Dark greens—such as spinach, chard, turnip greens, or arugula—quickly wilted with a splash of balsamic vinegar or lemon juice, plus a sprinkle of black pepper and toasted nuts on top.

- Crudités and a low-calorie dressing for dipping. Some delicious possibilities include mushrooms, snow peas, broccoli and cauliflower florets, and strips of bell pepper, zucchini, carrots, celery, and jîcama.

- Vegetables roasted or grilled alongside your one-dish-meal recipes: sweet potatoes, beets, rutabaga, carrots, cauliflower, eggplant, or brussels sprouts tossed with a bit of olive oil and seasoning before cooking.

- Steamed or microwaved asparagus or green beans tossed with lemon juice or dry mustard and herbs.

- Purees of cooked broccoli, cauliflower, zucchini, asparagus, sweet potatoes, or carrots (with a bit of cooking liquid, stock, or fat-free sour cream) for a creamy, comforting accompaniment reminiscent of mashed potatoes. You can also try using potatoes for half the mixture for a milder taste and creamier texture.

- Fruit salads or applesauce—scented with fresh or candied ginger and cinnamon—as desserts or starters. Layer them with fat-free or low-fat yogurt for parfaits.

- Fruit slices sprinkled with fresh mint and a splash of orange juice or liqueur as dessert or a stylish appetizer.

- Grilled kebabs of pineapple and other firm fruits, brushed with honey and served over fat-free or low-fat yogurt.

- Apples or pears cored and sprinkled with cinnamon sugar, lemon juice, and raisins or other dried fruits before baking.

- Fruit compote dessert made with fresh and/or dried fruits that have been simmered in a little fruit juice, lightly sweetened, and flavored with vanilla extract.

To help get the amount of carbohydrates you need each day, you'll want to accompany some one-dish dinners with a bread, such as one of these:

- Whole-grain roll or slice of whole-wheat bread;

- Corn bread or corn muffin;

- Whole-grain bagel or pita bread;

- Warm corn tortilla or whole-wheat or vegetable-flavor flour tortilla;

- Breadsticks.

Finally, if you need a serving or two of calcium-rich dairy foods, have a glass of fat-free milk or a cup of flavored fat-free yogurt with dinner.

one-dish path
to good nutrition and fun

Most of us grew up with a big hunk of meat as the center of attention at dinnertime. It filled our plates, and everything else was an afterthought. Many of the things we now know are necessary for good health were largely overlooked.

Does your brain ache trying to figure out if you've eaten the right amounts from every food group every day? That's one of the beauties of the all-in-one approach. It helps you make healthful changes to your diet without worry. The meals are based on grains, pastas, beans, and starchy vegetables, with a lavish array of colorful fruits and nonstarchy vegetables, plus a healthfully modest portion of protein. You'll find yourself loving these dishes, and not just because they're good for you. These one-dish meals will awaken your appetite and invite you to eat with all your senses. They're a wonderful combination of colors, flavors, aromas, and textures all in one great dish.

Fun to eat, one-dish meals are just as much fun to cook. Experiment freely, trying lots of new ingredients and combinations.

- *Have fun with flavor.* Spice the dishes up or down with different flavors from herbs, spices, and condiments. Seasoning boosts flavor without heaping on calories or salt.

- *Add fun colors and textures.* Add other seasonal vegetables and fruits that you love, found at the market, or can pick from your garden.

- *Try fun new foods.* Go ahead, get as exotic in your substitutions as you dare and your eating goals allow. Maybe you've been eager to try a game meat (lower in calories and fat than the meat called for in the recipe). Substitute lean bison or ostrich for beef, or venison for turkey breast. Perhaps the array of different Asian greens at the market caught your eye. Go ahead and try them in place of spinach or cabbage.

- *Substitute with the freshest and most available.* If cod or halibut is the freshest catch of the day, use it instead of the snapper called for in the recipe. If you have some leftover grilled salmon, use it rather than canned.

- *Humor your food preferences.* If you or your family enjoys buckwheat pasta instead of elbow macaroni—or earthy brown rice instead of wild rice—indulge in your favorites.

Whether you choose to follow the recipes in this book or have your own culinary adventures, you need never think of one-dish meals as boring. You'll notice something else: Your one-dish dinners will be a lot more healthful than those heavy meat-and-potatoes meals of yesteryear. And it couldn't be any easier.

give yourself the gift of more time

We all wish we had more time—to get in that daily exercise, putter in our gardens, take a long walk, watch the sunset, reconnect with loved ones, help the kids with their homework, curl up with a good book, or simply relax in a warm bubble bath. One-dish meals—with no elaborate cooking and no sinkful of pots and pans to wash afterwards—give us more time to do the things we want to do.

Here are a few other time-saving tips to include in your meal planning:

- *Plan meals at least a week in advance.* Using your week's menu, inventory what's in your kitchen and make a shopping list of ingredients you'll need. Shop just once a week rather than several times.

- *Avoid extra trips to the store.* Keep a notepad on your refrigerator. Write down things as you run low so you won't forget them on next week's shopping list.

- *Organize your kitchen and pantry so you can find ingredients easily.* When each type of food has a special spot, it's faster to keep track of it at a glance. Don't forget to rotate foods, using the oldest items first. You'll enjoy them at their best, and nothing will become outdated.

- *Keep a well-stocked pantry.* It's extra insurance that you'll be able to whip up dinner in a snap. With weekly menus and grocery lists, you'll quickly realize what foods you use most often.

- *Prep as you put away groceries.* For instance, when you get home from the market, grate the cheese for the recipes you'll be making later that week. You'll need to wash the knife, grater, and cutting board only once instead of each time you need cheese. (If time is really of the essence for you, packages of grated cheese and bags of precut and prewashed vegetables and salad greens may be worth the extra cost.)

- *Plan leftovers.* If you're grilling chicken one night, fix enough to use another time in a pasta dish or a salad. If you know you'll need cooked rice or green beans again later in the week, make extra. Cover and refrigerate for up to several days, or freeze for longer storage.

- *Get things ready ahead of time.* Do advance prep work and assemble as much as you can for tomorrow's dinner tonight. If you are already chopping onions for today and will need more tomorrow, chop enough for both days. Most dressings, marinades, and sauces can be made ahead of time.

- *Pick fast recipes.* When you're short on time, don't look at just the total time a recipe takes to cook. Quick-cooking dishes may require more of your undivided attention, while some longer-cooking recipes may cook themselves, allowing you to do two things at once. That's the ultimate time-saving technique!

- *Make one-dish meals ahead for emergencies and busy days.* Occasionally make a double recipe and freeze half to reheat when you don't have time to cook. You can even make several meals one weekend to stock your freezer. Divide the meals into usable-size servings and label them before freezing. Keep in mind that some foods don't freeze well. They include egg dishes; mayonnaise, yogurt, or cream sauces; raw vegetables such as lettuce, cucumbers, and tomatoes; and potatoes.

- *Freeze for ease.* Freeze one-dish meals in metal pans that can go from the freezer to the oven without fuss. To avoid having to buy extra pans, line them with heavy-duty aluminum foil before filling them. When the food is frozen solid, lift it out of the pan and return your pan to kitchen duty. When you're ready to heat the foil pouches, set them back into the pan to bake. You'll eliminate having to scrub the pan afterwards. Or you can freeze meals in disposable aluminum pans and simply toss them in the recycle bin when you're finished.

- *Shorten clean-up time.* While you cook, tidy up during a lull in the recipe, such as when a dish is simmering.

- *Delegate.* Many hands make light work. Sharing chores also brings other family members into the kitchen to catch up on the day's events.

more ways to save money

Around the world, one-dish meals traditionally have been a way for frugal home cooks to extend limited protein and create hardy meals from humble ingredients. Health benefits aside, you'll come to appreciate the money you can save with the one-dish-meal heritage—basing meals on economical plant foods, such as beans and grains, and using costlier meats, seafood, and poultry as flavorful condiments. By making it simpler to enjoy more homecooked meals, one-dish meals also conserve money you might have spent on more expensive fast food and take-out. Cooking dinner in one pot even saves energy dollars.

Here are some healthful ideas for further stretching your grocery dollars:

- *Minimize your grocery shopping time.* The longer you're in the store, the more money you are likely to spend. That's where planning weekly menus and making a grocery list really pay off. Stick to your list and try to resist impulse buying. Get to know the layout of your market and shop when it's the least busy so that you're in and out in a flash. The worst times to shop are Saturday mornings and when everyone gets off work. You can maximize your time by shopping when everyone else is home: weeknights after dinnertime or Sunday afternoons while the big game is on television.

- *Shop at a large supermarket.* Supermarkets have larger food selections and usually lower prices than small corner markets, convenience stores, and delis. Cooperatives, grocery warehouses, and day-old bread outlets may also save you money.

- *Don't shop when you're tired and hungry.* You'll buy more—especially tempting high-fat or sugary goodies—when your willpower is weak.

- *Buy in-season produce.* It's usually the freshest and least expensive. Not only will it offer the best taste and nutrition, it will last longest. Wilted vegetables and bruised or overripe fruit aren't good values. Buy only as much as you can use. Good produce gone bad is money thrown away.

- *Harvest savings from your garden.* Homegrown produce can be cheaper, especially when you grow higher-priced foods, such as fresh herbs, asparagus, snap peas, and specialty greens. Other sources of affordable produce are from generous neighbors who garden, farm stands, and farmers' markets.

- *Watch for sales and plan your menus around them.* In addition, learn when your store usually marks items down.

- *Try store brand and generic products.* They're often cheaper while comparable in quality and nutrition.

- *Buy in bulk.* Much of what you find in bulk bins is the most healthful, low-fat, high-fiber, nonprocessed food at the market. Items sold in bulk are typically cheaper than packaged items.

- *Clip coupons and turn in rebate offers.* But remember, they're only bargains if they're for products you need.

- *Play the "stock market."* Take advantage of sales to stock up on nonperishable items you use regularly. If you have freezer space, stock up on seasonal produce to freeze when it's at the peak of freshness and prices are the best. Watch for sales on meat and family packs of items for your freezer.

- *Emphasize nutritional value.* Low-cost foods high in protein include fat-free milk, chicken, and dried beans. Other inexpensive nutritious foods are grains, whole-grain breads and pastas, oatmeal and some other cereals, and fruits and vegetables. For the most nutrients, pick the most vibrantly colored produce, such as romaine, endive, or spinach, rather than iceberg lettuce. If fresh produce isn't at its peak, frozen or canned products may offer greater nutritional value. The goal is to use your grocery budget for the good stuff, not junk food such as packaged snacks and cookies, prepared foods, and sugary sodas.

- *Price shop.* Comparison shop by looking at the unit price—that's the price based on a product's weight, say a dollar per pound. By watching unit pricing, you'll also keep from being fooled by downsize packaging that leaves you with less for your money. Also compare prices of various forms of the same foods, such as canned, frozen, and fresh juices, seafood, and produce. Frozen fish is usually less expensive than fresh. You usually get more food value when you aren't paying for extra packaging and for amenities such as having someone else add the water to juice concentrate.

- *Make your own convenience foods.* You can save a lot of money by making many of the things you use often. You'll enjoy extra health benefits, too.

    —Do your own prep work. Clean and cut up your own fruits and vegetables, grate cheese, dry-roast nuts, cut up chicken, and mix spice blends and salad dressings.

    —Canned stocks and broths cost more than homemade and often are laden with salt and fat. Make your own without adding salt, using a soup pot or slow cooker. When the soup is cool, divide it into $1/2$- to 2-cup containers as desired, and refrigerate overnight or freeze. Before using the soup, lift off the solid fat at the top, and your stock will be low calorie and virtually fat free.

    —Cook a big batch of brown rice or another whole grain and freeze in desired portions.

    —Cook your own dried beans, such as pintos and kidney. Fresh cooked beans are richer in fiber—three times more than canned—and can be prepared without salt. Canned beans, by comparison, can contain almost 500 mg of sodium in a half cup! Cook a whole pot of beans in your slow cooker and freeze them in desired portions.

As you can see, taking a little time for planning can yield big rewards in saving money, time, and energy.

appendix c

SHOPPING INFORMATION

With your commitment to a lifetime of healthful eating well under way, you've planned your menus for the week and made a grocery list. Once you get to the supermarket, however, shopping can be a minefield of hidden calories, fat, and sodium. Packaged, canned, and frozen foods surround you in a dizzying array of brands and options. Look-alike products sitting side by side can offer vastly different choices for your nutrition and health. When shopping for prepared foods, your best defense is to become a savvy label reader.

making sense of nutrition labels

Nutrition labels on most U.S.-made products have been standardized by the Food and Drug Administration, so it's easy to compare items and to see at a glance how they fit into your eating goals. Those labels can be confusing, though, so here are a few clues to making them work for you.

Remember that single foods, every meal, or even an entire day's meals don't have to perfectly match guidelines. Healthful eating and good nutrition are the result of your overall diet and the food choices you make over time. The numbers are a tool that can help you balance what you eat and make more healthful selections so that you get enough, yet not too much, of what you need.

- Note the Serving Size and number of Servings Per Container. If a can is intended for more than one serving and you eat the whole thing, you'll need to multiply the nutritional values on the label by the number of servings.

- Note the Calories and the Calories from Fat. The closer the two numbers, the fattier the food. If one kind of cookie is 60 calories with 30 coming from fat and another variety of 60-calorie cookie has 5 of its calories coming from fat, the latter cookie can be a more healthful choice.

- Next comes a list of how many grams or milligrams of Total Fat, Saturated Fat, Cholesterol, Sodium, Total Carbohydrate, Dietary Fiber, Sugars, and Protein are in each serving. Each gram of fat supplies 9 calories, over twice what a gram of protein or carbohydrate supplies.

- To the right of those numbers is "% Daily Value." If your cookie's Total Fat is 30 percent, that doesn't mean the cookie is 30 percent fat. It means that the cookie supplies 30 percent of the total amount of fat you need for the *entire day* based on a 2,000-calorie diet.

Nutrition Facts		
Serving Size 1 cup (240mL)		
Servings Per Container 8		
Amount Per Serving		
Calories 90	Calories from Fat 0	
		% Daily Value*
Total Fat 0g		**0%**
Saturated Fat 0g		**0%**
Cholesterol 5mg		**0%**
Sodium 125mg		**5%**
Total Carbohydrate 13g		**4%**
Dietary Fiber 0g		**0%**
Sugars 12g		
Protein 8g		

Vitamin A	10%	• Vitamin C	2%
Calcium 30%	• Iron 0%	• Vitamin D	25%

*Percent Daily Values are based on a 2,000 calorie diet. Your daily values may be higher or lower depending on your calorie needs:

	Calories	2,000	2,500
Total Fat	Less than	65g	80g
Sat. Fat	Less than	20g	25g
Cholesterol	Less than	300mg	300mg
Sodium	Less than	2,400mg	2,400mg
Total Carbohydrate		300g	375g
Dietary Fiber		25g	30g

Calories per gram:
Fat 9 • Carbohydrate 4 • Protein 4

The percentages for the things in foods that give us energy (and supply calories)—fat, saturated fat, total carbohydrates, and protein—are all based on current governmental recommendations for a 2,000-calorie diet:

Total fat—30 percent of total calories (65 g)

Saturated fat—10 percent of calories (22 g)

Carbohydrate—60 percent of calories (300 g)

Protein—10 percent of calories (50 g)

Your daily calories may be more or less, so you may have to adjust the numbers proportionately. A 2,000-calorie diet is about right for moderately active women, teenage girls, and sedentary men. Children, sedentary women, and some older adults may need only 1,600 to 1,800 calories per day. Most men, teenage boys, and active women need 2,500. Some more-active people need 2,800 calories.

The daily percentages for cholesterol, sodium, and dietary fiber are the same for everyone:

> Cholesterol—less than 300 mg
> Sodium—less than 2,400 mg
> Dietary fiber—25 g

Currently, a general guideline is that if the % Daily Value is 20 percent or greater, that food can be considered a high source for that nutrient. Less than 5 percent is a low source.

· Four nutrients on the label—Vitamin A, Vitamin C, Calcium, and Iron—are simply the given percentages of the daily recommended intakes in each serving. Check with your doctor to learn whether these amounts are appropriate for you.

· There are two general types of carbohydrate: complex carbs found in high-fiber whole-grain foods (Dietary Fiber) and simple carbs (Sugars). Added sugars (4 grams equals 1 teaspoon sugar) supply energy, but too much can be a source of excess calories. When looking for good sources of fiber-rich complex carbohydrates, look for foods that have 3 grams or more of fiber per serving.

· Here is a look at what's ahead. Several years ago, the Food and Nutrition Board of the National Academy of Sciences changed the way scientists evaluate our diets. Instead of the Recommended Daily Amounts (RDAs) used for food labels, they now use Dietary Reference Intakes (DRIs), which basically change the focus from just preventing deficiencies to optimizing good health and decreasing the risk of chronic diseases. In the near future, experts will determine how nutritional labels may change in coming years to use the new DRIs.

deciphering label claims

The government also regulates the claims that manufacturers can make on package labels about their food. When you see the terms below, you know the food has met these legal standards:

· Free (fat-free, sugar-free, cholesterol-free, sodium-free, calorie-free)—less than 0.5 gram of fat or sugar, less than 2 milligrams of cholesterol, less than 5 grams of sodium, or fewer than 5 calories per serving;

· Low (low fat, low sodium, low cholesterol, low saturated fat)—3 grams or less of fat, 140 milligrams or less of sodium, 20 milligrams or less of cholesterol, or 1 gram or less of saturated fat per serving;

- Light or lite—one-third fewer calories, or at least 50 percent less fat or sodium, than the regular version;

- Reduced—at least 25 percent less than the standard version;

- Lean—less than 10 grams of fat, less than 4.5 grams of saturated fat, and no more than 95 milligrams of cholesterol per serving.

Finally, don't forget to look at the ingredients listed on the package. They're shown by weight, with the largest amount first and the smallest amount last. Knowing what's in the food can help you find where calories, fats, and sodium are hidden. For example, words ending in "–ose," such as sucrose or lactose, are sugars in disguise. Reading the ingredient list for a bread is the only way to know if it's truly a whole-grain product or just tinted brown to look more wholesome. Look for whole-wheat flour, not simply wheat flour, as the first ingredient.

american heart association heart check

We know it's not always possible to read labels when you're shopping. Some days you're in a hurry, the kids are crying, or you've forgotten your reading glasses. The American Heart Association's Food Certification Program can help you quickly and easily identify foods that can be part of a balanced, heart-healthy eating plan. Just look for the red heart-check mark on the package. It means that the product meets the American Heart Association's food criteria for saturated fat and cholesterol for healthy people over age two.

American Heart Association

Meets American Heart Association food criteria for saturated fat and cholesterol for healthy people over age 2.

appendix d
RISK FACTORS FOR HEART DISEASE

A healthful lifestyle is a good idea for everyone. The payoffs can be huge—feeling great and being able to do many of the things you want to do. Some news headlines may make you think the road to good heart health is difficult to navigate. Don't worry! You're in the driver's seat. There are many simple things you can do to help stay on course. Once you understand what factors contribute to your risk of heart disease, you'll know what route to take.

Some risk factors are not within your control. Your genes are one such factor. If you have an immediate family member (brother, sister, mother, or father) who suffered a heart attack or had other heart problems, you are at greater risk for heart disease. Hereditary factors can predispose you to high blood pressure, high cholesterol, strokes, or obesity. African-Americans appear to have a greater risk for heart disease than white Americans. Men have a greater risk of developing heart disease earlier in life than women, but it's still the main cause of death for both sexes. As you age, your risk increases.

The good news is that many things *are* in your control. By following a healthful lifestyle, you can reduce your risk of heart disease and other chronic diseases—simple things you can do for lifelong rewards!

1. **Quit smoking! Cigarettes and cigars aren't fashionable—unless you like sallow skin, yellow teeth, wrinkles, bad breath, and dulled taste buds. That's just on the outside. Inside, smoking doubles your risk of a heart attack and puts you at two to four times greater risk for sudden cardiac death than people who don't smoke.**

2. **Get moving! Being active is one very important way to help prevent heart disease. A sedentary lifestyle is a major heart disease risk factor. It's more important to be fit than sleek. Slim people who don't exercise can have the same risk of sudden cardiac death, heart disease, diabetes, and high cholesterol as someone who is obese. Physical activity alone, no matter what your weight, can cut your risk of heart disease and type 2 diabetes in *half*.**

Physical activity can make you feel great and may put a bounce back into your step. It can help you replace those worry lines from stress with smiles, sleep more soundly at night, feel peppier, and get more accomplished each day. It can even help turn that flab into fabulous abs.

You'll be doing your body even greater favors on the inside. Regular exercise reduces body fat and helps you maintain a healthful weight. Not only does exercise itself burn calories, but the more muscle you gain, the more fat you'll burn. Exercise also raises HDL (good) cholesterol and helps lower LDL (bad) cholesterol and triglyceride levels in your blood. Being physically active can also lower your blood pressure.

Forget grueling hours at the gym. The old adage of "no pain, no gain" is passé and was disproved long ago. Moderate-intensity walking or any other moderate to rigorous activity that's fun for you is effective for heart health. Strive for at least 30 minutes of activity on most days. You don't even have to do the activity all at once. Maybe two 15-minute or three 10-minute sessions work better for you. Think of it as snacking on exercise.

The more active you are, however, the more benefits you'll enjoy. It all adds up. Fortunately, there are plenty of easy ways to bring activity into your daily lifestyle. Another old adage says that variety is the spice of life. Here are some ideas for putting spice into your exercise plan:

· Walk the dog or go to a park with the kids and play ball.

· Learn a new dance, or take a yoga, Pilates, or strength-training class.

· Plant a garden. Dig in the dirt, hoe, and weed for beautiful flowers or delicious veggies.

· Park at the farthest parking spot, or get off the bus or train a stop early, and walk—briskly.

· Take the stairs instead of the elevator or escalator.

· Enjoy an invigorating walk during your lunch break.

· Clean the house with gusto.

· Pretend you are a kid again—ride your bike to the park or grocery store, and play sports with your friends.

· Be a pal and help your neighbors rake their leaves, move, clean carpets, or shovel snow.

· Lose the remote control; don't be a couch potato!

· Ditch the power lawn machines. Rake leaves instead of using a leaf blower, and push a lawn mower rather than ride one.

· Walk several laps enthusiastically around the mall.

· Walk the golf course instead of riding the cart, and swim rather than lounge at the side of the pool.

· Watch great videos or enjoy a good book while riding your exercise bike or walking on your treadmill.

· Take your favorite exercise tape along when you travel and work out in your hotel room, or stay at places with fitness centers.

- Play sports or walk around the field instead of lounging in the stands while your kids are playing.

- Plan family outings and vacations that include physical activity (such as hiking, backpacking, swimming, or walking through tourist areas and museums).

  If you've been parked on the couch for too long, are over the age of fifty, or have any medical conditions, please check with your doctor before beginning an intense exercise regimen.

3. See your doctor for regular checkups. Get tested for heart disease risk factors, including type 2 diabetes, high blood pressure, high total cholesterol levels (including high triglyceride and LDL cholesterol levels), and low HDL cholesterol levels. Then do your part to keep things at healthful levels.

- To keep your blood pressure in check (below 140/90), it is very important to maintain a healthful weight. A good way to do that is to keep active and physically fit. Emphasize vitamin-rich fruits and vegetables, whole-grain products, and fat-free and low-fat dairy products in your diet. Take time to relax and soothe the stresses from your day. Doing these things can help you reduce blood pressure, as well as lower your risk of heart disease and stroke. If they are not enough, your doctor may prescribe medications and/or a low-sodium diet for you.

- To help avoid high cholesterol levels, eat a heart-smart diet and exercise regularly. Doing those two things can also help lower LDL cholesterol and raise HDL cholesterol levels. Dig into vitamin-rich, whole-grain, and calcium-rich foods that are low in most saturated fats. If your doctor prescribes medication for you, take it.

- To help prevent or control diabetes, get regular exercise, follow your doctor's advice for weight and blood sugar management, eat a high-fiber diet, and minimize excess fat in your diet. If your diabetes requires medication, take it as prescribed and get regular follow-ups to prevent complications.

4. Eat right. As you learned in Appendix A: Eating for a Healthy Heart (page 273), the foods you eat can greatly reduce your risk of heart disease. Emphasize fruits, vegetables, whole grains, and fiber. Minimize saturated and trans fats. Choose monounsaturated and polyunsaturated fats instead, especially omega-3s. Drink no more than one alcoholic drink a day if you are a woman, two if you are a man. Balance the calories you eat with what your body needs.

5. If you can pinch a few inches around your middle, it's your wake-up call. High body fat, not just the number on your bathroom scale, may be the real health risk factor for both men and women. That's because excess fat is most often the result of insufficient exercise. Your risk of heart disease is also greater

when that fat's around your middle—women with waist measurements greater than 35 inches and men over 40 inches. Excess body fat can contribute to insulin resistance, high blood pressure, and high cholesterol.

Scientists often use body mass index (BMI) as a tool to determine overweight and obesity. BMI is simply your body weight (without clothes) relative to your height (without shoes), and in most adults it correlates with body fat. It's not accurate, however, for children, the elderly, or conditioned muscular athletes (since muscle weighs more than fat).

HEIGHT	OVERWEIGHT (BMI 25.0–29.9)	OBESE (BMI 30.0 AND ABOVE)
4'10"	119–142 lb	143 lb or more
4'11"	124–147	148
5'0"	128–152	153
5'1"	132–157	158
5'2"	136–163	164
5'3"	141–168	169
5'4"	145–173	174
5'5"	150–179	180
5'6"	155–185	186
5'7"	159–190	191
5'8"	164–196	197
5'9"	169–202	203
5'10"	174–208	209
5'11"	179–214	215
6'0"	184–220	221
6'1"	189–226	227
6'2"	194–232	233
6'3"	200–239	240
6'4"	205–245	246

Below 25—A BMI from 18.5 to 24.9 is considered healthy. BMIs less than 18.5 are considered underweight.

25.0 to 29.9—Overweight—BMIs in this range indicate a moderate risk of heart and blood vessel disease. A BMI of 25 translates to about 10 percent over ideal body weight.

30 or more—Obesity—This means a high risk of heart and blood vessel disease, with 30 or more extra pounds of fat.

40 or more—Extreme obesity.

People with BMIs between 30 and 40 are currently considered obese, and 40 or more is extreme obesity. Obesity is associated with increased risk for heart disease and stroke, as well as a number of other health problems, including type 2 diabetes.

Make good health, not looking good, your goal. Just because you look model-perfect doesn't necessarily mean you're healthy. You could be eating doughnuts and french fries and never moving from the couch! Remember, good health is determined by what you *do*. Being your healthiest and preventing health problems, no matter what your weight, means having an active lifestyle and eating a balanced, nutritious diet. It's never too late to get started and enjoy the results.

If you're at a healthful weight for you, stay there by enjoying regular exercise and eating wisely. Avoiding weight gain in the first place is an easier way to avoid health problems—an important consideration for parents who want to help their children develop lifelong healthful habits.

If your scale has begun creeping into overweight numbers, rather than dieting to attain that elusive ideal weight, adopt a healthful lifestyle—good diet and regular exercise. It's the soundest goal for most people. A wholesome diet and plenty of activity will boost your metabolism and turn your body into a better calorie-burning machine. Excess weight will melt off slowly and be more likely to stay off. Your body will achieve a weight that's healthy for you. Because you're exercising, you'll be losing that unhealthful fat. If you add some strength training to your exercise regimen a few days each week, you can replace that fat with lean muscle, which burns 50 times more calories!

If your BMI is already 30 or greater, or over 25 if you have health problems, we recommend reducing calories *and* increasing your activity to achieve a 5 to 10 percent weight loss. That's right—you don't have to achieve an "ideal" weight to reduce your risk of health problems or see improvements in your cholesterol levels, blood pressure, and insulin resistance. Remember, good health is your goal, and that's realistically in your hands!

healthful weight loss

If you want to lose weight, you may be able to do so by tipping the energy balance. That means burn more calories (be more active) than you take in (eat fewer calories). If that doesn't work, you may need a doctor's help.

Tortoises make the most successful dieters. Healthy, safe weight loss while eating a balanced, nutritious diet is slow and steady (no more than 1 or 2 pounds a week without a doctor's supervision). You can probably achieve that amount of weight loss by eating 500 to 1,000 calories fewer each day than you need to maintain your weight. (See pages 282–83 for your caloric requirements.)

Equally important is boosting your physical activity. That will ensure that you are losing body fat while maintaining or building lean muscle mass. You'll also be more likely to keep the weight off, which is indispensable in the long run. Do a slow burn: Every 3,500 extra calories you burn is a pound lost.

Many people are so preoccupied with being thin, they take extreme, expensive, and potentially dangerous measures to attain unrealistic goals. Rapid weight loss programs, fad diets that eliminate certain foods or insist on certain food combinations or expensive special food products, severe calorie restrictions (1,200 calories or less for women, 1,500 or less for men), or weight-loss supplements that promise quick and effortless results can be hazardous to your health. Remember, if it sounds too good to be true, it probably is.

diet tips to help you tip the scale down

Here are some very doable tips to help you get started if you want to lose weight:

- Calories count. Think fat makes you fat? Think again! It's the calories. Fat-laden foods, however, are more calorie dense, and eating less of them can help you cut unnecessary calories. Learn the calorie counts of your favorite foods —you may be in for a few surprises!

- Follow a healthful eating plan, such as the one outlined on pages 285–88. Enjoy a variety of foods, but eat less of them. Focus on fresh fruits and vegetables, whole grains, legumes, and foods low in saturated fat. Not only are they more healthful choices, but also they will fill you up for fewer calories.

- Servings have ballooned into Paul Bunyan–size portions in recent years. Eating smaller portions will help you not balloon as well!

- You don't have to clean your plate. It's okay to stop eating when you feel full.

- Eat breakfast every morning. It will boost your metabolism by about 5 percent, so you'll burn more calories all day and be less likely to overeat later in the day. Don't skip other meals, either.

- Slow down and enjoy leisurely meals. Savor each bite. Pay attention to the flavor, texture, and aroma of the foods you eat. Eating slowly gives your body time to feel full, so you're less likely to gobble more than you need or really want.

- Drink lots of fluids (but watch out for high-calorie sugary drinks) so that you feel full and don't mistake thirst for hunger.

- You don't have to deny yourself foods you love. Just don't overdo it. Many dietitians advocate the 80/20 rule as a way to balance splurges. Fill up on the good stuff 80 percent of the time, then allow yourself the occasional treat with the calories you've saved.

- Learn a few low-calorie cooking tricks. Here are some of our favorites:

—Use nonstick cookware so you can cook with less oil or margarine. Try a pump sprayer to spritz a minimal amount of oil on your pan, or cook foods in a small amount of flavorful liquid, such as broth or wine. Instead of frying, try baking, broiling, grilling, microwaving, or steaming whenever possible.

—Accentuate flavor. Explore fresh herbs, spices, hot peppers, and condiments. Other flavor boosters include lightly toasting spices, marinating lean meats and vegetables, making reductions of soups and sauces, and using splashes of citrus juice or various vinegars.

—Enjoy rich-tasting, creamy sauces and soups without unwanted fat. Puree a portion or thicken with potatoes, cornstarch, or flour. Substitute fat-free condensed milk or fat-free sour cream for cream. Lighten sauces and dressings by extending them with fat-free yogurt, ricotta cheese, or cottage cheese.

—Get the most "flavor mileage" from high-calorie ingredients by using them thoughtfully and moderately. Sprinkle cheeses on top of dishes where their flavors are most apparent. Use strong, flavorful cheeses and oils—a little goes a long way. Dry-roast nuts and seeds to heighten their flavors so you need less. Instead of using a large amount of regular chocolate chips, use a smaller amount of the miniature ones in your favorite desserts. Use cocoa powder instead of solid chocolate when possible.

—Let healthful eating become a reflex. Always take the skin off poultry, and remove excess fat from it and meats before cooking. Avoid slathering butter or mayonnaise on your bread. Try preserves, vegetable spreads, low-fat cream cheese, or other condiments.

—Snack smart. To satisfy the munchies, reach for fresh fruit, baked chips, fat-free or low-fat yogurt, and low-fat popped corn instead of candy or fried chips. Or walk around the block and perhaps you won't even want a snack when you return.

Living a healthful lifestyle really can help reduce your risk for heart disease and stroke. Now, that's good news.

appendix e
EQUIVALENTS

Here are approximate equivalents for some items you may use often. Keep in mind that some foods, especially produce, vary widely between regions and by season. This list is merely a guideline to simplify your shopping.

INGREDIENT	MEASUREMENT
Basil leaves, fresh	$^2/_3$ ounce = $^1/_2$ cup
Bell pepper, any color	1 medium = 1 cup chopped or sliced
Carrot	1 medium = $^1/_3$ to $^1/_2$ cup chopped or sliced, $^1/_2$ cup shredded
Celery	1 medium rib = $^1/_2$ cup chopped or sliced
Cheese, hard, such as Parmesan	4 ounces = 1 cup grated $3^1/_2$ ounces = 1 cup shredded
Cheese, semihard, such as Cheddar, mozzarella, or Swiss	4 ounces = 1 cup grated
Cheese, soft, such as blue, feta, or goat	1 ounce, crumbled = $^1/_4$ cup
Cucumber	1 medium = 1 cup sliced
Lemon juice	1 medium = 3 tablespoons
Lemon zest	1 medium = 2 to 3 teaspoons
Lime juice	1 medium = $1^1/_2$ to 2 tablespoons
Lime zest	1 medium = 1 teaspoon
Mushrooms (button)	1 pound = 5 cups sliced or 6 cups chopped
Onions, green	8 to 9 medium = 1 cup sliced (green and white parts)
Onions, white or yellow	1 large = 1 cup chopped 1 medium = $^2/_3$ cup chopped 1 small = $^1/_3$ cup chopped
Orange juice	1 medium = $^1/_3$ to $^1/_2$ cup
Orange zest	1 medium = $1^1/_2$ to 2 tablespoons
Strawberries, fresh	1 pint = 2 cups sliced or chopped
Tomatoes	2 large, 3 medium, or 4 small = $1^1/_2$ to 2 cups, chopped

appendix f
AMERICAN HEART ASSOCIATION
NATIONAL CENTER AND AFFILIATES

For more information about our programs and services, call 1-800-AHA-USA1 (1-800-242-8721) or contact us online at www.americanheart.org. For information about the American Stroke Association, a division of the American Heart Association, call 1-888-4STROKE (1-888-478-7653).

NATIONAL CENTER
American Heart Association
7272 Greenville Avenue
Dallas, TX 75231-4596
214-373-6300

AFFILIATES
Florida/Puerto Rico Affiliate
St. Petersburg, FL

Greater Midwest Affiliate
Illinois, Indiana, Michigan, Minnesota, North Dakota, South Dakota, Wisconsin
Chicago, IL

Heartland Affiliate
Arkansas, Iowa, Kansas, Missouri, Nebraska, Oklahoma
Topeka, KS

Heritage Affiliate
Connecticut, Long Island, New Jersey, New York City
New York, NY

Mid-Atlantic Affiliate
District of Columbia, Maryland, North Carolina, South Carolina, Virginia
Glen Allen, VA

Northeast Affiliate
Maine, Massachusetts, New Hampshire, New York State (except New York City and Long Island), Rhode Island, Vermont
Framingham, MA

Ohio Valley Affiliate
Kentucky, Ohio, West Virginia
Columbus, OH

Pacific/Mountain Affiliate
Alaska, Arizona, Colorado, Hawaii, Idaho, Montana, New Mexico, Oregon, Washington, Wyoming
Seattle, WA

Pennsylvania/Delaware Affiliate
Delaware, Pennsylvania
Wormleysburg, PA

Southeast Affiliate
Alabama, Georgia, Louisiana, Mississippi, Tennessee
Marietta, GA

Texas Affiliate
Austin, TX

Western States Affiliate
California, Nevada, Utah
Los Angeles, CA

index